PASTORAL CATECHETICS

PASTORAL CATECHETICS

EDITED BY JOHANNES HOFINGER S.J.
AND THEODORE C. STONE

HERDER AND HERDER

1964
HERDER AND HERDER NEW YORK
232 Madison Avenue, New York 16, N.Y.

Nihil obstat: Patrick A. Barry
                  Censor Librorum

Imprimatur: ✠Robert F. Joyce
                  Bishop of Burlington
                  April 27, 1964

Library of Congress Catalog Card Number: 64–19730
© 1964 by Herder and Herder, Incorporated
Printed in the United States of America

Contents

Introduction

In opening Vatican Council II Pope John XXIII asked God: "Renew thy wonders in this our days as by a new Pentecost." The assembled bishops at the council in their opening message to the world wrote: "We wish to convey to all men and to all nations the message of salvation, love and peace, which Jesus Christ, Son of the living God, brought to the world and entrusted to the Church. . . . In the course of our meetings, under the guidance of the Holy Spirit, we intend to seek the most efficacious ways of renewing ourselves and of becoming the constantly more faithful witness of the Gospel of Jesus Christ. . . . We will devote ourselves with all our energies, with all our thoughts, towards renewing ourselves and the faithful entrusted to us, that the image of Jesus Christ which shines in our hearts 'to reflect the splendor of God' (2 Cor 4:6) may appear to all people."

Until Pentecost the Church was a faltering witness. With the coming of the Holy Spirit she boldly manifested herself as the continuation of Christ. The first Pentecost was a beginning of the renewal of the face of the earth. We know the thrilling events that transpired: how Peter, standing up with the eleven, lifted up his voice and spoke out; how the first Christians "continued steadfastly in the teaching of the apostles and in the communion of the breaking of the bread and in the prayers;" how the "multitude of the believers were of one mind and one soul;" and how "with great power the apostles gave testimony to the resurrection of Jesus Christ our Lord." At the first Pentecost, through the special action of the Holy Spirit, the Church manifested herself as the continuation of Christ. She showed herself possessed of his power to communicate the Christ-life and to impart divine truth. A new pentecost in any age of history possesses the essential characteristics of the first Pentecost. In this era the Church must manifest herself, in a manner intelligible and meaningful to the nations, as the continuation of Christ, on fire with his power to save and sanctify.

To live out our Christian existence in a secular society and shine as witnesses, we need more than correct ideas and information about Christianity, however important this may be. If the Church is to be "the sign to the nations," as the first council of the Vatican explained in 1870, Catholics must live with a faith which is more than an ideology or code of behavior. It is therefore refreshing to see how the main emphasis in the pastoral efforts of the Church concentrates more and more on a personal, existential concept of faith which manifests itself as an acceptance, a conversion, a consecration, a communion between God and man in Christ.

The purpose of this book is to offer a richer and fuller understanding of the catechetical renewal and to show its pastoral role in the new pentecost which is descending upon the Church. It will try to present some of the ideas related to a more existential vision of Christian faith. Instead of stressing one-sidedly only one of the elements in Christian faith, for instance faith as truths to be believed or faith as profession, this collection of papers will emphasize other equally necessary elements, such as commitment and trust. It will attempt to present the full traditional view of faith, following the best theological tradition of St. Augustine, which explains faith as credere Deum, credere Deo and credere in Deum. We will also propose that living faith—personal communion between God and man in Christ —is the aim of religious education, the heart of the Church's prophetical mission.

In this book the catechetical apostolate will be divided into a threefold division, organically structured on the biblical concept of faith as a personal encounter between God and man in Christ. Part one will treat of God meeting man; part two will consider man meeting God in faith; part three will treat of the transmission of God's message in terms of this personal communion between God and man in Christ.

Part one, "God Meets Man," treats of divine revelation. Revelation is here considered not merely as the deposit of faith but as the personal expression of God's plan to insert the whole of mankind into his divine life. In this dynamic view revelation is more than the unfolding of religious truths; it is God's manifesting his very personality under the motivation of an intense love. Since God meets man in revelation and reveals himself through four major signs, these will form the frame of part one. Various aspects of the biblical, liturgical, witness and doctrinal signs will be discussed to clarify the relation of scripture, liturgy, witness and doctrine to the catechetical apostolate. In considering the biblical sign Richard Sneed O.S.B. will show the impact of the biblical renewal on the present-day catechetical apostolate. A concrete example of how the biblical renewal can be emplemented will be discussed by Gerard S. Sloyan. William Sherzer of Sacred Heart Seminary, Detroit will discuss the liturgical sign, showing its importance and intertwinement with Christ's prophetical mission. In his article on the role of witness in transmitting the message, Alfonso Nebreda S.J. will offer valuable insights concerning the witness sign in catechetics. The theological implications of the catechetical renewal will be examined by Bernard Cooke S.J. Finally, William Reedy will sum up part one of *Pastoral Catechetics* with a global presentation of the mystery of Christ in the light of the four signs through which the all holy God comes to man.

The second part of the book is concerned with faith: man's response to God's call in revelation. Faith is the meeting point of a series of major recoveries in the field of theology which are deepening and vitalizing the whole field of religious education. Living faith is precisely the aim of pastoral catechetics. In part two Alfonso Nebreda will discuss some of the recoveries in recent pastoral research which pertain to a richer concept of faith. He will show how these recoveries affect the field of catechetics in its very roots. In his article on the three stages in leading man to faith and their hole in the catechesis of the faithful, Johannes Hofinger S.J. will further clarify our understanding of living faith.

Part three will consider matters related to the communication of the Christian message. Religious sociology, psychology and anthropology, methods and techniques of communication, programs of training, catechetical structures, etc. fit into this third major area of catechetical concern, called "Transmission of God's Message." This third section hinges essentially on the previous two. For its content, features and characteristics are determined by the goal of catechetics, by the stages in the process of faith and by the mentalities and milieux which affect man's approach to God. Thus an integral part of the third section of catechetics is a constant awareness that living faith is the aim of catechetics; it is necessary to keep in view the characteristics of the three stages, and the psychological and sociological factors influencing personal encounter. Only in the combined light of the first two sections of catechetics, that is, God meeting man in revelation and man answering God in faith, do teaching techniques and methods obtain their importance and validity. In this part of the book John O'Sullivan and Andrew Greeley will discuss value patterns, mentalities and sociological factors which aid or hinder personal commitment. The remainder of part three will be devoted to a study of catechetical structures related to the training of seminarians, religious and laity. José Calle S.J. and Paul Brunner S.J. of the East Asian Pastoral Institute will present an important article on the program of pastoral theology for major seminaries. Frank Norris, S.S. of St. Patrick Seminary, Menlo Park will discuss the catechetical course for major seminarians. Sister M. Carol Frances B.V.M. deals with the catechetical formation of religious from her experience in directing Mundelein

College's excellent Religious Education Program. The chapter on the training of lay catechists by Raymond Lucker and Theodore Stone offer catechetical directors guidance for the structuring of catechetical training programs in the light of the three major divisions of catechetics. Lastly, Sister M. Virgine, M.H.S.H. will outline a survey course whose purpose is to introduce lay men and women to the catechetical apostolate.

We wish to thank the many people who have made this book possible. It is dedicated to the self-sacrificing lay men of holy Church who, in this new pentecost which is descending upon the world, do so much to bring God's good news to men. Plans are being made for a companion volume to *Pastoral Catechetics*. It will deal with the practical problems connected with the communication of the message.

JOHANNES HOFINGER S.J.
THEODORE C. STONE

PART ONE

GOD MEETS MAN

Revelation is more than the unfolding of religious truth. It is God unveiling his personality under the impulse of intense love and coming into personal communion with man. Through the biblical, liturgical, witness and doctrinal signs God comes to believers. Part one concerns the various aspects of the signs by which God meets man.

Biblical Sign

The Biblical Renewal and Its Bearing on Catechetics

RICHARD SNEED O.S.B.

VERY gradually the general public is becoming conscious of what readers of learned periodicals have known for more than a decade: the so-called "biblical renewal" in Roman Catholic circles is producing exceptionally distinguished scholars both in number and depth. The results of their research now form a vital and vigorous part of contemporary biblical scholarship.

Much of today's vitality in Catholic biblical studies results from the encouragement of the late Pius XII, whose encyclical *Divino afflante Spiritu,* issued in 1943, expressed the desire for "a deeper and more accurate interpretation of Sacred Scripture in our time."[1] In the same encyclical the pontiff recalled the immense labors undertaken by exegetes for nearly two thousand years "so that the word of God, imparted to men through the Sacred Letters, might daily be more deeply and fully understood and more intensely loved...."[2]

Moreover the motive for biblical investigation, whether ancient or new, was clearly set down. For as the pope insisted:

... the Sacred Books were not given by God to satisfy their curiosity or to provide them with material for study and research, but, as the Apostle observes, in order that these Divine Oracles might "instruct us to salvation, by the faith which is in Christ Jesus" and "that the man of God may be perfect, furnished to every good work" (2 Tm 3: 15.17).[3]

[1] *Rome and the Study of Sacred Scripture,* seventh ed., St. Meinrad 1962, 96.

[2] Ibid., 102.

[3] Ibid., 103.

Further attention need not be devoted to the cause and effect of Pius XII's impact on contemporary biblical studies, for this has been already analyzed.[4] Suffice it to say that the biblical renewal in the Church is an observable phenomenon of our times, and it can be defined precisely as an international effort to realize the directives of *Divino afflante Spiritu*. Frederick R. McManus has succinctly described the aims of this renewal: ". . . to study the written Word of God, to spread a knowledge of that study, and to encourage the hearing and reading of that Word."[5]

Where these aims succeed there are, *necessarily,* important implications for catechetics. Catechetics is after all the art of communicating God's message of salvation. Anything that bears upon that message, either with reference to its content or the method by which it is transmitted, necessarily bears upon catechetics. Sacred scripture is *the* word of God and is the Church's most precious source of the message.

This essay will attempt to single out certain major conclusions arrived at anew in recent years and their bearing on both the content and method of modern catechetics.

First of all, modern biblical scholarship has provided new emphasis upon the truth that the bible is the narrative of the progressive saving encounters of God with man. As preserved for us by the sacred writers these encounters are not isolated actions; today, in the perspective of time, they can be seen as a continuous series, a unity revealing a progressive plan culminating in the definitive encounter of God and man in Jesus Christ.

The narrative of the continuity of God's dealings with man and on behalf of man has come to be known in the biblical renewal as Heilsgeschichte or salvation history. It is, as Roland E. Murphy has said, "the record that sees Yahweh revealing Himself in the historical fact."[6] Salvation history is not only the

---

[4] Jean Levie S.J., *The Bible: Word of God in Words of Men,* tr. S. H. Treman, New York 1961.

[5] "What Is Being Done?" *Sunday Morning Crisis,* ed. R. Hovda, Baltimore 1963, 48.

[6] "Promise and Preparation," *The Gospel of Jesus the Christ: A Symposium,* South Orange, N.J. 1962, 11.

17

recognition of God's hand in human affairs, it is also a partial discovery of his nature: his goodness and his will to save.

Salvation history encompasses two ages: a time of *preparatory* encounter and a time of *definitive* encounter. The period of preparation for the definitive revelation of God in his Christ is more easily seen as a unity from the perspective of its realization. Hence we approach the panorama of the divine encounter with man from the wrong end of the telescope: from the perspective of the New Testament.

Like us St. Paul was the privileged recipient of the completed revelation of God's loving design for us. In a preeminent way it was his special mission (Rom 1:1) to proclaim the saving plan of God in its fullness. And Paul's proclamation is the apostolic message, the message:

> concerning the Son of God,
> promised beforehand through the prophets (Rom 1:2),
> who was David's descendent in his human nature (Rom 1:3),
> by whose blood we are reconciled to the Father (Eph 1:7),
> who was constituted instrument of divine life for us
> by his resurrection (Rom 1:4),
> Jesus, the Christ, our Lord.

The decisive entry of God into human history in the person of Jesus Christ is however the end-term, the culmination of a whole series of gracious actions, instructive and preparatory. After all, we live in the age of fulfillment. But fulfillment presupposes promise and preparation.

A total view of the span of God's dynamic activity in history is neatly summarized by the author of the letter to the Hebrews:

> When in times past God spoke to our fathers,
> he spoke in fragmentary and varied fashion by the prophets,
> but in this the final age,
> he has spoken to us by his Son,
> whom he has made heir of the whole universe . . . (Heb 1:1–2).

The saving action of God "in those times past when God spoke to our fathers in fragmentary and varied fashion" can now be seen from the perspective of fulfillment. Faith can *now* perceive God's continuous dealings with ancient Israel as a *series* preparing for and leading to the end-term: his definitive saving action in his Son. That definitive saving action in his Son, which we today share, can best be understood only in connection with the preparation. St. Paul formulates this idea succinctly when he describes the Old Testament as a "tutor charged with guiding us to Christ" (Gal 3:24).

Hence the extreme importance of Israel's written reflections. The Hebrew scriptures are not simply an anthology of fascinating literary forms, nor do they merely constitute a fanciful history in song and story of an obscure people's religious and political culture on the fertile crescent bridge. Rather, for the Christian, the Old Testament is primarily and essentially the narrative of the progressive action of the Lord of history, caring for his people, dealing concretely in the life of the community and in the life of the individual.

True, God spoke to our fathers, as the author of Hebrews declared, but he spoke to them in saving actions, by way of *events*. And if modern catechetics is to aim at personal and communal dedication to the loving design of God in all its richness, if it is to lead to a full experience of the dynamic activity of God in his Christ, then an integral part of modern catechetics must be in terms of God's own guidance in that series of preparatory events preserved for us in the Old Testament, the "tutor charged with guiding us to Christ."

When we refer to the series of God's actions in ancient Israel's experience, we certainly do not mean to limit the divine care to a catalogue of spectacular interventions. Contemporary biblical study espouses no such view, and neither should catechesis. Rather it was the genius of the Israelite community to recognize in events the steadfast love of the Lord of history. Indeed, in every age this Lord chose from his people spokesmen who communicated the significance of events, the concrete evidence of the Lord's loving kindness.

But in addition to the living voices of God's spokesmen, or prophets, there existed in ancient Israel a special means by which the community kept constantly aware of God's gracious care: her worship. For example, at the harvest festival the worshiper presented the first fruits of his labors at the sanctuary and there gratefully acknowledged the Lord's gift of the land and his bounteous blessings. That acknowledgment was rendered especially in a credo, a profession of fidelity to the Lord who gave meaning to events. The very words of such a liturgical recital are preserved in the book of Deuteronomy:

My father was a wandering Aramean who went down to Egypt
with a small household and lived there as an alien.
But there he became a nation great, strong, and numerous.
When the Egyptians maltreated us and oppressed us,
imposing hard labor upon us,
we cried to the God of our fathers,
and he heard our cry and saw our affliction, our toil, and
our oppression.
He brought us out of Egypt with his strong hand and
outstretched arm,
with terrifying power, with signs and wonders;
and bringing us into this country,
he gave us this land flowing with milk and honey.
And behold now I bring the first of the fruit of the ground,
which thou, O Lord, hast given me (Dt 26:5-10).

Note the articles of faith in this creed. They are not abstract formulations. The doctrines of *this* creed are historical realities, events:

The *God of our fathers* has made good his promises!
The same God who delivered us from slavery
and made us a nation
has given us the land.
That the Lord is faithful, provident, and powerful is evident
from his deeds
which we have experienced
and continue to experience!

20

The credal formula of Dt 26 is merely one example illustrative of the empirical nature of Israel's faith. Similar formulations are easily adduced, as for example in the litanies we call Psalms 134 and 135. The point is that through her experience Israel came to know a faithful, loving, powerful God who willed to save. Thus from the community's reflection on the Lord's dealing with her there emerged a growing consciousness of a *plan* of salvation.

Is it possible to designate as pivotal any single experience of Israel that more especially explains her consciousness as a *people* in a divine *plan?* Is there some definite turning point in her history that gave meaning and continuity to the past and hope for the future? Most assuredly there is. That *decisive* encounter is preserved for us in the book of Exodus.

Embracing as the exodus does the entire encounter from deliverance from Egypt to union at Sinai, this is the pivotal experience which shaped a *people* of God aware of a past and of a destiny. Henceforth Israel's God, the God of Abraham, Isaac and Jacob, is known and worshiped as the Lord who brought his people out of the land of Egypt, as the prologue to the ten commandments insists: "I am the Lord your God who brought you out of the land of Egypt, out of the house of bondage" (Ex 20:1).

Israel's God is no theological abstraction, but a God who acts, who deals lovingly with his people, whose hand is visible in the events that determine her future.

At Sinai the community is reminded of the loving care of the God who saves with *power:*

"*You have seen* what I did to the Egyptians, and how I bore you on eagles' wings and brought you to myself (Ex 19:4).

Given this concrete evidence, Israel now hears a solemn invitation:

Now, therefore, if you will obey my voice and keep my covenant, you shall be my own possession among all peoples . . . you shall be to me a kingdom of priests and a holy nation (Ex 19:5-6).

21

To the loving invitation of the Lord the assembly responds:

All that the Lord has spoken we will do (Ex 19:8).

A commitment has been made, and now it is sealed:

And Moses wrote all the words of the Lord. And he rose early in the morning and built an altar at the foot of the mountain, and twelve pillars, according to the twelve tribes of Israel. And he sent young men of the people of Israel, who offered burnt offerings and sacrificed peace offerings of oxen to the Lord. And Moses took half of the blood and put it into basins, and half of the blood he threw against the altar. Then he took the book of the covenant and read it in the hearing of the people; and they said, "All that the Lord has spoken we will do, and we will be obedient." And Moses took the blood and threw it upon the people, and said, "Behold the blood of the covenant which the Lord has made with you in accordance with all these words" (Ex 24:4–8).

Among the ancient Hebrews blood was considered practically synonymous with life. Because the gift of life was from God and belonged to him alone, blood was regarded as sacred, not for man's taking or consumption (Lv 17:10–14; Dt 12:23). Once one grasps the Old Testament significance of blood as life, the Sinai rite becomes intelligible. An altar is constructed. Animals are immolated, and the lifeblood collected in basins. The pact or covenant is then sealed by the blood-sprinkling ceremony: the blood is dashed on the altar and then upon the people. The Lord and his people now share a common *life.* They have become, as it were, "blood brothers" or, better yet, the covenant bond is so intimate that Israel has become the Lord's son: "When Israel was a child, I loved him, and out of Egypt I called my son" (Os 11:1).

One simply cannot arrive at the complete picture of God's dealings with ancient Israel unless he recognizes the pivotal nature of the Sinai covenant. Neither can one arrive at the heart of God's plan in Christ without reference to the covenant event. The Christian mystery, the encounter with God in Christ, is precisely the Sinai covenant brought to perfection, and a biblically centered catechetics will emphasize the fact.

For Jesus himself is the new covenant, the bond that intimately unites God and man. No longer is that union by way of external symbol only. It is a reality in terms of the lifeblood of Christ that unites the community to the Lord and its members to one another. Moses said of the blood of the immolated victims: "Behold the blood of the covenant" (Ex 24:8). Jesus says: "This cup is the new covenant in *my* blood" (1 Cor 11:25).

The definitive encounter at Sinai made Israel a people with a community commitment. The new covenant in Christ means a new people with a community commitment. Moreover, just as Israel continually renewed her covenant, so too does the Christian community, for every Mass is a covenant renewal in Christ Jesus. Obviously then the biblical theology of the covenant has tremendous bearing on catechetics.

We know from the books of Deuteronomy, Josue, Judges and 1–2 Samuel the story of Israel's vacillation regarding her covenant commitment, how she repeatedly faltered as she took possession of her inheritance. But God's people continually renewed their trust in their Lord. They were confident of the Lord's will to save. It was a live trust conditioned by the concrete circumstances in which the people found themselves. This trust in the Lord's will to carry out his promises, this hope shaped by everyday realities facing an emergent community are what scholars call messianism or messianic faith or hope. Here again there are important implications for catechetics, especially in the treatment of what is called messianic prophecy.

For instance, after the year 1000 B.C. Israel found herself rather firmly ensconced in Palestine, a nation among nations with a king among kings. The nation's experience with the great monarch David gave rise to a new form of that trust in the Lord who makes good his promises. This messianic trust was in the Lord who would provide a king who would save Israel forever. Thus was born what is often referred to as royal messianism, the hope for a royal Messiah.

Royal messianism finds lucid articulation in the prophet Nathan's oracle announcing an eternal covenant between the Lord and the dynasty of David. From this time not only is the community in a son-father relationship, but the Davidic king, who sums up the entire nation in his person, is God's son. His dynasty will be established forever:

> I will raise up your seed after you,
> the issue of your own body
> and I will establish his kingship. . . .
>
> I will be to him a father,
> and he a son to me . . .
>
> Your house and your kingship
> shall be made sure forever before me,
> your throne shall be established forever (2 Sam 7:12,14,16)

The so-called royal psalms furnish a similar vision in which the sonship of the king is emphatic: "I will proclaim the decree of the Lord: The Lord said to me, 'You are my son; this day I have begotten you'" (Ps 2:7).

Perhaps most familiar of all from the tradition of royal messianism are the beautiful Isaian passages dealing with the Emmanuel sign (Is 7) and the Prince of Peace (Is 9).

Royal messianism in Israel did not die, and we have only to read the very first page of the New Testament to find the conviction that Israel's confidence was fully justified.

We have emphasized the fact that Israel was able to recognize in events the guiding hand of the Lord of history. We have seen that especially as a result of the community commitment to the Lord at Sinai the nation was constantly aware of an identity and a destiny. In addition the nation's experience with the monarchy gave new precision to her trust in the Lord.

But continued infidelity to the covenant brought ruin and destruction—this time in Babylon. Through suffering and humiliation however a certain purification was effected, and another dimension of trust in the Lord's will to save emerged. This new insight came to be formulated in the concept of a mysterious figure, the suffering servant. The self-oblation of the Lord's suffering servant brings redemption to all:

> Truly he bore our wounds,
> our pains he made his burden,
> and we esteemed him as one smitten,
> struck down by God and afflicted.
> Yet he was wounded for our sins,
> crushed by our iniquities. . . .
>
> and by his stripes we were healed.
> Though oppressed,
>   he submitted and opened not his mouth,
>   like a lamb led to the slaughter,
>   like a sheep dumb before his shearers,
>   for he opened not his mouth. . . .
>
> He shall see a posterity,
> he shall enjoy length of days,
> the good pleasure of the Lord shall prosper at his hand. . . .
>
> By his knowledge shall my servant justify many,
> and their sins shall he bear.
> Therefore I shall apportion him many,
> the multitudes shall he receive as booty
>
> (Is 53:4–5,7,10–11).

Thus Israel's vision of salvation was broadened and deepened. Without relinquishing the hope of the covenant fulfillment in the person of a messianic king, the nation now looked to a purification through the suffering servant of the Lord.

Yet another facet of Israel's confidence in the Lord's will to save merits attention: the notion of the heavenly Son of Man. Once again the articulation of the nation's trust was conditioned by historical circumstances. The centuries immediately preceding the inauguration of the Christian era were marked by unrest, strife and even bloodshed. Therefore the nation yearned for the victory of God over the world's power. This longing gradually transformed itself into a hope for the transcendent Son of Man:

> In visions of the night I saw,
> and behold,
> with the clouds of heaven there came one like
> a son of man,
> to the Ancient of Days he came
> and was presented before him.
> And to him was given dominion and glory and a kingdom,
> that all peoples, nations, and languages should serve him;
> his dominion is an everlasting one,
> which shall not pass away,
> and his kingdom one which shall not be destroyed
>
> (Dn 7:13–14).

We have dealt at length with God's plan that gradually revealed itself through his dealings with his people Israel. It is our thesis that the apostolic message which we outlined at the outset is not fully comprehensible without an understanding of the continuity of the two testaments, and it is the apostolic message that is the core of modern catechetics. For this reason we have attempted to touch upon some of the major themes testifying to Israel's recognition of the dynamic presence of the God who plans, the God who is faithful to his promises to save Israel, who prepares Israel for that salvation by way of a covenant, by way of a trust in a royal Messiah, a suffering servant, a heavenly Son of Man.

These themes converge on the person of Jesus of Nazareth and, indeed, are brought to a perfection far surpassing their original significance. This is the way that the Lord of history has chosen to speak to man. It is to the credit of contemporary exponents of catechetics that they are drawing deeply upon the resources of the biblical renewal. For is it not true that the catechist, whose task it is to lead Christians to a realization of what the divine plan is for him personally in Christ, can hardly improve upon the divine pedagogy of the Old Testament, God's own "tutor charged with guiding us to Christ?"

But the notion of preparatory encounter and the themes of covenant and messianism are only a few of the emergents of the biblical renewal bearing upon catechetics. Among many others we should like to choose one which, perhaps, has not received sufficient emphasis in catechesis. It is the soteriology of St. Paul, the theology of the redemption according to the apostle to the Gentiles. Or more accurately, it is one aspect of Paul's theology of redemption.

Faithful to the primitive preaching (Acts 2:14–36; 10:34–43), Paul ascribes to Christ's resurrection its essential role in man's redemption (Rom 1:4; 4:25). The death and resurrection of Christ are for the apostle theological realities inseparable in their efficacy. The researches of J. Schmitt, Lucien Cerfaux, F. X. Durrwell, S. Lyonnet, and David M. Stanley, to mention but a few, demonstrate a restoration of the proper emphasis on Christ's resurrection as an efficient *cause* of man's salvation. This is one of the great rediscoveries of the biblical renewal, and it must be said that modern catechetics has rapidly assimilated this long neglected truth of revelation, even if certain manuals of dogmatic theology do not reflect a similar appreciation.

What perhaps has not received an adequate place in contemporary catechesis is Paul's view of Christ's sacrificial bloodshed (Rom 3:21–26),[7] a view brought out clearly as a result of the painstaking work of Moraldi and above all of Lyonnet.[8]

[7] At least one catechetical presentation that incorporates to a large extent the results of Lyonnet's work is William F. Hogan's *Christ's Redemptive Sacrifice* in the Foundations of Catholic Theology Series, Englewood Cliffs 1963. Perhaps this is the long awaited precedent.

[8] One of the best expositions of the current work on the Pauline concept of Christ's sacrifice is that by E. F. Siegman C.PP.S., "The Blood of Christ in St. Paul's Soteriology," *Proceedings of the Second Precious Blood Study Week,* Rensselaer 1960, 11–35. Father Lyonnet has published in a number of periodicals pending the completion of his *Theologia Biblica Novi Testamenti,* Rome 1957-, two parts of which have been published. See also "Conception paulinienne de la rédemption," *Lumière et Vie* 7 (1958), 35–66; "La sotériologie paulinienne," *Introduction à la Bible* II, Tournai 1959, 840–889; "De munere sacrificiali sanguinis," *Verbum Domini* 39 (1961), 17–38. *Theology Digest* has provided English summaries of many of his studies. See especially in the present connection: "The Saving Justice of

The problem is that God's redeeming encounter with man in Christ has too long been presented almost exclusively in terms of a theory of juridical compensation, vicarious substitution and meritorious causality. Apart from the possible value of presenting the redemptive work of Christ in this *mode,* the fact is that Paul expresses the efficacy of the bloodshed of Christ in totally other modalities, i.e. in biblical modalities.

The point is that for St. Paul Jesus' bloodshed is not viewed as man's juridical penalty paid vicariously to an angry God who must be appeased in rigorous justice, but as an expression of Christ's infinite love and obedience which could find its term only in reunion with the beloved. How widely this differs from many a current presentation of the mystery of Christ's sacrificial death will become apparent if we outline briefly the apostle's thought.

To enter into the mind of the apostle we have only to return to the Old Testament categories that Paul employs to communicate the redemptive character of Christ's atoning death.

We have reviewed already the Hebrew concept of blood, not as a symbol of death, but of life, that which is from God and belongs to him alone (Lv 17:10–14). Moreover we have seen in the Sinai rite that sacrificial blood, blood released, "life" released, had as its function the effecting of a union. The blood unites God and his people.

So too in later Old Testament sacrifices the death of the victim was a *condition,* a means of releasing the "life" which then served to reunite or reconcile God and the offerer, to resume the union that had been severed by sin. Indeed Moraldi[9] has amply demonstrated that this reuniting was, properly speaking, the function of bloodshed throughout Old Testament sacrificial the-

---

God," *TD* 8 (1960), 80–82; "St. Paul and a Mystical Redemption," 83–88; "Redemptive Value of the Resurrection," 89–93; and "Scriptural Meaning of Expiation," *TD* 10 (1962), 227–232.

9 *Espiazione sacrificiale e riti espiatori nell' ambiente biblico e nell' Antico Testamento,* Rome 1956.

ology. In other words the death of the sacrificial victim was not a substitute for the death penalty the offerer owed as a result of sin or crime, but rather a means of releasing life (blood) which by its nature belonged to God and to which the offerer united himself. Hence, since the offerer identified himself with the blood of the victim, and the blood of the victim "returned" to its source, so too the offerer "returned," i.e. was reconciled. Sacrificial bloodshed therefore effected reconcilation or union which had been interrupted by sin. Thus the death of the victim was not a penalty; nor was there question of vicarious substitution. Rather the death of the victim was a condition for the release of life that, according to the Hebrew mentality, made possible a return to the Lord because of its very nature.

Therefore when Paul comes to speak of the sacrificial death of Christ, of his atoning bloodshed, as a Hebrew he simply draws upon his Old Testament heritage to articulate the function of Christ's bloodshed. This is forcefully expressed in Rom 3:23–25:

... all have sinned and are deprived of the glory of God,
they are justified by his grace as a gift,
through the *reconciliation* which is in Christ Jesus,
whom God set forth as a *kapporeth* by his blood,
to be received by faith.

The Greek term we have rendered reconciliation is apolytrosis. Technically it means a liberation, but in the Hebrew sense of liberation *for* something or someone, or a deliverance *to* something or someone. Some translators prefer to use atonement in the etymological sense meaning union, i.e. at-one-ment. Hence Paul is saying first of all that man is justified by reason of the union effected by the blood when God publicly set forth Christ Jesus as a kapporeth.

Kapporeth is the Hebrew name for the gold covering of the ark of the covenant and is generally translated mercy seat or propitiatory. This part of the ark of the covenant the Israelites looked upon as the Lord's throne and special place of presence (Ex 25:22). On the day of atonement, the Yom Kippurim, the high priest sprinkled sacrificial blood on the kapporeth, thereby reconciling with God the people and their possessions which had been separated from him by the defilement of sin (Lv 16:11–19).[10]

Thus in Rom 3:25 Paul speaks of the reconciliation effected by Christ's bloodshed in Old Testament thought patterns, and specifically in terms of the Yom Kippurim rite. Christ is the new kapporeth where men are returned to the presence of God by reason of his own blood that purifies and unites man to God. Other passages could be multiplied of course to substantiate further that this is Paul's view of Christ's sacrificial bloodshed. The work of biblical scholars, especially those that have been cited already, has demonstrated beyond reasonable doubt that such is the mind of Paul. Their careful analyses are readily available to the world of catechetics.

What we wish to emphasize here is that there are in Lyonnet's synthesis tremendous implications for catechetics. In fact Father Lyonnet's researches mark a turning point in the theology of redemption and must not be overlooked by any theologian, as Father Siegman has pointed out.[11] The same obligation holds for the catechist as well.

Far richer is this *biblical* view of the sacrificial death of Jesus. In a total surrender of self, in a movement of infinite love and obedience, he freely gives his own lifeblood, divine life released. By reason of his solidarity with all humanity, mankind, objectively speaking, returns to the Father, is reconciled to God from whom it had been estranged by sin. Accepting this sacrifice of love, the Father then constitutes this man Jesus (Rom 1:4) instrument of divine life now accessible to all men.

This view differs radically from the usual presentation of

---

[10] Lv 16:20–21 speaks of the famous scapegoat to which the sins of Israel were ritually transferred. It should be observed, as Father Siegman has noted (op. cit., 32, n. 14), that a) this ritual is *not* a sacrifice; b) the sins are carried away, not expiated by vicarious death; and c) the rite is quite exceptional, not having any other Old Testament parallel.

[11] Op. cit., 33.

Jesus' death as an act of infinite compensation demanded in strict justice which God chose to require and which could be paid only by a divine person. Such a view, that of the appeasement of God by a penalty suffered vicariously, is not hereby rejected or contemned. But one cannot help but wonder whether such a presentation today effectively transmits the mystery of Christ's redemptive death as its proponents intend it to. One wonders if it would not be better to return to those biblical categories of thought in which the inspired authors worked.

This much is certain: the current emphasis upon the efficient causality of the resurrection, as preserved in the scriptures, does not fit easily with the later modes of expression which are employed to communicate the meaning of Christ's death. Even a cursory examination of theology manuals that have attempted to incorporate more fully the redemptive character of the resurrection reveals difficulty.

If however the sacrificial death of Christ is seen as it is presented in St. Paul, as a loving return of humanity to its God in the person of Jesus whose blood reconciles, then the effect of the resurrection is clearly seen as the divine response to Christ's loving surrender on the cross. The response is one of acceptance articulated in the glorification of the man Jesus, the gift of the Spirit of which Christ is constituted the instrument. Hence the death and resurrection of Christ are truly presented for what they are: two aspects of the same reality: the redemption of mankind, in which every individual participates who commits himself to Christ by faith and baptism.

The present essay has attempted to single out some of the major results of the Catholic biblical renewal. There are other results, not even mentioned, that are equally significant for today's catechetical revival. One has only to think, for example, of the bearing on catechetics implicit in the recent advances in the understanding of the gospel tradition by means of the judicious application of the form-critical method, or of the insights

31

furnished by the growing recognition of the literary character of Gn 1–11.

Yet it is evident that no essay can hope to touch on all facets of the biblical renewal relevant to contemporary catechetics. What every reader can confidently expect however is that the present catechetical renewal, so obviously the work of the Spirit of God, will continue to utilize the best of the biblical renewal. Biblical scholars everywhere must surely rejoice, knowing that their labors are truly useful to God's people, that their efforts are indeed bearing fruit, since their fellow laborers in the Lord's vineyard are working diligently, that the divine oracles, as Pius XII insisted, "instruct us to salvation" (2 Tim 3:15).

What Should Children's Catechisms Be Like?

GERARD S. SLOYAN

THE fate of the religious formation of the young—and therefore of the adults they become—is intimately tied to the fate of the catechism.

The connection is not a necessary one. Historical studies have shown the various modes of transmission of the Church's faith, chiefly a living liturgy and a Christian atmosphere or culture, before ever handbooks of this sort were devised.[1] Still, the summary catecheses that long preceded the late medieval wall charts, and the pre- and post-Reformation printed booklets in question-and-answer form, also have a vigorous history.[2] From the break-up of the catechumenate, which in turn was caused by the barbarian invasions and the dissolution of the Roman Empire, the summaries of Christian faith proposed by bishops in synod and council to their (barely literate) clergy were the chief means of passing on the Church's faith. Despite the cataloging of revealed data in multiples of seven and other such unimaginative techniques—mnemonic in intent but also based on a shallow concep-

[1] See J. A. Jungmann S.J., "Religious Education in Late Medieval Times," Gerard S. Sloyan (ed.) *Shaping the Christian Message,* abridged edition; Glen Rock, N.J. 1963, 46–99; Part III, "The Fundamentals of Liturgy and Kerygma," *Pastoral Liturgy,* New York 1962, 325–416.

[2] See W. Croce S.J., "Contents of Catechesis: The Message of Salvation," *Lumen Vitae* 11 (September-December 1956), 595–604; for citation of these medieval summary catecheses, see the present writer's essays in *Shaping the Christian Message,* 30–45, and *Modern Catechetics,* New York 1963, 95–101; L. Bopp, "Katechese," *Lexikon für Theologie und Kirche,* vol. 8, Freiburg 1961, 27–31; J. Hofinger, "Katechismus," ibid., 45–50.

tion of the nature of God's revealing Word—these summaries had the virtue of being lineal descendants of the creeds.

The creeds have been shown by Cullmann,[3] Schreibmayr[4] and others to have been recitals of sacred events in the history of the Christian people rather than mere "religious propositions," as they were widely thought to have been until these researches were accomplished—and still are in circles where "propositional faith" is anathema. The creeds are formulated *kerygmata* or joyous announcements of all that God has done to save his people, both from their sins and for eternal life. The creedal phrases are largely biblical in origin: indeed, they took their rise from the same declarations of faith that provided the framework for the gospels as we know them.[5]

It is not ultimately helpful, however, to assert that the catechism answer is cognate with gospel material, even though at two or three removes. It is widely realized that it is not sufficiently cognate. The fact that this is so is almost a definition of what is wrong with catechisms. First, however, we must discuss the situation in which the "religious truth" or "proposition" finds itself in today's Christian world, for this is at the root of the whole question.

Catholics are convinced that a formulation of doctrine in human words can be a genuine deliverance of Christian faith, e.g. "Jesus Christ is true God and true man." The Church in ecumenical council, territorial synods of bishops, theologians, and authors of catechisms are all capable—though obviously at different levels of spiritual authority—of speaking true faith in their own (i.e., nonbiblical) words in a way that will be consonant with biblical faith. In the case of bishops their state-

[3] Oscar Cullmann, *The Earliest Christian Confessions,* London 1949.

[4] Franz Schreibmayr, "The Faith of the Church and Formal Doctrinal Instruction," *Modern Catechetics,* 45–62; see also J. N. D. Kelly, *Early Christian Creeds,* London 1950, 1–61.

[5] See P. Benoit O.P., "Remarques sur les 'sommaires' des Actes II, IV, et V," and "Les Origines du Symbole des Apôtres dans le Nouveau Testament," *Exégèse et Théologie,* vol. 2, Paris 1961, 191–211.

ments will *be* Catholic tradition; theologians and catechists, on the other hand, hope to write in a way that accords with Catholic tradition. It should be evident from this that a positive sanction attaches to any book composed of numerous such formulations, whether done with pedagogical skill or not. The chief norm will be fidelity to creedal phrases, and after that, similarity to popular theological formulations, whether good, bad or indifferent.

If, on the other hand, such formulations are thought to be essentially injurious to the reality of a meeting with God in the person of Christ, then their multiplication will necessarily be viewed as an evil. The better framed the statements of divine truth are in the order of human thought, the more imperiled will the reality of the encounter be. Such is the outlook of certain Protestant Christians, whose evangelical commitment makes them view any departure from the inspired page of scripture as a danger to the dialogue between God and men. Certain thinkers among them have even dispensed with the bridge of the bible because its symbolism is no longer "relevant."

Catholics tend not to have heard of these problems for historical reasons (though they are acquainted with a popular mentality that feels it can do without the bible—un-Catholic though this outlook is). Yet the catechism as a potential stumbling-block to encounter with God is a problem for the Catholic, and an important one, in light of the renewals in the Church that the Holy Spirit is achieving in our time. The doctrinal supposition among Catholics is that, despite God's infinity and mysteriousness, he can both be known and spoken of as known. The two possibilities are necessary conditions of Catholic faith. God's dealings with us escape our full comprehension, but we describe them freely. Jesus did so; so did St. Paul, and on a different plane St. Augustine and St. Thomas Aquinas; so do we.

That these attempts to speak about God, about his attributes and his love for men, should be looked on with suspicion as "merely human formulations" and therefore fallible in the way

35

men are fallible surprises the Catholic. On hearing the notion he is prone to reject it as some sort of religious skepticism or, if not that, as incompatible with his commitment to the infallible truth the Church is committed to voicing.

The problem is real, however. God has first of all spoken a Word to men through his deeds, not through human summaries of the meaning of those deeds. When the Word of God came to hearers on Moses' lips, or Isaiah's, or in a unique way through the speech of God's only-begotten Son, this speech of God always threw light on the meaning of his deed. The ten commandments help us know something of the meaning of the mystical experience of Moses on Sinai and the people's awed reaction to it; they are not by any means the whole meaning of Sinai. Similarly, the Sermon on the Mount and all the parables and sayings of our Lord are not the fullness of God's Word to men. Jesus, the speaker—Lord and Christ, as Catholic faith holds him to be —is that act of God which is a Person among us; he and only he is the fullness of the divine Word. In his utterances he gives himself to us in fragmentary and varied fashion, somewhat as God spoke to our fathers through the prophets. The Word incarnate is available to the whole Church and to individual believers not merely on the pages of a book—even though it be an inspired book—but in terms of a meeting with him which is a real event in one's life. Notice, we did not say he could not be met through private scripture reading, for clearly there is a sense in which he lives in its pages. What we said was that he speaks to members of the Church, as members of the Church, through his action in their lives. He does this in a unique way through his presence to his people in the liturgy.[6] The activities they engage in daily can

[6] "To accomplish so great a work [that of our salvation], Christ is always present in his Church, especially in her liturgical celebrations . . . every liturgical celebration, because it is an action of Christ the priest and of his body which is the Church, is a sacred action surpassing all others; no other action of the Church can equal its efficacy by the same title and to the same degree." Constitution on the Sacred Liturgy of the Second Vatican Council I, §7.

be a means of encountering him—charitable acts in a catechetical class as between teacher and pupils; the experience of pain, or of a major setback. The Lord Jesus is everywhere, and everywhere active to be in touch with us in the power of the Holy Spirit.

We seem up till now to have omitted the chief point at issue. Does not Christ act constantly in pupils' lives, or students', as adolescents prefer to be called? In a living catechetical situation where Jesus Christ, whom the true and only God has sent into the world, is spoken of lovingly and correctly, why should he not be active? What is to prevent living contact? Does not everything favor it?

In order to attempt to isolate our response, let us first set aside those factors extrinsic to the problem we have posed for ourselves:

—we assume the presence of love in the catechetical situation; nothing lasting is taught about values apart from a climate of love, and Christianity's sole concern is with values; we may not, of course, forget that the use of a badly composed catechism is objectively a sin against love, however inadvertent the offense;

—we assume the validity of protestations that the Catechism of the Council of Trent and all the classic catechisms up to the one done under the patronage of the German bishops (1955) were composed for adults, and that children's and adolescents' books were (and are) to be made from them; the claim is hard to credit when young people's catechisms consistently employ the wording of the adult handbooks, but in itself it is a correct claim: children should not be made to use grown-ups' books;

—we assume, finally, that the case for a printed catechism in every child's hand is not definitive; like the missal, the catechism grows more important as the lived experience of Jesus Christ is more difficult to re-create, and less important.

Let us turn now to the words and ways in which we speak and act about God, and about Christ, in catechisms.

In his opening address to the second session of the Second Vatican Council on September 29, 1963, Pope Paul VI addressed himself to his predecessor, Pope John XXIII. He said in an extended apostrophe that the latter had called his brothers together to make them realize that, in unity with the pope and deriving strength and leadership from him, they were to "safeguard 'the sacred heritage of Christian truth, and expound it with greater efficacy.' "[7] John had said that the council Fathers had not gathered primarily to discuss fundamentals of Catholic doctrine, "but to study them afresh and reformulate them in contemporary terms. For this deposit of faith, or truths which are contained in time-honored teaching, is one thing; the manner in which these truths are set forth (with their meaning preserved intact) is something else."[8]

The present pope went on to provide the Church with some unimpeachable catechetical principles. "An article of Christian doctrine," he wrote, "is not merely a truth to be investigated by reason in the light of faith, but is also an efficacious, life-giving Word."[9] The Church's magisterial authority is not purely speculative nor wholly negative, hence the council must do more and more to "demonstrate the power and dynamic quality of Christ's teaching."[10] Once again he quoted Pope John, this time to the effect that we are not mere curators guarding the treasure of Catholic doctrine in a museum, but men who "must work out ways and means of expounding these truths in a manner more consistent with a predominantly pastoral view of the Church's teaching office."[11]

The individual catechist could not ask for better help in prosecuting his task of adaptation. He may be limited theologically, hence unable to say why certain creedal or conciliar phrases are no longer as satisfactory as they once were. He may know of the

---

[7] Pope Paul VI, "At the Opening of the Second Session of the Vatican Council (*Salvete, Fratres*)," *The Pope Speaks* 9, 2 (1964), 128.

[8] Pope John XXIII, "The Council—At the Threshold of a New Era (*Gaudet Mater Ecclesia*)," *TPS* 8, 3 (1963), 212f.

[9] Pope Paul VI, loc cit.

[10] Ibid.

[11] Pope John XXIII, op. cit., 213.

fluidity of human speech and of developments in the history of ideas, but be unable to provide the substitute expressions that will serve for the next five hundred years. It is the task of theologians, both bishops in council and others working privately, to hammer out terms like "consubstantial," "transubstantiation" and "primacy of jurisdiction," which see service for a millennium or so. The Christian reality behind the terms cannot change. The human expressions themselves cannot be expected to survive.

Because of this radical fluidity of expression the catechist is always safest in instructing in terms of the bible. There will be times when a cultural phenomenon from the ancient Near East will not say much to moderns, modern children especially. Certain religious concepts are elusive for our contemporaries, such as eschatological thought of any sort or "totality-thinking" (e.g. human solidarity in guilt and innocence). In general, though, the biblical revelation is couched in basic language and ideas available to the majority of men. The great building blocks of God's dealings with his people are death and life, light and darkness; water, sky, earth, fire; joy, peace, anger, hatred, forgiveness. One does not get very far away from these ideas in catechizing, and one takes flight in "person," "nature," "species," "preternatural," "near occasion" only in pursuit of subtle heretics who have been there first.

It would be foolish to say that the bible yields its meaning to the man of good will at a single reading. Obviously it does not. An even less meaningful mode of speech than the biblical is of little help in understanding the bible, however. That is why the theological component of catechizing (which is something analytical, discursive, in its essence) contributes little to a biblical understanding already available.

"He who eats my flesh and drinks my blood will not taste death forever" is the starting-point of a thousand eucharistic difficulties. It is also the beginning and end of Catholic faith in the food for eternal life and pledge of bodily resurrection. The words

39

of Jesus have an evident and plain meaning antecedent to all subtle inflections that can be levied against them. When his words are said in the spirit of the Church's faith, by believers to believers, a thousand thousand heretics recede into the abyss of nothingness. A point comes fairly soon in the Christian child's existence when he does not need the help of the Gnostics, Arius, the Cathari, Hus, Zwingli, or the Lollards, to hear a saving truth or enunciate it.

He needs to have said in his hearing and himself say and sing:

—"My commandment is that you love one another as I have loved you."

—"If you love only those who love you, what reward can you expect? . . . And if you greet only your brothers, what is there extraordinary about that?"

—"I am the Lord. This land where you are I shall give you for you and your children. I shall protect you wherever you go."

—"The Lord is not in the wind . . . The Lord is not in the earthquake . . . The Lord is not in the fire . . . But after the fire a whistling, as of a gentle air."

—"Which one of the three was neighbor to the man who fell among robbers? . . . Then go and do as he did."

It does not help much to say that there would be little to choose among catechisms prepared for Catholic, Protestant, and Orthodox children if only the words of the Savior or of inspired scripture were provided as the answers to be memorized. This presumably is a benefit, not a drawback. From a Catholic standpoint, biblical faith and Catholic faith are indistinguishable. One does not promote the Catholic cause by alleging those matters "where Catholicity differs." This burden may be felt somewhere, but it should not lie on Catholic shoulders.

What, then, of development in faith: the necessary work of theology, the Church's many encounters with doubt and denial, the explications that have come with the centuries? Take questions and answers like the following, culled at random from the

French national catechism. Do they not reflect the Catholic reality better than quotations from Exodus or St. John's gospel?

199. What things are necessary to receive Confirmation worthily [*bien*]?

To receive Confirmation worthily, one must be in the state of grace and know the principal Christian truths.

260. What does it mean to gain an indulgence?

Gaining an indulgence means obtaining from God a lessening of the punishment we must undergo for our sins, or its complete removal.

It may not seem fair to choose questions such as the above for testing purposes. Others in the same catechism on confirmation and on penitential discipline are undoubtedly more biblical. The point is that questions like the above two abound in children's catechisms, and the problem posed by such books is not being faced unless they are taken into account. "Knowing the principal Christian truths" either is or is not a prerequisite for receiving the fullness of the gift of the Spirit. The Church's faith in indulgences either can or cannot be derived from biblical sources.

Let us affirm unequivocally that the first matter is in the realm of western Church discipline. The second is a doctrinal question of some importance (although not nearly so much importance as when this type of catechism was coming into full flower). And both matters could profit immeasurably by having better questions substituted for the ones asked.

Is this, then, a plea for questions that can be answered exclusively in biblical terms?

In effect, yes. A given response may of course be a coupling of biblical texts, or a "human" answer framed in a biblical paraphrase, or if it concerns some twentieth-century problem like housing or nuclear war, a straightforward response in a biblical spirit. In any case, when we speak God's Word to children in terms other than those he uses to address us, we do so at our peril. We should beware the pitfalls that surround the attempt. Infidelity to his Word lurks on every hand.

41

He is not trying to catch us at doctrinal inexactness, needless to say; we need not fear that. But the folly of preferring our words to his should strike us very forcibly. As things stand, it does not seem to occur to us at all. In the delicate business of determining what verbal "sacraments" shall stay in memory for a lifetime as signs of the reality of God's love for us, we need to have an anxious care about any attempts at improving on the divine gift.

The Holy Spirit has said: "My God, you know me to my depths. You know when I sit down and when I stand; from afar off you read my thoughts" (Psalm 138). A real obduracy of spirit is required to prefer: "God *does* know all things, even our most secret thoughts, words and actions."

We have expressed a strong preference for the Word of God over human words, going on the assumption that students will be asked to commit some living speech to memory always. The assumption is a correct and a good one. It is the tucking safely in the fissures of the cortex verbal formulas that once were living but now are dead, or that never lived, that is the wasteful procedure. "Oh, but they will mean something to them one day." As the French say, it is able to be. But it is not worth chancing. Teach children words that are spirit and life, and they will mean something to them one day because they mean something to them now.

Should, then, a question elicit the divine Word in every case? For example: "What did Jesus promise to those who would receive him in the Holy Eucharist?" "He who eats of this bread shall not taste death forever." Or: "What was the prayer of Jesus in the garden?" "Father, if it be possible, let this cup pass from me. Nevertheless, not my will but yours be done."

Again, we hope we have not prejudged the issue by inept examples. The difficulty is, once it is decided that a living Word of the Savior should fittingly be part of a Christian's mental fabric throughout his life, any cue or stimulus decided upon to elicit it seems hollow and contrived. In fact, Christ said these things in specific situations in his own life. They should be learned in the context of those situations. Then he may, equally in fact, say them to us in numberless situations in our own lives. To learn them as pat answers to questions the child has not asked (i.e. difficulties he has not experienced) may destroy forever the possibility of God's speaking to him when he needs to hear him.

The last step in our inquiry involves asking why, ultimately, a child's catechism must be God's living speech put into the context of his life. It is too shallow to say: "The scriptures are inspired. We should esteem them." It does not change the argument to speak about a two-edged sword that cuts to the point where joints and marrow, soul and spirit meet. What is the intrinsic reason that biblical speech is the great "type" of God's Word addressed to man?

The answer is that Christian theology and catechizing are reflections on what God has done in human history; but what he has done at a certain peak of importance in our history is testified to in the scriptures. As he acted before, so will he act again. As he came to meet humanity in the person of his Son Jesus, so will he meet each of us, and we him. There will be encounter only because there has been encounter, and on precisely the same terms. The child cannot discover God unless he develops some sense of how men have met him before.

To say that Jesus is Lord, or that God is all-powerful and all-merciful, is to say very little. Rather, all it is to do is *say* something. What did Jesus *do* that made the early Church experience his Lordship? How did the Israelites see Yahweh in action so that they said: "Our God is power. All his ways are mercy."?

Biblical theology is recital of God's mighty acts for our salvation, not a philosophical presentation of the attributes of the divine Being. God is known by what he has done, and the proclamation of what he has done is the basis of Christian theology.[12]

[12] Alan Richardson, *The Bible in the Age of Science,* Philadelphia 1961, 139f.

43

When we say that the essential character of the bible is historical witness, we do not thereby escape the perils of abstractness in catechizing. A dull historical recital can be as meaningless to youth as a revelling in formulas. Witness the general ineffectiveness of lessons in "bible history." Conversely, catechetics or dogmatic theology *can* be brought to life by translating biblical faith into the nonbiblical language of another age.[13] Neither will come alive, however, if the reality of God's action in the events of world history is set aside. He is the Lord of history. He is known by his acts. Any description of his divine *status* is somehow untrue to the God who has revealed himself by his *deeds*.

The Australian national catechism sees what is at issue here by entitling certain early lessons, "God Looks after Me," "God Loves Me," "My Father is the Holy God."[14] Even though the authors falter at times, they do depart consciously from any mere treatment of attributes and discuss God's activity in Israel's life and in the child's life. Interestingly, the second book (for upper elementary students) represents a decline. There we are back with "God All-Wise, Almighty," "God Holy and Just," and "The Living God," with static-type questions, and answers to match, though the lessons are in with biblical material and could be salvaged by being pulled inside-out like a fractious coatsleeve.[15]

Yet there is a difficulty deeper still which keeps catechisms from speaking God's Word to his people. It is the supposition—largely unspoken but no less real because of that—that biblical language is unsatisfactory because poetic, symbolic, figurative. There is a better mode of human expression, in this hypothesis. It is the language of analysis followed by concepts in synthesis, an improvement on that untidy universe where all reality is described in terms of breath, life, water, the cross, presence, glory.

[13] G. Ernest Wright, *God Who Acts,* London 1952, 108.
[14] *Catholic Catechism,* Book One, Issued and Prescribed for Use in the Catholic Schools of Australia by the Australian Hierarchy, 1st September 1962, Sydney 1962, 15–24.
[15] Ibid., Book Two, 1st September 1963, 23–29.

44

God will almost surely fail of his purpose in speaking to us as he has done (it is thought). Therefore we take precautions at our early opportunity. We hope to hear his message faithfully by translating it into a quite different set of categories than the ones he uses in addressing us.

Yet any such assumption is, prima facie, *not* the one in possession. Surely he is God and knows what he is about. The language of human propositions which transmit the content of the biblical revelation is simply another set of verbal symbols. Is it so clear that we men will have a firmer grasp on the symbols we choose than the ones he chooses?

Yes, we say, but we *fix* our meanings. "Substance" means thus and so, neither more nor less, whereas "Son" and "Father"— analogies with the human situation in the first place—can mean anything and nothing. They are, of their nature, "error-prone."

Recall why it was that definition and distinction were necessary in the first place, why recourse was had to nonbiblical terms like *ousía, hypóstasis* and *hénōsis:* infidelity to the Word of God, a departure from the clear meaning the biblical words had when they were read out and listened to in faith in the Church.

The reader should not suppose that a case is being made here against the Church's need for theology. Ignorance of the true nature of God's Word has spawned heresies without number; subtlety in orthodox faith is needed to respond adequately to subtle denial. Nonetheless, the language of the biblical revelation, although marked by historical particularity, is also universal:

. . . not . . . in the sense of enunciating philosophical generalizations about the world and human nature at large, but in the sense that it is relevant to the predicament of every individual person coming into the world . . . who is . . . aware of himself as in rebellion against the purpose for which he exists . . . a creature whose mortality . . . creates in him that anxiety which [is] the symptom of his estrangement from his own true being and destiny . . . The biblical symbols possess truth because they are universally adequate to the religious situation in which

45

they were created. They "speak to the condition" of men in all lands, and in every age of history, including the age of science.[16]

We must have strong Catholic faith in that idea, stronger faith in the bible than in the creeds, councils, and catechisms that derive their power of utterance from it. We must, in a word, have a rebirth of trust in those biblical images of speech which reflect the divine deeds described in the holy books.

Q. Well, shall we then have catechisms or shall we not?

A. If we have the right kind we shall have them; otherwise we shall not.

Q. (Weakly) The right kind?

A. Yes, made up of the bible chiefly, and scaled down to little people's speech without a qualm, where necessary.

Q. Any questions?

A. Probably not. Just answers to questions that are skillfully made to come up, by the catechist.

Q. Any other requirements?

A. Great art. Terribly important. Oh! that means graphic art that conveys both the transcendent and the demonic, and literary art of an equally high order. That means lots of children's catechisms. No fixed national museum of formulas.

Q. Who, pray, will write these catechisms?

A. Readers of *Pastoral Catechetics,* whether as yet born or unborn. God knows.

[16] Richardson, op. cit., 156; see also A. M. Farrer, *A Rebirth of Images,* London 1944.

Liturgical Sign

Liturgy and Catechetics: Inseparable Partners

WILLIAM SHERZER

As long as people have been able to think, they have wondered and worried about the attitude toward them of the power that controls the universe. All the ancient offerings and sacrifices were efforts to learn the mind of the lords of all things toward us here in this world. At length God speaks a word—Christ, and we learn that God is love, that God is favorably inclined toward us, that he is inviting the whole human race to enter into new relationships of love with him. This revelation of God's paternal love, this invitation to everlasting union is renewed daily in the liturgy.

The work of the Church is carried on through catechetics and liturgy, which are closely related but not the same. Catechetics tells us about the gift which is Christ, liturgy actually gives us the Savior. In the former we learn what it means to be a Christian, in the latter we are made Christians. Catechetics then is the servant of liturgy. If catechetics plays its role in the Church effectively, the Christian comes into the liturgy prepared to gain what Christ is waiting there to give him. The Christian is born at holy baptism, but birth is not the whole life; it is only a beginning. The infant has before him a long process of growth which will take place through liturgy. He must grow to a maturity of faith, hope and love; and if he does not so grow he remains religiously childish. If his faith, hope and charity are childish he will not come to the fullness of manhood in Christ which is God's plan for him. Faith, hope and love

48

which are exercised in liturgy will bring religious maturity; but liturgy cannot serve this purpose unless the Christian has been prepared by catechetics to find in liturgy what is there for him; that is, to find Christ.

Because faith has to function upon a known object, man cannot believe in God until he knows God. Thus if a man does not know what is revealed in liturgy, if liturgy is only a holy blur, a something out of focus, then it will not serve his faith. Faith develops by exercise, and it is exercised chiefly by his participation in the sacramental actions of the Church.

Again, hope cannot develop through liturgy unless the Christian understands that he meets in the liturgy Jesus, his mediator, the One who takes away the sins of the world. How can the Christian have confidence in a salvation he does not recognize? Once we know that our Lord is acting in the liturgy right here and now to save us from our sins, we can grow in hope by renewing at Mass our confidence and trust in his living purpose to preserve us.

Furthermore, since the sacred liturgy is the sacramentalization of the death and rising of the Lord who gave himself unto death for love of us, it constantly challenges us to answer this love with love; to escape imprisonment in our little egoism, pettiness, selfishness; to turn from self to God and neighbor; to make God's interests paramount in our lives rather than our own; to enlarge our hearts until there is room in them for all those gathered with us at the altar and even for all those throughout the Church who are one with us in faith, charity and hope.

Jesus, Our Priest

The liturgy of the holy Catholic Church begets sons and daughters to the heavenly Father and makes us brothers of Jesus and of all our fellows who have also been reborn of water and the Holy Spirit; and it gives foundation to our hopes for eternal life. In the liturgy Jesus Christ, now risen from death, saves us by sharing with us his conquest of hell, sin and the grave. By his own passage through death to the new life of the resurrection he has broken the power of Satan; and Christ's power to destroy our sin and renew our life, the power of his death and resurrection is at work in the liturgy of the Church. The sacraments are signs, signs of death and new life, signs both of the passage of the Lord through death to life and of the passage of the Christian people, his followers, from the kingdom of Satan into the kingdom of God—which the preface of the feast of Christ the King tells us is an everlasting kingdom of truth and life, of holiness and grace, of justice, love and peace. The priest does not offer *his* Mass or sit in *his* confessional; rather the priest is the instrument of Christ so that Christ offers the Mass and Christ sits in the confessional. The pen does not write; the man writes. The ambassador does not act in his own name or of himself; he acts in the name of the president and by presidential authority. Christ is not locked into the historical past; but what he did in Palestine—die and rise, ascend, and send the Holy Spirit—all these events of our redemption he continues in the twentieth century Church by sacred symbolizations of these precise saving events of his own life. These symbolizations are of course the sacraments. Through the sacraments our Lord acts to destroy sin in us and to raise us to the life of grace; he raises us to a participation in the very life of heaven; he sends the Holy Spirit. We want our students to believe that baptism has been for them an act of the living, risen Lord sharing with them his victory over death and hell; that the Eucharist is an act of the same Lord uniting us to himself and through himself uniting us to the heavenly Father; that confirmation is Christ imparting to us the supreme gift of his Spirit; that marriage is Christ creating among us a living sign in husband and wife of that wondrous union that binds Jesus to his Body, the Church; that holy orders is the action of Christ making men living symbols of the invisible Lord and forming out of sinful men his personal instruments of salvation for the human race; that penance is the loving act of the merciful Christ who restores his brothers to their place in the family of their common Father. Truly the sacraments are not things to be received, but sacramental renewals and continuations of those very actions of the Lord which had their historical occurrence nineteen centuries ago in Judea. Since the holy signs which are the sacraments of the Church are therefore actions of our Lord himself, we say that they will inevitably bring us the gifts of mercy which they promise if we will only approach and enter into these holy actions, these holy meetings with our Savior with real openness to God, with faith, trust and love. It is the work of catechetics to serve the faith of the Christian, to bring it to maturity, by explaining to him the liturgical texts and signs so that he may profit fully from these sacred actions; to form his attitudes of reverence, gratitude, to stir his sense of mystery, to awaken his sense of membership in the community of the Church.

Levels of Meaning

These catechetical tasks are taken up by the Christian teacher who shows his students that each liturgical action, especially each sacrament, has three levels of meaning: the natural, the Old Testament and the Christian. The responsible catechist will explain baptism by clarifying the relevant natural meanings of water: to wash, to irrigate, to drown. For baptism does contain these natural significances. It does wash, cleanse, purify us from sin; it does bring new life to men; it does drown the "old man" of sin and bring us to the new life in Christ. The catechist will go on to unfold the Old Testament events which pre-figure baptism: the water of the Red Sea which slew the evil men of Egypt and saved the people of God; the water Moses drew from the desert rock—again a means of rescue and salvation. For baptism does contain these scriptural significances since through its holy washing we do pass from the kingdom of Satan into

51

the kingdom of Christ, from slavery to sin into the freedom of the sons of God wherewith Christ has made us free. The water of baptism is a miraculous saving fountain springing up in the desert of this world at the command of Jesus, the new Moses. The teacher must then go on to show that the central New Testament event, the saving death and resurrection of Jesus Christ, is also symbolized by the sacramental water which signifies our death to sin and that world which is the enemy of God by burying us in the water, and which signifies our salvation and renewal of life by bringing us forth as if from a watery grave.

The effective catechist will take his students to a baptism in the parish church in order to add this concrete experience to the learning process. He will connect the asperges rite and the holy water basin at the door of the church with baptism and urge the student always to use the holy water with a deep sense of gratitude for his faith and membership in the Church, for his hope of heaven. He will point out the tradition among us that our baptisms take place on Sunday, the day of the resurrection of the Lord; he will make sure that the student realizes the relationship between baptism, Sunday and the resurrection. The instructor in divine truth will explain to the student how baptism gives us God as our Father, the Church as our mother, Christ as our brother, the Holy Spirit as our friend and protector, and all our fellow Christians as our brothers too. He will help his pupils to understand that only the baptized may come into the eucharistic assembly of the Church since only the sons and daughters of the heavenly Father have the right to sit at his table and partake of the holy food. He will point out that the new life given us by God at baptism can only grow to maturity through multiplied acts of faith, trust and love directed toward God and through a constant sacrificial, loving service to our fellows. He will not permit his students to pass from his care without realizing that the true motive for having oneself baptized or for bringing one's children to the saving waters is filial love and gratitude to God for his wondrous offer of mercy for our sins and of friendship with himself. Too often we have allowed ourselves to think that the motive for baptism is simply to keep the canon law which lays the legal obligation upon parents to see to the prompt baptism of their children.

Similarly the modern teacher of religion will make his students aware of the natural, OT and NT meanings of eating a meal, of anointing with oil, of the imposition of hands, of the marriage union. For this awareness is essential for a true understanding of the other sacraments. He must be especially careful to provide this treatment to the Eucharist for this is the sacrament which many Christians participate in daily and which all Christians deserving of the name participate in Sunday after Sunday. And the faith of the people will develop by meeting Christ in this great sign of his and his Father's love only if for them the eucharistic meal is truly a recognizable sign unsurpassably rich with its triple meanings of natural food, the manna of exodus and the death and resurrection of the Savior.

Mass as Transformation

The Mass is not simply a way in which Christ becomes present. And yet if some Catholics are asked: "What happens at Mass?" they will say that our Lord becomes present, that the bread and wine are transformed into the body and blood of Christ. A further question then has to be asked: "Why? Why is he present?" "Why is he come?" Catechetics has to show the Christian that Christ is in the Eucharist to work a transformation in us, that the action of Christ is not just to come and to be there as if that were the end of it. He is come to change you and me.

We then go on to ask: "How does he change us?" That the action he is performing is one of change is clear from the fact that the bread and wine are changed into the body and blood of Christ; this is sacrament, this is symbol; so that if the bread

53

and wine are changed into the body and blood of Christ, this also tells us what is happening to us. We too must be changed into men of God, into Christ; the action of the Mass is not just to transform bread and wine: it is to transform people, and those people by the Mass itself are given the task of transforming families and transforming places of work, places of recreation. The task that the Mass places upon us is a work of transformation, a going out from it to transform the world in which we have to live. But this transformation that is symbolized to us by the changing of bread and wine into the body and blood of Christ is seen in all its implications only when drawn out by catechetics. The people must not think that the whole transformation is complete at the consecration. They have to see that they must be changed and that, if they leave the Mass without being changed into better men of greater faith, hope and charity, then the Mass has not achieved its full purpose in them, even though it is true that Christ did become present. Furthermore they have to see that if they leave the church and go out to their homes and the world and their homes and the world are not places of greater faith, hope and charity, then again the Mass has not achieved its full purpose.

Now this transformation is fundamentally a changing of minds and thoughts so that people will think what God wants them to think, so that they will have God's outlook on life and its problems. It is a work of transforming their hope so that their hope will not be in money, in worldly success, prestige, power. Their hope is in Christ; their hope is in what God offers, not in what the world offers. They are transformed by becoming men whose hearts are open to God and open to other people. And this is the work of the Mass; this is what the Mass is saying to them; this is what the Mass is accomplishing in us: we have to be transformed and are being transformed in mind and heart and principles.

It is the work of catechetics to let us see that this communion meal is not a cafeteria situation, just a group of individuals being fed, but that it is a family being fed by its own Father. Now this truth has earth-shaking implications. For then we see that this holy communion is not only union with God, but besides it is communion with everyone else present; it is communion with the whole Church; it is union with the communion of saints; and, potentially, it is communion with the whole human race. Unless the people have been taught through catechetics to realize this in the communion, there remains the anomaly of good Catholics going to Mass, receiving holy communion daily and still harboring racial prejudice, resentments, not understanding that these are incompatible with the Eucharist, not understanding that the action of receiving holy communion is a profession of our belief in the unity of mankind in Christ. Many of our people simply do not see this relationship, and so until catechetics does its job the liturgy cannot do its job. One has to be prepared for participation in the sacred rites of the Church in order to be transformed by them.

Finally we must realize that the communion implies that we be concerned about the problems of the world, especially the spiritual problems, especially the problem of men not knowing God, but beyond that the other problems that have to be solved if men are even going to listen to men of God. And so the whole social apostolate of the Church is contained, at least by implication, in the social act of communion, and our people have to be helped to understand this. They must be led to realize that the "Ite missa est" at the end of Mass is a mission; it is a true commissioning of men to go out into the world and to do this work of transformation. It is a true commission to men to go out and live their prophetic role given by confirmation. Unless they see the "Ite missa est" in this way they will only think it a signal that everything is all over and that "Deo gratias" is just a "thanks to God that it is all over—now I can go home." Yet the meaning of this phrase is truly profound. At solemn Mass it is sung so solemnly because it is a most solemn moment. It is like the moment in a missionary society when people are given their mission crosses, given their mission assignments. The Church is here assigning her people to go out and transform the world, to be the leaven that will remake the world. Yet most of our people walk out with little sense that the Church has placed on them an apostolic mission. Most Catholics do not leave the church with the idea that there is some unfinished business that they have to get busy about because catechetics has not made this clear to them. Even men of good will do not understand their Christian role.

True Worship Is Personal Worship

The Catholic religion with its many ceremonies, its use of exotic religious clothing and its Latin language unintelligible to the worshipers is very liable to misunderstanding. Ever present is the possibility that our people will stop at the point where true worship begins. This danger is realized when Catholics think of the liturgy as the action of God without understanding that it is also the action of the Church—that is to say, the action of each member of the Church. We have a multitude of believers who do not think it strange that they do not answer the priest at Mass when he speaks directly to them; who do not think it strange to hear the word of God read to them in a language they do not understand; who do not think it strange to accept the heavenly Father's invitation to the sacred meal which is the Mass without any intention at all of partaking of the holy food there set before them for eating. A sound catechetical program will try very diligently to make clear to our people that we must take our proper part in the liturgical prayers which accompany each sacrament, that we must hear the word of God intelligibly, that we must receive the body and blood of the Lord if we are truly to participate in the eucharistic sacrifice. The Christian people must pray, not just watch the priest pray; must hear the word of God, not just watch the priest read it to himself; must share in the holy communion, not just watch the priest consume the sacred food.

The statement that the sacrifice of the Mass is the same sacrifice as that of the cross because both have the same priest and the same victim is very much in need of important qualifications. On the cross our Lord acted alone. In the Mass our Lord acts in union with the whole Church. On the cross Christ was dying; at Mass Christ is risen and immortal. At Mass the whole Church is both priest and victim; on calvary our Lord alone was priest and victim, or perhaps we should say our Lord and his holy Mother . . . in whatever sense the Church will finally come to understand the union of Son and Mother in the redemptive action on calvary.

If the liturgy is to develop and to bring to maturity the Christian's faith, hope and love, the believer must be provoked by the liturgy to profound acts of belief, of trust and of service. To participate in the liturgy is to give over oneself to self-sacrificing service of God and of the human family. And our daily living, if it is Christian living, is simply a sincere day-to-day effort to see life as God sees it, to put our hope for happiness in God rather than in sin and worldliness, to sacrifice ourselves for others rather than sacrificing others for ourselves. Thus true Christian living confirms and tests the sincerity of the liturgical prayer of the Catholic.

Covenant and Commitment

The catechist then wishes the student to involve himself with Christ and with Christ appreciated as brother, friend and Savior each time he enters upon an act of holy liturgy. The teacher wants his pupil to know that sacraments are not received but are acted. Christ is there to offer us mercy for our repented sins and his friendship. The Christian is there believing, trusting, loving and accepting the gracious offer of divine largess. What now are we really saying except that each act of liturgy is for the believing participant a renewal of the new and eternal covenant between God the Father and his Church, his people, which exists through the reconciling death and resurrection and ascension of Jesus Christ? In covenant God and man meet in mutual self-giving. Thus on Sinai God gave himself to the Jews as their God and Moses and his followers gave themselves to God as his people. This mosaic covenant was sealed with sacrifice, and memorialized forever in the book of Exodus. After Sinai the Jews knew themselves as a people who had covenanted with God, who had promised with solemn rites to keep his law. When the student has read Exodus he has some background to bring to his wrestling with the words of the consecration of the Mass: the new and eternal covenant. Now the student can more readily be led to know himself as a man who also has covenanted with God. The birth, death, resurrection, ascension of Jesus and his sending the Spirit-comforter to us are a divine proclamation to men of God as father, lover, friend. Jesus has given us the law of the new covenant by which those faithful to the covenant will be able to be recognized; this, the Christian law, is simply love. The sincere Christian man has not yet solved his problem of self-identity until he knows himself as a man involved in covenant with God which can only be kept by constant positive sacrificial love of God and man. The modern religious teacher, parent or professional, will ask himself whether his students yet know that their baptism has made them members of a holy people and partners with God himself in a covenant of charity; whether they yet know that the Eucharist offered and received—in fact every act of liturgy—is an explicit renewal of the Christian covenant-pact.

The Two-Headed Monster

What we are trying to say is that liturgy helps us to avoid legalism and formalism by demanding of us the personal gift of self. Once we begin to understand the liturgy and to participate lovingly with our Lord in his Church in its sacred actions, we no longer come to baptism, to confession, to Mass or keep the fasts of the Church only out of a sense of law. Rather we come to baptism because we desire union with God; we come to confession because we cannot stand the thought of being estranged from our Father in heaven; we come to Mass because our filial devotion makes us unwilling to spurn the invitation of our Father to come with great joy to the festal meal at which we will celebrate the victory, over hell and death, of our brother, God's Son. For we sense that this victory is our victory, and this cause for joy is our cause for joy. We come to pledge again our loyalty, our love; gratefully aware of God's breathtaking favor, we come to give thanks. And the fasts of the Church are neither unpleasant duties nor stoic heroics but gestures of sorrow, repentance and reparation.

Again, to participate knowingly and lovingly in the sacred liturgy is to move beyond a semi-Christian worship which contents itself with the perfection of ceremonial and glories in the dramatic effects of elaborate ritual. Such participation would mean an end to communionless Masses, to lengthy opaque forms, to Masses without preaching, to excesses in vesture. In other words an end to mere formalism from which the Spirit has been long departed.

In our catechetical proclamation of Jesus Christ we must contend with and overcome the two-headed monster of legalism and formalism. The saving of men by the death and resurrection of our Lord is the great central event of history, and the Church within which salvation reaches us is both mother and teacher. Laws, forms, definitions, rules and reasons have their place in the life of the Church, but they must not obscure her mission given by her divine Savior and Head to speak to all who will listen the glad tidings of great joy that there has been born for us a Savior which is Christ the Lord; that death and sin are vanquished; that there is hope; that Jesus is truly risen, the first-fruits of them that sleep. But the catechist will teach the

59

child that Christianity is a message of hope, redemption and joy with too little effect if the liturgical life of the parish church does not reinforce the picture given the child in the classroom. The Catholic child should learn in class that Sunday is the joyful weekly celebration of the defeat of death and of Satan by the Head of the Church, but the child should also experience the joy of the resurrection-victory in the joy of the parish Sunday Mass. The decorations of the church, the adorned altar, the flowers, the candles, the lights, the exultant music, the theme of the homily should impress the child that this is truly a great day of great glory and great joy. In parishes in which Mass is offered in silence with no songs or acclamations from the people, in which two and three collections are taken up within a half-hour period, in which the sermons are rather like classroom instructions or are commentaries upon the morals of the congregation, it will be difficult to teach the children their religion as joyful good news.

Education in Prayer as Preparation for Liturgy

Again, catechetics has an important task to perform in preparing the child for liturgical prayer. The teacher by his awe-filled reverent manner of speaking of God and of all holy things, by his care in making the sign of the cross, in genuflecting, in bowing his head at the holy name, by his way of holding his hands and head while praying, of handling the rosary, religious statues and pictures conveys to his pupils a sense of reverence without which there is no sincere prayer. By acting with reverence we teach reverence. At Mass we have the child stand for the entrance of the celebrant and for the gospel, kiss the sacred text after the scripture reading, kneel, bow and adore at the consecration, walk to the altar for holy communion with solemnity, remain in prayer for a few moments after Mass. In addition we want the child to learn to respect the image of God in each human fellow. Accordingly we help him to see God in black and white, yellow man and brown man, to see in each man his brother—especially those who are of the household of the faith. To learn to reverence God without learning to reverence man is to falsify our religious life. The teacher must teach respect for man by respecting the dignity of each child before him. We cannot teach love except by loving.

For a true liturgical prayer man must bring a sense of his debt to God. The classroom helps create in the child this attitude of gratitude by leading him in an expression of his thanks to God as part of the lessons on the incarnation and the redemption. The teacher moves from formal explanation of doctrine into prayer of thanksgiving in order that the student may learn to raise his heart in thanks to God whenever he hears mention of the great saving events accomplished by the Father through Jesus Christ. Each time the child sees the crucifix sentiments of praise and thanks spontaneously arise within him if he has been well taught. Only then can he transfer his grateful response to the message of mercy as spoken by his teacher and to the sacred image of crucified love to the sacramental proclamation of this same message and renewal of this same image—the Eucharist—the Mass. To the child prepared by his teacher for the experience of liturgical worship the great eucharistic action almost inevitably provokes his faith to express itself in an outpouring of thanks to God.

Our teaching on thanksgiving must not stop with arousing a sense of gratitude for such blessings as good homes and parents, health and opportunity; rather the child must always be brought to see that even the boy who has few opportunities, little money, no parents and no home still has reason to give thanks to God. For he too has been saved from his sins, from hell, from death. Gratitude is not fulfilled by a casual "thanks a lot" to a benefactor. The virtue of gratitude is present only when we remember what has been done for us, when we reciprocate favor for favor. Gratitude does not forget and looks for a way to respond with more than words. The child who has learned the full meaning of thanks will find it natural enough that the Eucharist is our great way of remembering what Christ has done for us and of offering the return gift of ourselves to the Lord who gave himself for us.

Again, since what is done will be more influential than what is said, both in doing and saying we must stress that Christian prayer is a word spoken to the heavenly Father through Jesus Christ and in the Holy Spirit. For this is the way the liturgy prays. Even on the great marian feasts of the assumption and of the immaculate conception the Church begins the prayer of the day "O God" and does not address the Blessed Virgin directly. If the child hears only "Hail Marys" before and after class he will not be prepared for the liturgy. Classroom prayer and instruction ought to be to the Father, through the Son, in the Holy Spirit, and with the Blessed Mother and the saints. Perhaps our idiomatic use of the phrase "to pray to the saints" could with benefit to us all be changed to "pray with the saints." For is not all prayer really to God?

If our children are to enter the eucharistic congregation of the Church attuned to the spirit of the occasion, they must come to Mass with a sense of mystery unimpaired by overly rationalistic teaching. At times we may have given the child excuse for thinking that everything can be explained in the categories of human logic. An over-enthusiastic apologetics course can leave the child with a diminished awareness of his need for faith. We must confront the child early in life with the fact that man cannot comprehend God. My ways are not your ways, says God. How incomprehensible his judgments, how unsearchable his ways, says St. Paul.

A further point: our classroom teaching must give to the student a sense of his membership in the Church. He is not an isolated man with an individual connection to God. Rather he is a child of a family of which God is the Father, in which all Christians are brothers, of which the holy Church is mother; the parish church is the place of family gatherings in the house of

62

the Father; the altar is the family table at which the Father feeds us all. We do not pray alone ever. . . . We always pray with and in the Church. Jesus always prays with us as do all the company of heaven and all the Church on earth. By encouraging the children to bring their personal needs to the prayerful attention of the whole class, we develop a sense of ourselves as a family of God with all the mutual responsibilities of brother for brother. Only when this teaching has been presented successfully will the child be ready for liturgy. For liturgical prayer is always the prayer of the community, of Christ and his brothers.

Use of Liturgical Texts

A final matter in our discussion of relating catechetics to liturgy is that the very texts of the missal and the ritual have to become material for catechetical instruction. We cannot teach people about Mass in the abstract only; we have to lead them into the missal and show them that these truths are expressed and lived there.

As an example let us take the first prayer of the canon of the Mass which starts out "Te igitur, clementissime Pater." Here the child learns to see God as the "clementissime Pater," the most kind, most loving Father. This is the way the Church speaks of God to the child. The missal goes on: "per Jesum Christum, Filium tuum Dominum nostrum." These words are packed with meaning! Through Jesus Christ, who is your Son, who is therefore related to God and therefore our Lord. The whole incarnation! "We pray you and beseech you that you will accept our gifts." We must make clear to the child the symbolism of giftgiving. What does it mean to give a gift to somebody? How is it that our own heart and self have to be involved in giftgiving?

Now these sacrifices that we offer are for the whole Church. Thus the rest of the prayer brings out the unity of the Church! "Grant her peace and unity." Who? The holy father and the bishop are mentioned. Well, are we truly Catholic if we are not in peace and communion with our bishop? If we are not in peace and communion with our bishop we are not Catholics, and if we are not in peace and communion with the apostolic see of Rome we are not Catholics. We have endless groups of people who say Mass and go through all kinds of Catholic ceremonies, sprinkle holy water, and give benediction, and hear confessions, but they are not Catholics because they are not united with the apostolic see of Rome. Here it is, right here in the missal, that the unity of the Church is our unity with Rome and with our bishop. Right here are the marks of the Church: unity, apostolicity, catholicity, holiness. If these texts are not studied the child may read them through often but quite miss their meaning.

Take also the prayer after the consecration. It starts out "Unde et memores," and from this prayer the child learns that we are remembering something. Who is? We! Your servants and your holy people: the notion of the Christian as a member of a special people. What are we doing? We are calling to mind the passion of Christ, your Son, our Lord, his resurrection, his ascension. So we are calling to mind the "mirabilia Dei," the great deeds of our salvation. (This is similar to the Jew's calling to mind of their delivery out of Egypt and slavery.) Then the prayer says: ". . . we offer to your supreme majesty . . . of the gifts you have bestowed on us." Next we offer *what?* "Christ the unblemished victim, the sacred bread and the chalice of everlasting salvation." And it goes on in the following prayers to bring out the whole mediation of Christ: ". . . that these gifts may be carried to the altar on high and that all of us who shall receive the most precious body and blood of your Son may be filled with every heavenly gift and blessing." This means that if we do not partake (to turn it around) we will not receive "every heavenly gift and blessing." Thus the child can be impressed with the necessity of communion right from this prayer itself: that those who *partake* will be filled with every heavenly gift and blessing, not those who just *come.* If the child begins to see this

64

truth he begins to see the Mass as a meal. He begins to see how improper it is to accept this invitation to dinner and then to refuse to eat when he arrives there. One just does not do this sort of thing. And so if the Christian has come to a sacred meal to which God has invited him, he does not refuse to eat. If there is a liturgical answer that should be given to the question of why we should receive holy communion when we come to Mass, it is that it will not only do us good but that the very logic of the Mass demands eating. For if the Mass is a sacred meal to which God invites us then the conclusion is quite evident: one does not receive an invitation to dinner and then refuse to eat when one arrives there.

Liturgy is a great help to catechetics but catechetics is an indispensable help to the liturgy. The treasures that liturgy contains cannot profit the people, and their faith, hope and charity cannot come to maturity, unless catechetics prepares them for worship, gives them a right perspective and approach and takes them beyond a legalistic, impersonal, formalistic religion that all our people will admit does not transform them and does not lead them to any sense of urgency about transforming the world around them.

Witness Sign

Role of Witness in Transmitting the Message

ALFONSO NEBREDA S.J.

Introduction

THE New Testament expresses the Lord's missionary command in three diverse ways. According to Mark, Christ said: "Preach the gospel to every creature" (Mk 16:16). Matthew expresses the command in the following words: "Go, therefore, and make disciples of all nations" (Mt 28:19). Luke offers another formula: "You shall be witnesses for me" (Acts 1:8). Despite three modes of expression these texts are complementary. Christ's command is to announce a message (Mark) which aims at making disciples (Matthew) and which consists in bearing witness (Luke).

If we analyze the best record of primitive evangelization, the Acts of the Apostles, we will immediately detect how witness remains at the core of the transmission of the message. The Acts of the Apostles forcefully presents two types of witness: the direct witness of the apostles and indirect witness of the community and of individual Christians. The apostles witnessed by *word* under the strength and guidance of the Spirit:

> And when they had prayed, the place where they had assembled was shaken, and they were all filled with the Holy Spirit, and spoke of God with boldness (Acts 4:31; cf. 1:8; 4:19–20; 10:33).

In addition they witnessed by *signs* which confirmed the words:

> Now by the hands of the apostles many signs and wonders were done among the people. And with one accord they all would meet in Solomon's portice (Acts 5:12; cf. 2:43).

67

The persecutions accompanying such catechizing and especially the joy in accepting these trials belong intimately within this direct witnessing of the apostles.

> So they departed from the presence of the Sanhedrin, rejoicing that they had been counted worthy to suffer disgrace for the name of Jesus (Acts 5:41).

The indirect witness of the community, namely of those who obey the Spirit (cf. Acts 5:32) centers around the holy life, full of joy and charity, of the first Christians.

> And they continued steadfastly in the teaching of the apostles and in the communion of the breaking of the bread and in the prayers. And fear came upon every soul; many wonders also and signs were done by means of the apostles in Jerusalem, and great fear came upon all. And all who believed were together and held all things in common, and would sell their possessions and goods and distribute them among all according as anyone had need. And continuing daily with one accord in the temple, and breaking bread in their houses, they took their food with gladness and simplicity of heart, praising God and being in favor with all the people. And day by day the Lord added to their company such as were to be saved (Acts 2:42–47; cf. 4:32–35; 5:12–16).

This is the way the message was transmitted. The apostles preached the life-giving message and by it they were transformed. And the life of the Christian community confirmed this transformation by showing in action the meaning and power of the gospel.

Why is Christianity transmitted by witness? In order to understand the importance and implications of witness in today's transmission of the message, we propose to look at the problem from the three major points of view which constitute the frame of this book, namely *revelation:* God meeting man; *faith:* man meeting God; and thirdly, the problem of *transmission.*

Being a missionary the author might be permitted to present the role of witness mainly in terms of missionary approach.

Today we seem to be at the crossroads of a new missionary conception. The idea of missions is no longer restricted to foreign and home missions. Instead the whole Church is looked upon as being in the state of mission, in that she is to bear witness to Christ everywhere among those who do not believe.[1] So understood it is evident that the mission of the Church does not limit itself to so-called missionary countries, but covers the whole field of pastoral activity in the world. Concentrating on a richer concept of Christian faith which goes beyond mere holding of certain truths of revelation to a personal commitment involving the whole man, we are led to reexamine our pastoral methods among the many Christians who, although baptized, have never been led to make such a personal commitment. The recovery of this personal characteristic of faith, of which the Church becomes again more and more conscious through her missionary activity, is a constant reminder for pastors and catechists that special attention must be given to preparing the ground for the message, taking into account both the human elements for the faithful transmission of the divine message and the concrete situation of man in his response to God. This will be therefore the perspective from which we intend to examine the role of witness in the transmission of the message. Even in the case of *catechesis proper,*[2] which presupposes a personal global conversion, the main concern remains to stress the approach and ways of proceeding which help deepen that conversion. Conversion, after all, must be a permanent dimension of Christian existence.

[1] This and several other points raised in this article will be explained in further depth by Father Nebreda in his article in part two: "Living Faith: Major Concern of Religious Education"—ed.

[2] Three stages can be distinguished in the process of faith. The following terms used in this article and elsewhere in the book refer to these stages: *Pre-evangelization:* that stage in the process of faith which prepares the ground for conversion. *Evangelization:* that stage in the process of faith in which the kerygma is proclaimed. The person, already disposed, is challenged to accept Christ as the Lord and Savior. *Catechesis proper:* that stage in the process of faith which presupposes conversion and belief. Religious education for members of the Church commonly falls in this category.

1. REVELATION: GOD MEETING MAN

"Persons can be known only by revelation. We have no access to personal intimacy except through the free witness of the person. And persons do not witness of themselves but under the inspiration of love."[3]

It is against this background that we wish to explore the meaning of Christian revelation. God's revelation is not intended as cold information on a series of abstract truths. It is essentially the self-manifestation of his intimacy—the opening of his heart. Everything in Christian revelation can be summed up as follows: God reveals himself as the Father who in his Son through his Spirit invites us to share in his divine life. This is precisely what the theology of the New Testament, especially St. Paul, calls the mystery of Christ. The word mystery here does not mean a problem or a puzzle which baffles the intellect, stimulates and mortifies curiosity. It is a warm welcome inviting one to catch a glimpse of the intimacy of a *Person*.

More than by what we say do we reveal ourselves in our way of looking, in our tone of voice, in a gesture, in our whole behavior. The same applies to God. More than by his words he speaks to us through his wonderful deeds (mirabilia Dei), which culminate in his Word-Made-Flesh for us and for our salvation. Words have only a subsidiary role: explaining the sense of those deeds and especially the Person of his Son. In fact the content of revelation is but God's providential plan of salvation in Christ. And it is above all in realizing this plan that God reveals to us who he is and the communion to which he calls us.

Christianity then, centered and summed up in the mystery of Christ, is not a system, an objective interpretation of nature, a philosophy of life. It is essentially a message of salvation, the proclamation of the good tidings of God coming to us in Christ. No wonder that it can never be transmitted by mere

[3] R. Latourelle S.J.: "La revelation comme parole, temoignage et recontre," *Gregorianum* (1962), 48–49.

words. Values cannot be taught: they must be shown as operative in an incarnate witness. Christianity in its ultimate analysis is a Person—Christ. We do not enter into contact with a Person through words or arguments but by a phenomenon of communion.[4]

This insight shows already the importance of Christian witness in the transmission of the message. Witness, involving the whole personality, places man on the level of personal relations. It forces the modern positivistic mentality, which tends to reject speculation on ultimate origins, to confront Christianity as a fact. It leads him to discover the radical difference between the realm of things and the world of human beings, giving him a sense of the person which will bring him to face God as Someone rather than as a Something. This thought introduces us to a discussion of faith as man's personal answer to God's call.

2. FAITH: MAN MEETING GOD

The following recounts one of the most interesting experiences of my eight-year stay in Japan. For several hours one day I had been discussing religious ideas with an old Buddhist bonze[5] of a Zen monastery not far from Tokyo, when I asked him: "How do you manage to convey to your novices your spiritual ideas?" The venerable old monk smiled. "Thus far," he said in a typically polite Japanese way, "I have been admiring the excellence of your Japanese. If I were blind, it would have been difficult for me to tell that you were not Japanese. And yet this question of yours, even if I had been blind, would have immediately told me that you were a westerner. How can you transmit a religious experience in words? Only by a spiritual contact, by 'rubbing,' so to say, two persons with each other, will the disciple perceive the message...."

---

[4] This point as well as the personal structure of the act of faith has been masterly studied by J. Mouroux, *I Believe,* New York 1959. See also from the same author *From Baptism to the Act of Faith,* Boston 1963.

[5] Bonze: a Buddhist monk of the far east.

Never have I been given closer insight into the biblical meaning of the word knowledge. Only by purifying our western intellectualist conception of knowledge can we grasp the all-embracing humanism of biblical anthropology.[6] Eastern psychology, in which the different faculties in man are not so sharply distinguished but merged and blended in a more global and inclusive operation, is certainly closer to the concept of Old Testament "knowing." It casts a remarkable light on the words of our Lord recorded by St. John: "Now this is everlasting life, that they may know thee, the only true God, and him whom thou has sent, Jesus Christ" (Jn 17:3).

As far as pastoral theology is concerned, the emphasis on a richer conception of Christian faith is perhaps the most significant result of recent research.[7] Also in the field of catechetics the awareness of this deeper concept of faith has brought about definite progress: this emphasis moves from the object (what to believe) to the subject (how faith affects the believer both in mentality and behavior), finally concentrating on interpersonal communion between the believer and God.[8]

These three levels belong essentially to the knowledge of faith. Faith must be objective since it is concerned with the facts and truths which constitute divine revelation. This is why catechetics implies a task of *instruction* or information. Faith demands acceptance of a new hierarchy of values. For this reason catechetics also involves the role of *formation*—shaping a man's mentality and behavior into a Christian personality. But faith is above all an entering into that personal communion with God to which divine revelation invites man. This last definition points to the highest task of catechetics: *initiation* into the

[6] Biblical anthropology refers to culture, customs, physical and mental characteristics, etc.

[7] See the works of F. X. Arnold, especially *Dienst am Glauben,* Frieburg 1948, and "Faith as Assent and Commitment," *Lumen Vitae* 2(1956), 571–582.

[8] See M. van Caster S.J., "Teaching, Formation and Initiation," *Lumen Vitae* 9(1956), 612–17.

mystery of God who acts in man and makes himself known in Christ living in his Church.

The catechetical evolution during the twentieth century could give the impression that the above chronological order is the logical way of proceeding, as if information was the point of departure leading to formation, and finally blossoming into initiation or communion with God in Christ. And yet, as Father van Caster stresses, the reverse is more accurate. Contact with God is not to be found at the end of an impersonal instruction and an anthropocentric formation. There is not first a revelation of abstract ideas; on the contrary the "ideas are the result of reflection on the living knowledge accorded by God in a contact with Him. . . . As soon as the catechist really presents a sign of God, it is God making Himself known in this sign and introducing man into a dialogue with Him."[9]

The growing insistence on personalistic lines in present-day philosophies casts a significant light on the point we are discussing. There is a radical difference between knowing an object and knowing a person; and one of the saddest consequences of our technical civilization seems to be the blurring of this distinction and the tendency to objectify all our knowledge of persons. We are keenly aware and jealous of the unique characteristics of our personal identity. And yet we feel the fundamental inadequacy of words and concepts to express this identity.

Words, being the common heritage of a given culture, become worn out by usage. Having to rely on words for our self-expression, we feel imprisoned in the tight and rigid enclosure which they force on us. If we were to describe adequately our personal feelings we would almost have to invent new words and expressions. This is why in moments of privileged self-consciousness or of deep personal emotions, words fail and we have to recede into silence.

The same inadequacy applies to concepts. We are justly proud

[9] Ibid. 613–14.

of our power to reason and to build up universal concepts. This power constitutes the basic difference between man's way of knowing and the way inferior creatures know. And yet it is precisely here that our limitations appear. To know by abstraction is to siphon from unique concrete things common features which can then be applied to any individual, yet without being able to represent any of them in their striking originality. It is like the biologist wanting to analyze life by dissecting it. If this inadequacy holds true of any existing reality, how much more does it hold true of the most wonderous being—a person?

A person can never reveal himself or be known in mere words or concepts. Words and concepts will at most help in knowing about him, but "to know about a person" and "to know a person" are things basically different. We may have heard or read thousands of things about someone. But unless we meet this person we will not know him. A simple example may illustrate this point. Imagine a well known personality in the field of literature or science. Among his many students there is a brilliant young man who had studied under him for long years and has even written books on the achievements of his master. Who knows better the thinker as a man: this brilliant student who possesses such a wide and deep amount of knowledge about his master, or the learned man's wife? And yet, if we ask the wife about her husband, she will most likely come out with a series of clichés and platitudes, and eventually be at a loss of what to say. But the fact remains that she knows her husband as no one else. Many years of intimate communion have given her an insight so deep and unique that it cannot be conveyed in words. In confronting human situations she will, by intuition, judge correctly about her husband's personality.

Meeting a person *as a person* thus implies an involvement wherein all the faculties of a man are opened in an effort to look at the other and understand the other as the other. Such involvement, which we might call "sympathy," "communion," "encounter," enkindles in man his latent powers of intuition and opens in him unused eyes which are essentially eyes of love. This is why, in dealing with persons, it is not accurate to say that knowledge brings about love. The reverse is more correct. It is love which brings about knowledge. And this is not only true of the person seeking to know, but also and especially of the person who is to be known. As we have stressed before, persons can be known only by revelation—through their free witness. But persons do not witness of themselves except under the inspiration of love. If a person is to be known as he is, he must feel that we approach him with an attitude of understanding. Otherwise he will instinctively refuse to show himself as he is, and we will be left with a picture of him which is, perforce, a caricature.

It is hardly necessary to stress how all this applies to the knowledge of God. One of the great intuitions of Cardinal Newman was the decisive role of the moral attitude of the seeker in the process of faith. We cannot understand justice unless we love justice; we cannot understand peace unless we love peace; we cannot understand a person unless we love the person. Father de la Taille has presented this truth in a beautiful way: "The light of faith, although residing in the mind, does not enter man through the mind but through the heart. There is its door of entry, there is the passage through which God pours it more or less abundantly, more or less alive, according as love itself lives in us beyond any other affection or, on the contrary, according as self-love dominates over or oppresses love of God."[10]

Now we perceive more clearly why we cannot attain even the level of true instruction (information) in catechetics unless the task of initiation is duly performed: stressing from the beginning the need of a spiritual openness which is to lead to true encounter with God. It is precisely here that the role of witness reveals its importance. Showing beyond words and concepts how faith affects and transforms a living man, witness focuses attention

[10] M. de la Taille S.J., "L'oraison contemplative," *Recherches de Science Religieuse* 9 (1919), 279.

on the realm of persons. It invites, almost compels others to see this faith-in-action as an interpersonal relation between the witness and God. By its power of radiation it gently involves others in an atmosphere of religious contagion where God is more deeply grasped as the Father who invites us to share his friendship and his life in Christ.

3. Witness: Meeting Point of Man and God

God meeting man in revelation and man meeting God in faith are the two predominant mysterious lines which converge in Christian existence. And yet these two lines need a meeting point where Christian faith takes its birth. God could have provided otherwise; but he who has lovingly decided to need man decreed to make use of human mediation. St. Paul proclaims this fact: "Faith depends on hearing" (Rom 10:17).

God adapts man from within so that he might welcome the word of salvation presented to him in historical mediations. His interior grace, "enlightening every man that comes into this world" (Jn 1:9), receives in scripture different names. It is called revelation (Mt 11:25), attraction of the Father (Jn 6:44–46,66), enlightening of the heart (2 Cor 4:6), witness (1 Jn 5:10). But together with this interior witness there is a divine message presented in human words, expressing from without the call which the Spirit utters within man's heart. In Christ, the great Witness, the basic law governing the transmission of Christianity was promulgated. It is the law of the incarnation. In his Son-Made-Flesh God made clear again and this time in unique fashion how seriously he took mankind. Christ is as truly man as he is truly God. St. Paul has stressed the full implication of this guiding principle of Christianity: "Jesus, who though he was by nature God, did not consider being equal to God a thing to be clung to, but emptied himself, taking the nature of a slave and being made like unto men" (Phil 2:6–7). The same law applies in the prolongation of the

76

incarnation, by which the Word of God becomes flesh in a son of man to make him a Son of God. If God accepts the human word as channel of transmission, this means, by the same token, that he accepts the condition and dynamism of words: that they be truly human, that is, meaningful. This condition implies that we speak to man, not simply at him. This is the root of the transcendent importance of the work of pre-evangelization, bridging as it does the gaps in and preparing the ground for a truly human dialogue.[11] But the word alone, even if duly purified, is insufficient. Never before, perhaps, has man been made so painfully aware of the pitfalls of human words as he is now. We are confronted daily with a flood of words whose main purpose seems not communication between man and man but a distortion of what man actually thinks. The finest words have been abused to convey the most hideous realities. No wonder that modern man is incurably suspicious of ideologies and words.

But there is a total existential word, a word full of truth and free of ambiguities. It is the living word of the man—his whole life, his attitude toward things and persons. It is here that witness takes root and shows its decisive importance, especially since that which is to be transmitted is not a theory of abstract and impersonal truths but a message of life, an ensemble of values all centered upon a Person and addressed to persons.

Within the trinitarian life—fountainhead of all Christian existence—we know the identity of the divine persons by the testimony each one gives of the other. We know the Father by the Son:

> The hour is coming when I will no longer speak to you in parables, but will speak to you plainly of the Father (Jn 16:25; see 3:11;3:32–34).

Jesus is shown to us as the Son by the testimony which his Father gives to us:

---

[11] See our *Distinguishing the Different Stages in Missionary Preaching,* Rome 1962, 23–26.

77

A bright cloud overshadowed them, and behold, a voice out of the cloud said, "This is my beloved Son, in whom I am well pleased; hear him" (Mt 17:5; see Mt 3:17; Jn 12:28)

The Holy Spirit is known by the testimony of the Son:

But when the Advocate has come, whom I will send you from the Father, the Spirit of truth who proceeds from the Father, he will bear witness concerning me (Jn 15:26).

Christ stresses again and again that he is the witness of his Father:

For I have not spoken on my own authority, but he who sent me, the Father, has commanded what I should say, and what I should declare. . . . The things, therefore, that I speak, I speak as the Father has bidden me (John 12:49–50).

The witness of Christ consisted in transmitting to man the truths which he has contemplated in the bosom of the Father:

No one has at any time seen God. The only-begotten Son, who is in the bosom of the Father, he has revealed him (Jn 1:18).

This is the witness which must be prolonged by the Church. As Christ transmits to her what he saw and heard from his Father, so she in turn is to transmit what she saw and heard from her Lord:

Even as you have sent me into the world, so also I have sent them into the world (Jn 17:18; see 20:21).

But the force of Christ's preaching resides in his works and in his whole personality more than in his words. The same applies to the Church. There are two ways by which she transmits her message: by her words (*verbal* evangelization) and by the witness of her life (*factual* evangelization). In both ways the same core of the message is proclaimed: the paschal mystery of the Lord—dead, risen and living forever. This mystery, as St. Augustine explains, can be considered either in the Head (Christ), as the apostles presented it, or in the body (the Church). The apostles saw Christ and believed in the Church.

78

We see the Church and believe in Christ. The history of conversions shows that they start very often from experience of the paschal mystery in the encounter either with a true Christian or with a fervent community. Thus it is the factual evangelization (witness) which confronts man with the risen Christ. Then and only then will the verbal evangelization have a meaningful impact on the mind and the heart.

According to Vatican Council I the Church is "the sign raised up to the nations."[12] And yet the image of the historical Church appears so distorted in the eyes of the unbeliever that one wonders whether it is a sign or a countersign. Looking as he does from the outside through spectacles colored with all sorts of prejudices, is it not only to be expected that the nonbeliever feels repelled by the façade of an institution which, at best, belongs to the past and very often is associated with dark and oppressive memories? For him only the small sign of a Christian making present and accessible at his own level the true meaning of the living Church will work the miracle. This is the power and tremendous responsibility of Christian witness: to prolong and actualize the witness of Christ in his Church.

Christ, the great witness of God, has within him the two essential ingredients of witnessing. He is both transcendent and immanent to his milieu. He belongs essentially to his people: he is a true Jew of his time; he thinks like a Jew, he speaks like a Jew, he eats like a Jew; he is a Jew. And yet he cannot be reduced to his milieu. There is something in him which points to his heavenly origin. He is a living reminder of God's greatness and goodness, the embodiment of the kingdom of God.[13]

The same ingredients hold true for the Christian witness. He must belong to his environment, be a true citizen of his nation and his time, love his people, love his times. Nobody should be able to denounce him as a stranger to any truly human enter-

---

[12] Denz., 1794.

[13] Yves de Montcheuil S.J. in his *Problemes de la vie spirituelle,* Paris 1945, 21–47, explains this concept beautifully.

prise. And yet, being in Christ, he will be a beacon revealing to his distracted fellowmen the reality and value of the true life hidden in the heart of the Father.

4. WITNESS IN CATECHESIS PROPER

If the main role of the catechist is to foster a true communion with God—to introduce God to man and man to God—it is obvious that the indispensable requirement for such a task is that the catechist know God and also be sufficiently acquainted with the man whom he wants to introduce. In catechesis proper everything should rest upon the global faith and conversion which was attained at the stage of evangelization. In the catechesis proper everything should be directed to a development of this same personal faith. More than a time for convincing or arguing, catechesis proper is the time for a truly religious atmosphere, breathing the pure, happy air of the Christian community. The tone of the instructions should be more akin to that of a good spiritual retreat than to that of a classroom. In a truly religious environment the student should begin to feel himself at home as he progressively takes part in the worship of the Christian community. In instructions the main emphasis should not concern an exhaustive treatment of every detail of the creed and all precepts of moral observance; one should try, rather, to build up the Christian personality, that sense of Christ which the apostle extols.

Catechesis proper should indeed make full use of the biblical and liturgical signs. The word of God, incarnated in the bible, not only communicates divine revelation but also puts man in contact with the saving actions and power of God. However the saving actions of God, handed over in the bible to the Church, are not merely records of sacred history; they are made present and actualized in our midst through the sacramental signs of liturgy. It is in this context that the sign of witness should be incorporated and fully stressed. A subtle yet forceful use of the

80

lives of saints, an intelligent use of the growing literature of conversion, will help personalize and interiorize the Christian message in a fashion perfectly adapted to the psychology of the students. Yet, the all inclusive immediate witness will be the religion teacher himself. The religion teacher will show what it means to be a true Christian in today's world by what he is more than by what he says.

To be a Christian is not just to keep a series of laws—to go to Mass on Sunday, or to refrain from meat on Friday—so that one will be "in line." A Christian is not "in line," he is *in Christ.* In the Son of God he has become a new creature; he has entered a new life—a life of faith, hope and charity. He is one who cries with St. Paul: "I live in the faith of the Son of God who loved me and gave himself up for me" (Gal 2:20). In everything the Christian tries to see the hand of God.

The Christian knows and confesses himself to be a sinner because, as St. John so forcefully declares: "If we say that we have no sin, we deceive ourselves, and the truth is not in us . . . If we say we have not sinned, we make him a liar, and his word is not in us" (1 Jn 1:8–9). But he remains basically a man of hope, who acknowledges in deep gratitude that he has been saved by the merciful power of God in the blood of his Son (see 1 Jn 1:7).

The Christian is above all someone who knows God, one who loves him with his whole heart, and with his whole soul, and with his whole strength, and with his whole mind, and his neighbor as himself (see Lk 10:27), because "he who does not love does not know God; for God is love" (1 Jn 4:8). He is the man who sees God in everybody and everybody in God.

Finally the Christian is one who knows himself to be a living cell of the wonderful organism the body of Christ, and who feels himself involved in the responsibility of collaborating to make it healthier and to grow into "the mature measure of the fullness of Christ" (Eph 4:13).

If such is the catechist, then everything which he has to say will carry the weight of his Christian witness. His students might forget what he says, but the image of what he is will accompany and guide them in their journey through life.

5. WITNESS AND THE NONBELIEVER

If witness is so important at the stage of catechesis proper, in a sense its role is even more decisive in the first approach to the nonbeliever. Witness is truly the core of pre-evangelization. It will be worth remembering that many of our baptized youngsters and adults, so far as their commitment in faith is concerned, are at a level where they require a thorough pre-evangelization before they can be led to a real conversion which will turn their notional assent into a real adherence to God in a personal communion.

When we consider therefore that the difficulties which hinder the dialogue with the nonbeliever are not so much merely intellectual problems, but rather total, existential prejudices which set us as persons in a doubtful light and a suspect position, we realize that what we are, or seem to be, counts for much more than what we merely say. Against such prejudices there is no power in mere words. The nonbeliever's opinion is anchored to his prejudices; our words will not budge it. If *we* are a doubtful quantity, anything that comes from us will be equally suspect. There is no other way to communicate with the nonbeliever than to wait patiently until our witness, that is, the weight of our whole personality, shines through our deeds and words warmly enough to melt away the prejudices.

Collective witness must surely be used whenever possible. But this supposes the existence of a Christian community so radiant that it touches the life nerve of the nonbeliever. If the community witness is not strong or bright or wide enough to reach sufficiently into the lives of those who approach us for the first time, then we ourselves must be the incarnation of the witness of Christ. If we were to describe the basic character of Christian witness, we would say that it results from the sense of God, the sense of the mystery of man and the sense of our own misery, these senses all blended into a conscious religious attitude.

Sense of God

God is not an object but a most personal Being who constantly obliges man to break the mold of his tiny conceptions, for God does not let himself be imprisoned in any category. Reverence for the mystery of God must shine through every glance, every gesture, every word of the Christian who wants to welcome the nonbeliever in truth. His whole personality must radiate a permeating sense of the divine majesty, the transcendence of grace and God's mysterious working within him. Moreover he must be a sincere and admiring ambassador of divine discretion which respects the sanctuary of a conscience created free by the Almighty:

> Behold, I stand at the door and knock. If any man listens to my voice and opens the door to me, I will come in to him and will sup with him, and he with me (Ap 3:20).

Even from a psychological, human point of view, who can tell the beneficial effects of such reverence in the dialogue with a man who in the darkness gropes for the passage leading to a mystery as yet dimly perceived? When such a reverence does not remain merely at the level of human relations, but is the spontaneous fruit of a deeply religious sense of God, it can constitute the first spark which suggests something beyond this world, unsettling man and attracting him to the mystery of God.

Sense of Mystery of Man

This sense of mystery is a logical consequence of the sense of God. No man is an island closed upon himself. Rather he is a sponge, little by little impregnated by God—a creature of God's

83

love, carrying in his every cell the image and likeness of his Father who makes him capable of knowing and loving in order to beatify him with his own happiness, to make man his son in his Son. The mystery of human liberty demands a special meditation on the part of the Christian witness. The mystery of liberty, hallowed, accepted and contemplated in the mystery of God who wants man to be free and who communicates with him in utter delicacy and discretion, is the natural complement of the mystery of divine grace at work in the depth of human conscience. Mystery of grace, mystery of conscience—these words suggest what reverence and respect should constitute the climate of a true Christian witness.

God does not ignore the history of a man, his past, his social, psychological conditioning, his culture, his environment. It is precisely here that God wants to incarnate his word as a living and actualized prolongation of his substantial Word who once "was made flesh and dwelt among us" (Jn 1:14). Amid the bafflement and indecisiveness of a man's life, the Lord works in him with a constancy and patience which reveals infinite love, so that he may finally take possession of this heart immersed in its human conditions.

Consciousness of One's Own Misery

In an authentic religious experience, awareness of one's own misery is the very reverse of the sense of God. This is a precious indispensable element, one belonging to the attitude of a true Christian witness. Even though a man knows himself as messenger of God he understands that he will never be God's plenipotentiary. God is too jealous to yield his prerogatives to anyone. But if God, being as he is the Creator and Almighty, respects to such an extent the free will of his creature, what should be said of him who remains a poor servant and a sinner? The humble image of John the Baptist, true ambassador, comes to mind: "He must increase, but I must decrease" (Jn 3:30). If

Christ the Lord calls himself and willingly behaves as "servant of Yahweh" how much more must be the Christian who is conscious of his poverty and sins?

As a corollary to our reflections on the mystery of the sense of God, it would be good to remind ourselves that we do not *possess* truth, since truth is God and God is not a thing to be possessed, but a Person. It is more true to say that we are *possessed* by Truth, to the extent that we go out of ourselves to make room for Love—to the extent that we enter into communion with God and "practice the truth in love" (Eph 4:15). The well known biblical attitude of the "poor" (anawim), growing from a deep sense of the grandeur of God and an awareness of one's own lowliness, could serve as the best description of a true Christian witness.

A man habitually breathing the air of the three elements described above will not find it overly difficult to find the correct approach in his dialogue with the nonbeliever.

Sympathy and Understanding

The problem here, more than one of merely suggesting practical rules or techniques for the dialogue with nonbelievers, is above all one of sensibility, of spiritual insight so that we might establish harmony in our relations with another soul. At the outset the primary task of witness is not to impart knowledge or to correct erroneous consciences. Rather it is a time to allow another to discover in the warmth of a sympathy full of respect and veneration something of God's love which will be a seed of the greater revelation of God's goodness and kindness. Thus, existentially, witness develops its proper dynamism and begins to take root. The secret is to attain in depth a spiritual agreement of hearts. In the atmosphere built up by the sense of God and the sense of the mystery of man, such a communion will spring spontaneously. This will lead the witness first to *accept* everything good which is to be found in the other's situation, not only what appears on the surface but even what lies hidden to the other's consciousness. The first response to sympathy on the other's part will come through of itself when he feels well wishing eyes and a loving regard being directed toward him in an honest effort to do him justice—when we accept without ambiguity or paternalism whatever is good and noble in the man's life. It is this desire of justifying others from within as far as possible which best characterizes the approach of the Christian witness to the nonbeliever. "Justify from within" means a sincere effort to put oneself in the other's place, to try to see things through his eyes, to feel with the other's heart. Here also we must remember an elementary fact of human psychology: if we love it is not primarily because we understand; but we understand because we love. This understanding, indispensable climate of a welcoming witness, issues only from a sympathy which is already the fruit of love. This is why we have to purify continuously our own witness and try to look at man through the eyes and heart of God the Father. Only by loving as God loves will we succeed in discovering, even in someone aggressive and hostile, the amiable features of a person who was made by Love to love.

Although we may justify the other beyond what the actual situation would allow, positive fruits will accrue, fruits of truth, loyalty and softening of attitude. Now is not the time to discuss, much less to refute or correct; it is not even time to teach. It is rather the time to bear witness to the Love of God and the basic goodness of man. As for things which cannot be justified an understanding and discreet silence will suffice.

Thus when the other sees himself welcomed, and finds in us an echo full of goodness and openness, he will feel in turn a gentle but imperative invitation to understand us. The circle of mutual understanding is now complete. From its center, more existentially experienced than intellectually perceived, will blossom forth the promise-filled discovery: God is good and invites man to open his heart to love.

86

Doctrinal Sign

Theology and Catechetical Renewal

BERNARD COOKE S.J.

ONE of the things that augurs best for the continuing development of the catechetical apostolate in the present-day Church is its deep grounding in the contemporary developments of theology itself. Because of the growth of biblical studies and consequent biblical theology, because of the development of liturgical and sacramental theology, as well as fresh theological understanding of the Church, there is a great reserve of deepened faith—understanding that can feed into a reevaluation of religious education. This present essay will try to describe this impact of theology on the development of catechetical instruction.

There are of course many ways one might study the influence of theology on contemporary catechetics. For example one might sketch the increased theological attention to the sources of faith, especially scripture and sacramental life, and show how this has caused a new selection of material both for theological writing and research and for catechetical instruction. Unquestionably this summation would do much to clarify the relationship between these two areas of growth, but it is also something that has been done fairly well a number of times. This particular essay will attempt rather to study the various elements in theology which impinge upon catechetics, keeping the catechetical point of view as its guiding norm. The paper will try to discuss three elements: 1) the theological developments which touch upon God as communicating himself to man; 2) theological developments regarding man as seen by faith; 3) theological developments which touch upon the Church or, if you will, upon the community aspect of Christianity.

God as Communicating to Man

As is often being remarked, one of the most promising features of present-day theological development, both in Catholic and Protestant circles, is the emphasis on the mystery of the resurrection. While this emphasis has been rooted very largely in the recent development of New Testament theology, it is being incorporated into the whole synthesis of systematic theology and promises to play an increasingly important role in this area. Perhaps the aspect of the resurrection which touches most importantly on catechetics is the fact that it draws attention to the *continuing revelation* of the Father in the mystery of the risen Christ.

Christians have always known that Jesus of Nazareth, who lived in visible historical form two thousand years ago, is still alive and with us; but for the most part little attention was drawn to this fact, and few conclusions drawn from it either in theology or in religious education. Particularly since the appearance of Durrwell's work on the subject,[1] both theologians and religious educators have now drawn attention to the presence of Christ, not only divine but also human, in the mystery of the Church. Moreover they have emphasized that resurrection means not only the fact that Christ is no longer dead, but also that he lives now with *new life*. Resurrection means not only a coming back to life, but also the beginning of an entirely transformed way of human existing.

There are many ramifications of this particular emphasis in theology—in our notion of the Church, in the idea of grace, in the understanding of faith—but perhaps most important is the recaptured sense of the presence of Christ in those who are the

[1] F. X. Durrwell C.SS.R., *The Resurrection: A Biblical Study*, New York 1960.

members of his Church. While Catholic theology has lost none of its sense of the importance of the eucharistic presence of Christ, there is a regained awareness of the presence of Christ in those who form the Christian community. Not only theology and religious education but also Christian prayer are deeply affected by this awareness that Christ abides with those who make up the Church at any given period of time.

This theological emphasis is only now beginning to be felt on a wide scale in the Church's thinking; but it has already influenced catechetical theory and practice, and will do so even more. Catechetical leaders, grounding their own practice in the pedagogical methods of the primitive Christian community (as we find them reflected in the Acts of the Apostles), are making the mystery of the resurrection the core of their presentation of Christianity. Once again, as in the early days of Christianity, the gospel is seen to be "an announcing to the world of the good news" that death has been overcome in the person of This Man who, having passed through the portals of death, lives now no more to die.

One can easily see the reorientation of emphasis which this return to the doctrine of the resurrection is bound to have. While religious education will continue to center upon the figure of Christ as it has tended to do in more recent times, it will point not to Christ of two thousand years ago but to the Christ who is present in his followers at the present moment. Thus the importance of the new emphasis on the risen Christ is not just that this element of revelation will receive new stress; this emphasis creates a whole new context or atmosphere for the communication of the Christian faith. It creates a sense of immediacy, a sense of reality; it prepares for that impact which comes through direct encounter with the Person of Christ.

More is contained in this mystery of the resurrection than the fact that Christ has not left his Church but still abides with it. The heavenly Father who sent Christ into this world still speaks to the men of our day in and through this Son become

90

man. In his Son the Father is at the present moment revealing to the men of our own day his providential and fatherly love and his desire to communicate himself to them in his Word, this Word which alone can adequately express him. The Father works creatively to transform both the understanding and the being of men, changing them truly into sons of God.

Mention of the Father's continuing revelation to mankind brings us into contact with a second area of theological development which is of considerable import for religious education: the study of the divine Word's function in salvation history. At the present time there is a great deal of theological discussion and research in the area of what one might call "supernatural communications." That process by which God unfolds to mankind an understanding of himself is being examined in the light of contemporary developments in fields of knowledge such as anthropology and psychology. All of the traditional categories which bear upon this particular area—revelation, tradition, inspiration, prophecy—are being examined anew and seen in a somewhat fresh and deeper way.

As biblical studies draw continuing attention to the importance of the notion of salvation history, theologians are increasingly aware that "revelation" must be considered in a much broader context. It is essentially in the events of what is called sacred history that this God has manifested to mankind the kind of a divinity he is in their regard. However the events themselves are not sufficient to convey to man the understanding which God intends; in conjunction with these events certain special understanding has been given to individuals such as Moses and the prophets—and above all to Christ in his humanity—in order that they may communicate to others the deeper message which the divine action contains. It is the combination of these elements, the special divine activity in history and the special understandings of these events given by God, which make up the process of supernatural revelation.

Supernatural revelation is retained and developed within the social existence of that community (ancient Israel or the Church) in which the events occur. Over the centuries the recollection of God's deeds and the faith understanding of these deeds was preserved and handed on from generation to generation, not just by specialized groups such as prophets and priests but by the entire social structure of the people in question. While this process of handing on (tradition) has jealously preserved the sacred truth entrusted to the community, there has been a constant process of applying to the understanding of this deposit of faith the understandings of life which man has acquired in the course of his historical existence. Thus revelation has been guarded for us up to the present moment, and this in a dynamic and developing process which, always faithful to the original faith insights, included evolving clarification.

At given points in history, in order to guarantee the authenticity of this process of tradition, certain individuals have been specially directed by God (by what we call inspiration) to write down the traditions of the community as they then existed. Such scriptural inspiration does not necessarily involve new insights into revelation or any further clarification of the revelation as already understood by the community, but rather a genuine reflection of these two in written form. Issuing to quite an extent from the community situation, the inspired writings were recognized by this community as the special word of God and gathered together into what we now call the Old and New Testaments.

Contemporary theology sees the process of divine communication to man as a complex reality that involves the entire history of the people of the Old Testament as well as of the New Testament people of God. While no essentially new event has entered the picture since the end of the apostolic period, the processes of tradition have continued to the present day and will do so until the end of time. The focus of this community preservation of the word of God is to be found in the sacred scriptures and in the teachers officially deputed to preserve and explain them; still there is a valid application of the word tradition to the entire on-going life of the present-day Christian community.

Into this larger picture of the preservation and development of revealed truth religious pedagogy is situated. It is one of the functions, and a very important function, of the Church in safe-guarding an accurate understanding of divine revelation and in communicating it to succeeding generations. The fact that religious education finds itself so situated dictates to it the guide-lines of its own pedagogy.

Man as Seen by Faith

The immediacy of the risen Christ to the Church would indicate a highly personal context for the communication of religious understanding in contemporary catechetics. This new context is gradually being realized and the realization will be further intensified by the present theological investigation into what one might call the "personal aspect" of revelation. Under the impact of many factors, among them the awakened understanding of the human person in modern thought, contemporary theology is deeply concerned with studying the key elements in relevation from the point of view of their personal implications.

This trend is seen in present theological understanding of the mystery of grace. Moving away somewhat from the post-Reformation emphasis on grace as justification or on the role of actual grace in making human moral behavior efficacious, theologians are concentrating on the role of sanctifying grace in the life of the individual Christian as well as in the Christian community. One of the most fascinating developments is suggested by the studies which indicate that grace consists basically in a relatedness of the Christian to the three persons of the Blessed Trinity. Because of this new reality (grace) the Christian finds himself in a situation of son-ship, a situation which relates him differently to each of the three divine Persons and permits him to enter into a truly personal communication of knowledge and love with them.

Seen in this way, grace is not something superimposed on the human person but something which enters into him to transform and fulfill him as person. The supernatural order in no way detracts from the orientations of man to personal development and achievement, but truly opens up the capacities of his personal being to yet fuller participation in knowledge and in love. If persons develop in terms of their mature relatedness to other persons, the fact that grace sets up a situation of friendship with the three divine Persons means that entirely unprecedented possibilities of human maturity and growth enter the picture.

Seen in this way the life of grace is an integral element in human existing. Its development is not a question of peripheral and superadded practices, somewhat detached and apart from the normal course of human living; rather that which is the highest expression of the life of grace, charity, is found at the very center of all true human activity. When one says that a person develops in proportion to his capacity to love, one is stating in another form the oft-repeated truth that one's sanctity is measurable most properly by the extent of one's charity.

It is quite apparent how this approach to the understanding of sanctifying grace is of immense importance for the catechist. It points to the fact that grace is not to be explained primarily in terms of a reality given to man in order that he may be more correct in his ethical behavior. Rather grace is the foundation for the mystery of friendship with the three divine Persons. Grace is seen as something given the individual so that he can become more truly the person he is meant to be. Thus there is an openness, a sense of freedom, a sense of personal importance, rather than the sense of restriction and imposition sometimes found in the older emphasis on the ten commandments and on conformity to law as being the essence of the life of grace.

Another element closely associated with this recent understanding of grace is the theological development, in the years following World War II, of the notion of faith. Aware of the danger that one can understand faith in an excessively subjective and therefore relativist sense, Catholic theology until very recently laid great emphasis on the intellectual or rational elements in the act of faith. In the past couple decades, while in no way denying the intellectual nature of faith, Catholic theologians have been much more open to what one might call the "personal commitment" aspects of faith. Today in most contemporary theological literature one reads that faith is to be seen in terms of personal acceptance of the mystery of Christ, that it is the response which occurs in encounter with this Person who is the Father's Word come into history, that faith is a commitment one makes to become involved in the practical living out of the mystery of Christ in the community of faith.

More keenly than ever before, faith is seen to be what Vatican Council I already declared it to be, an act of freedom. It is essentially a choice which a Christian makes of a way of life, a choice made at baptism, reiterated in confirmation and re-expressed in each celebration of the eucharistic mystery. It is this choice which is at the very center of the development of the life of grace. Thus grace and personality develop integrally, for mature exercise of free choice is also the necessary condition for the growth of a genuine person. This theological understanding of faith is essentially and necessarily a religion of freedom. Any instruction with regard to development of Christian life must emphasize the growth of the ability to choose.

All this points out for the catechist the need of communicating the Christian faith in a way which leads to authentic Christian self-commitment. Mere informational acquisition is insufficient if it does not lead to the understanding that one must become Christian. The process of choosing Christ, of converting from an insufficient expression of Christian living into a more genuine giving of self, is a continuing thing in the Christian's existence. True catechesis must therefore make it possible for the student to find himself in that situation of faith-encounter which will challenge and motivate him to the profound personal choice of the Christian way of life.

Correlative with the theological development regarding grace and faith is the deepening understanding of sin. Partially because of contemporary growth in the psychological understanding of guilt, theologians are clarifying the fact that sin is self-denying, self-destroying. Just as grace is the development and fulfillment of the human personality, so sin is seen to be an evil because of what it does to the human person. It is a denial of the essential finality of a person to open out onto reality and above all onto other persons. Sin leads to a perversion of self-expression, leads to a gradual deterioration of the person's capacity to confront reality with authenticity and to open out in generosity to other persons. More profoundly sin is seen to be a denial of the divine offer of friendship. Biblical theology, with its insistence upon divine vocation as a call to participation in familiarity with the three divine Persons, has done much to highlight the nature of sin as a rejection of friendship, as a fundamental infidelity.

While moral theology has not abandoned the investigation of sin as opposition to law, it has deepened this very notion by insisting that sin most basically denies acceptance of the fundamental law of charity.

This theological development has done much to highlight the persistent problem of forming a mature conscience in the Christian. Considerable discussion during the past couple decades has been directed to this practical theological question, a question that is of particular importance for the religious pedagogue. It is to this latter that in large measure the informational aspect of developing of conscience is committed. It is the religious pedagogue who must give those understandings of human behavior and human development which will permit the Christian to advance consciously in the development of himself as a deciding being.

Clearly this says much about the way in which catechesis must present the whole mystery of evil in human life, how it must outline for the Christian his responsibilities in the moral order. While the elements of conformity to law and fear of a just God can never be neglected, still in the formation of conscience fear cannot become the governing motivation. Rather the context of love and freedom dictated by the renewed understandings of the resurrection, of grace and of divine Fatherhood must be preserved in teaching the evil of sin. Maturity in conscience must develop as maturity in power of Christian judgment and decision. One of the major tasks of present-day religious education is to develop an effective approach to conscience formation.

The last aspect of contemporary developments regarding man as seen by faith touches man's function in the historical process. Man in history, more specifically the Christian in history, is the bearer of divine wisdom and love. To him has been committed the task of witnessing to the intervention of God in human history, to the continuing work of the three divine Persons as they guide man in his historical existence toward the destiny of sharing in divine life. Not just individual human beings but the whole process of human life, the societal existence of man, is meant to be Christianized. This Christianization will be a redemption of all that makes up the context of human living; this redemption must be accomplished by the Christians who live in the midst of men, who witness to the life-giving Word of God and who transform by their own love the patterns of human choice and behavior.

Contemporary theology has advanced much in developing what may eventuate as a true theology of history. As never before theologians are aware of the importance of the historical dimension of divine revelation and divine activity. History as a necessary and characteristic context of Christianity is being investigated as an element of Christian truth which must be understood in order that it may then be sanctified.

97

Drawing from this theological emphasis on sacred history and the Christianization of present-day history, the religious educator has a task of directing the student outward to the Christian task which faces him. The catechist must prepare his student for life, life which because Christian is essentially apostolic and missionary. It is not enough for the catechist to give his students those elements of understanding which will allow him to develop and perfect his own individual existence: he must make clear to the student the responsibility which he bears because of his baptismal entry into the mystery of Christianizing the world. Until fairly recently there was an individualism in Christian thought and in Christian instruction which somewhat belied the orientation given Christian life by Christ himself. In our own day there has been an awakening to the need of seeing Christianity as the social mystery which it really is, and the catechist shares most importantly in the task of reawakening the Christian people to this wider frame of reference. This task leads us naturally into our third major portion of discussion, theological developments with regard to the Church.

Theological Developments Regarding the Church

Our modern world is one that is marked by awareness of the unity of mankind. Because of developments in the realm of communications, of travel, of information, the world has become increasingly one. While this oneness raises certain problems in the religious sphere, it opens up, really for the first time in the history of western Christianity, the potential for creating a Christian community embracing all peoples of the earth.

Reflecting this contemporary situation, the theology of the present day has developed most importantly its understanding of the mystery of the Church. Basing itself on a return to biblical understandings, Catholic theology is studying the Church less in terms of its canonical aspects, its institutional structure. Rather it is examining the Church as a community, as the new people of God. The Church is seen as a mystery in direct continuity with the mystery of Old Testament Israel, as fulfillment of those centuries of preparation which were carried on in the context of a religious community. The Church as a people is seen to be not so much a grouping of teachers and taught, of rulers and ruled, but rather as "the family of God."

This perspective raises for religious educators the question of how most validly to present the mystery of the Church. It is important that their students obtain a true and meaningful insight into the community reality of the Church, and that they feel themselves to be part of this mystery. It is important too that while they retain a correct understanding of the institutional side of the Church, a genuine and mature respect for the elements of authority and law, they still learn to regard the Church for what it is: a community of believers, a community gathered in worship around the altar of God.

In this understanding of the Church as something dynamic, something growing and developing, precisely because it is a community of persons in history, the whole notion of salvation history seems increasingly important. If the Church is a reality in history, a reality essentially historical in its being, then somehow or another historical methods must be utilized in providing this sort of insight. If the Church is to be considered an outgrowth of the history of salvation which preceded it and which is itself a continuing mystery of God's workings in the midst of mankind, then salvation history must be considered a reality which is not just of the past but which continues through the present into the future. To teach the Church in this way means that one must teach it in its roots and in its present existence, but also in its movement toward the future, toward its eschatological realization.

In our own day theology has reemphasized the notion that the Church is the body of Christ, that it is somehow an organic and vital reality, a living and developing reality. Organized under authority into a society the Christian community is in its depths the mystery of the abiding presence of Christ in the Spirit. It is that which as "body" expresses Christ, "translates" him meaningfully to the men of our present day as it has to the men of the past two thousand years. The Church's life of faith and charity embodies the mystery of Christ himself as Wisdom and Love in our contemporary world.

Not only is the Church as a society seen by present-day theology in this more vital fashion, but the individual Christian himself is seen to be a living part of this mystery. Christians are, as St. Paul would say, "the living stones" out of which this growing, developing temple of the spirit is fashioned. Each Christian, as well as the total Christian community, is meant to be a sacrament of Christ, manifesting externally to the men of our day the continuing mystery of Christ in our midst. The Christian community must continuously announce the mystery of Christ overcoming death in resurrection. Its charity is meant to touch all mankind and transform it. In and through the Christian community Christ himself abides in our world, re-creating it so that it becomes a truly Christian world.

Again, the catechetical task seems rather obvious: to present the Church as a static organization is to betray the task which confronts us. Only when Christians understand the living reality of the Church alive because of the risen Christ in its midst, sharing in this spiritualized existence which he has, will a real understanding of the Church flow out into deepened Christianized life and worship. Before Catholics can understand the task of witnessing to the present mystery of the risen Christ they must understand who they are in this mystery and how they are meant to function. The religious pedagogue must find the means of clarifying the sacramental world of each individual Christian as well as the larger sacramental task of the community as such. This he cannot do by himself, for the true realization of the living community can come to its members only in the experience which is proper to the Church of Christ: eucharistic sacrifice. However it is the catechist's task to prepare those whom he instructs for the experience, meaningful and practical, of vital liturgy.

It is apparent then that one of the most important areas of instruction which must be given by the catechist is that which deals with the Christian sacraments. Here again there are important developments in present-day Catholic theology from which religious education can and must draw. Few if any areas of theological investigation are developing as rapidly as is sacramental theology. Sacraments are being understood more profoundly than ever before as actions, actions simultaneously of Christ and of his Church, actions which have their efficacy precisely because they are acts of the risen Christ expressing himself through the instrumentality of his Body.

Since sacraments, and above all the key sacrament of the Eucharist, are the actions of Christ working in the Church at the present time, they are privileged situations for encountering Christ. It is in the sacraments that Christians come into contact with the risen Christ in his contemporary operation. It is in the sacraments that most totally Christ speaks to the modern world his transforming wisdom and love. For this reason it is only in sacramental actions that the experiential understanding of Christianity can be fully achieved. It is only in this situation of direct encounter with the mystery of salvation that the faith of the Christian community can be both professed and deepened.

Not only are sacraments actions of Christ, they are also actions of the Christian community. They are the actions which profess its acceptance of the reality of Christianity and its commitment to the task of Christianizing the world. Sacraments are the situations expressing that charity which is meant to be a bond of vital union between Christians and which directs them toward the salvation of their fellow men. For this reason sacraments are not only fulfillment of religious obligation as they have so often been considered by Catholics; they are the very wellspring of Christian activity and Christian faith. However they are "words," that is to say, actions which express meaningfulness; and in order that they have the meaning which they are intended to possess, meaning which may be effective as cause of grace, the Christian community must be made more conscious of its actions so that it can perform them with truer inner meaning.

To put it another way, one can say that meaningful liturgical ceremony, meaningful liturgical life is intrinsically dependent on correct catechesis in sacraments. For a Christian community consciously to offer the sacrifice of Christ's death and resurrection, it must be conscious of the way in which the action it performs at Mass is truly sacrificial. In order for Christians to commit themselves in this moment of supreme decision, they must be instructed with regard to the way in which the Mass is a context of decision and instructed as to the implications of this decision. The task of the religious educator with respect to liturgy is one of capital importance. If he succeeds in making the sacramental action an understood reality he has in very large measure succeeded in the task which is his in the mystery of the Church. On the other hand if he has failed to direct those whom he instructs toward a more meaningful participation in the liturgical ceremony, he cannot satisfy his conscience with regard to his catechetical function.

However it is at this point that the catechist must give way to the liturgical ceremony itself as the supreme occasion for religious education. While he can prepare his students for this sacred action, it is the action itself performed with meaning and with sincerity which instructs most importantly with regard to the meaning of Christianity. Faith is an act of understanding which is essentially experiential; it is an assent to the real and personal context of the Christian mystery; it is an assent to the on-going mystery of the death and resurrection of Christ as shared by each individual Christian and by the community of the faithful. Only in the liturgical ceremony itself can such an experience really be encountered; for this reason there must be a most important conformity and integration of religious in-instruction and liturgical practice. At this point religious theory and pastoral theology merge and become almost indistinguishable one from the other.

One last point regarding theological developments in the area of the Church might be mentioned because of its widespread importance in the religious life of our Catholic people. This is the theological investigation of the mystery of Mary. Few if any periods of the Church's theological life have seen as intensive a development of mariology as our own century. But not only has there been a quantitative development. There has also been, and that with marked emphasis, a redirection of theological study of Mary, a reintegration of mariology with ecclesiology. Increasingly, the mystery of Mary is seen to be part of the mystery of the Church. Her role, her grace and her person are studied in relationship to the wider community of the faithful. Mary is viewed not as a mystery apart, as if she were parallel to the mystery of Christ as object of the Church's devotion and study, but as part of the mystery of the Church itself. Mary is seen to be within the Church the perfect Christian, the exemplar of Christian sanctity, prayer and activity.

This point is of great practical importance for catechetics because of the orientation it provides not just for Christian understanding but for Christian prayer and life. Devotedness to Mary has always been one of the hallmarks of genuine Christian life, and it is essential for the authentic development of the Christian spirit that an accurate devotedness to Mary be provided our Christian people. Mary as exemplar of what a Christian should be in the mystery of the Church must be provided so that there will be an entry into the practice of Christian life which retains all the warmth and familiarity connected with her motherhood and which yet retains the profound mystery of her grace. To neglect an accurate and realistic catechesis of Mary would be to deprive the Christian faithful of an ideal of Christian life which they require for their integral development, an ideal provided them by God as a guide to a truly personal entry into relationship with Christ himself.

Conclusion

If there is one thing that stands out in this rather complex development of contemporary theology and its impact on modern catechetics it is the awakened interest in the divine action in history. This divine action, as a process that develops over the centuries, continues into the present and is directed into the future, is that to which our understanding must be directed and our activity conformed. This divine action is the basic pattern for the development of the Christian community and for the development of Christian understanding. As one examines what it is that God has been doing with the human race over the past millennia, one begins to realize what elements of divine pedagogy have been functioning to give man that understanding of himself and of his God which God wishes.

For this reason genuine catechesis must become increasingly aware of this divine process which instructs the faith-life of man. What is this divine process of transforming a human into a son of God? If it is not to work at cross purposes with the divine activity catechesis must conform itself to the divine pattern of action. The laws intrinsic in the process of revelation for the development of faith must become the principles guiding our modern catechetical reconstruction. Truly perceptive theology of this divine action is a necessary guide and source for the catechist in the reappraisal of his own activity and in the construction of a truly valid and effective catechesis. As we mentioned earlier in this essay, the function of the religious educator fits integrally into the present-day action of God in the mystery of the Church: through community life, sacramental encounter and religious instruction. God works to Christianize his people and those whom they meet. The process of religious education must conform itself in its own development to this divine direction or pay the penalty of being a disruptive and limiting force rather than a true instrument of the Spirit of God.

The Mystery of Christ

WILLIAM REEDY

God's Eternal Plan

GOD speaks to men in concrete ways, not in abstract propositions
or definitions. The wonder and mystery is that he should speak
to men at all! Yet he does. He makes known to us his plan,
conceived before the very foundations of the world were laid, observes St. Paul. This plan is to share with men his very own life
by grace.

In carrying out his plan God became man in Christ, that all
who are incorporated into Christ by faith and baptism may begin
now in time to live the divine life in a human way. The meeting
with Christ through faith is a person-to-person contact with the
living God. In fact God became man that men might become
God-like. Thus the wonder and mystery of faith is the transformation which takes place in us. We become new creatures in
Christ through baptism. Our encounter is with Christ through
whom we go to the Father.

From all eternity God intended to unite men to himself in life
and love. The plan began in heaven, out of time; continued on
earth in time; and will be completed in heaven—again out of
time. St. Paul, speaking of God's plan for us, uses the expression
"mystery of Christ." What he means is this: God has a plan
for the salvation of the world which is centered in his Son our
Lord Jesus Christ.

In making this plan known to us, and in revealing himself to us, God has spoken in the concrete facts and events of history. He has intervened from time to time in human events to form a people of his own: Israel in the Old Testament; the "new Israel" in the New Testament, which is the community of the baptized. It is in the context of a sacred history that God has revealed himself to us. It is in this same context that his message of salvation in Christ is proclaimed. This is his "method:" to speak to men a divine message—in the words of men—and in the persons and events of the course of history into which he himself has entered.

The Overall View of St. Paul

Unable to contain the overflowing joy and wonder roused in him by the good news of our salvation in Christ, St. Paul ecstatically and enthusiastically proclaims the plan of God for men. He would get to the *whole* plan first, for to see this magnificent whole before examining any one of its interrelated parts is a joyful compulsion which the great apostle cannot avoid. He announces this whole plan especially in his epistle to the Ephesians. It contains the core-curriculum of religious education, the "what it is," which as messengers of God we catechists must proclaim in his name—Christ acting in us as we hand down the message from above (Katakein).

The opening lines of the epistle (Eph 1:3–14) have been called "the hymn of redemption." Even before he speaks of the creation St. Paul speaks of redemption. From a heart full of faith he joyfully sings out the good news of our rebirth in Christ and of the overwhelming love of God in having from all eternity a plan to share divine life with beings other than himself.

The whole of what we are to teach, says St. Paul, is the *mystery of Christ,* God's redemptive plan for man centered in his Son. "Blessed be the God and Father of our Lord Jesus Christ, who in Christ has blessed us with every manner of spiritual blessing in the heavenly realm" (Eph 1:3). God's infinite generosity must be spoken of again! "These blessings correspond to his choice of us in Christ before the foundation of the world, that we should be holy and without blemish in his sight" (Eph 1:4).

If there be any willingness to listen in him who does not at first grasp the impact of this proclamation of God's plan to unite men to himself in life and love, St. Paul will reiterate the mystery of Christ: "Out of love he predestined us for himself to become through Jesus Christ his adopted children, conformable to the good pleasure of his will, to the praise of his resplendent grace, with which he has adorned us in his beloved Son" (Eph 1:5).

This "adornment" is a total encounter with Christ. For St. Paul it is to "put on the Lord Jesus Christ" (Rom 13:14). For him "to live means Christ" (Phil 1:21). "It is now no longer I who live, but Christ lives in me" (Gal 2:20). The personal encounter of the baptized with Christ, who transforms them by grace, is spoken of repeatedly by St. Paul in such expressions as "in Christ," "through Christ," "with Christ."

This personal encounter of man with God in Christ unfolds in the magnificent story of salvation, which for each of the apostles is the framework of his own proclamation of the one eternal plan of God.

St. Paul further presents this plan centered in the one redemptive act of Christ, his death-resurrection, in which all those who are baptized share. "In him we have our redemption through his blood, the remission of our transgressions in keeping with the riches of his grace" (Eph 1:7).

If there be any one thing to which all the apostles witness, it is the central event in salvation history: the death-resurrection of Christ. Now St. Paul presents our involvement in this "passover" from death to new life in Christ, speaking of baptism which like a great wave (water being a sign of life to the ancient people of Israel) inundates us, completely destroying the "old man" of sin and re-creating the new man in grace.

107

"With this grace he has inundated us . . . making known to us . . . the mystery of his will" (Eph 1:8). It is now time for the climax of St. Paul's pronouncement. Eight times already—in a different way each time to avoid the monotony of "sameness" in repetition—he has spoken of God's infinite goodness in calling us to share the divine life in Christ. He speaks now of the heart of the plan: the mystery of Christ.

"And this . . . he decreed to put into effect in Christ when the designated period of time had elapsed, namely, to gather all creation both in heaven and earth under one head, Christ" (Eph 1:9–10).

God's plan to unite men to himself in Christ began in heaven, continued on earth in two phases: one of preparation in the Old Testament, and the other, "when the designated period of time had elapsed," of fulfillment in Christ.

"In him we have been constituted a Chosen People . . . predestined to be devoted to the praise of (God's) glory—we who before Christ's coming had hoped in him. You, too, after you had heard the message of truth, the Good News proclaiming your salvation and had believed in it, in him you have been sealed with the promised Holy Spirit who is the first installment of our inheritance" (Eph 1:11–14).

The *first* installment? Yes—for there is more to come. Christ continues to live now in his Church as the head of that body of which we are living "Christ-ened" members. He who is the "firstborn of every creature" (Col 1:15), Christ, will come again to renew the heavens and the earth, and present this "new creation" to the Father, giving him more praise and glory than he received in the first creation.

This will be the third and final phase of the story of salvation, when the kingdom of God will be completed and God will be all in all. Meanwhile we are members of his kingdom on earth, born anew of water and the Spirit. Christ is continually acting in us, working to complete the kingdom. With him at the lead we are on our way heavenward to our true home.

"The final purpose of thus being sealed is our redemption as God's possession to the praise of his glory" (Eph 1:14), and thus St. Paul concludes this "hymn of redemption," this capsule overall view of God's plan for us centered in Christ—central figure in the history of God's working among men to form a people of his own—the Lord of history: Son of God: Savior.

The Mystery in Further Depth

Since it is the mystery of Christ, God's plan of redemption, which we are to proclaim, St. Paul will many times—always in fact—unfold more of this "mystery," reveal as much as we can see in the light of faith.

In the second chapter of Ephesians the apostle does more than proclaim; as every catechist must do he *explains* in terms understood by his hearers the content of what is proclaimed, each of its parts being seen as so many individual doctrines emanating from Christ as rays from a central source of light.

"But God, who is rich in mercy, was moved by the intense love with which he loved us, and when we were dead by reason of our transgressions, he made us live with the life of Christ. . . . Yes, it is by grace that you have been saved through faith; it is the gift of God; it is not the result of anything you did, so that no one has grounds for boasting. We are his handiwork, created in Christ Jesus in view of good deeds which God prepared beforehand for us to practice" (Eph 2:4–10).[1]

Scripture speaks of God as the rock of our salvation; and as the rock in the desert when struck by the rod of Aaron and Moses sent forth living water, so also is Christ the rock of our new life, from whose side when struck by the rod of the cross there poured a "fountain of water welling up into eternal life" (Jn 4:14).

Carrying this concrete image of the rock further, St. Paul will refer to us as stones fitted into Christ the cornerstone, the cement

1 That is, God decreed that we perform freely and willingly.

of love and life, binding us to him and to each other. The Old and New Testaments are summed up in Christ. All men are made one in him.

"Now in Christ Jesus you, who were once far off (from God by reason of sin), have been brought near through the blood of Christ . . . he it is who has made both Jew and Gentile one . . . that of the two races he might create in himself one new being. . . . He came and announced the good news of peace to you who were afar off, and of peace to those who were near, because by one and the same Spirit through him both of us have found entrance to the Father" (Eph 2:13–19).

It is St. Paul's office—it is the office of every catechist—to make known God's plan and so proclaim the mystery of Christ. And the essence of this plan, the individual doctrines which comprise it, are found in the New Testament kerygma. This is the essential body of truths which God meant to be proclaimed specifically and emphatically as the core of our teaching, the bedrock of truth, the hub of a wheel of dogma into which individual doctrines are fitted as spokes. It is this kerygma which forms the backbone upon which the epistles, gospels and creeds were later built, for the kerygma was proclaimed before it was confined to writing (Pentecost being a gift of tongues, not of pens).

We may summarily state the kerygma drawn from the New Testament in these truths:

Out of his infinite goodness and love (no merit on our part), God the Father has invited us to share with him his own divine life through Jesus Christ, whom he gave, a ransom for sinners (Eph 2:7; 1 Pet 5:10; Jn 17:21; Rom 8:29).

Born anew of water and the Spirit we are transformed into the likeness of Christ who acts in us by grace so that we, living God's life in time in the Church which is Christ, do good works under the lawful direction of the superiors he has appointed for us (Rom 6:3; 1 Jn 4:10; 1 Cor 12:13; Acts 20:28).

As children of God we have been sent the Spirit so that we will be enabled to render a service of love and a continuous sacrifice of praise to the Father through Christ. Thus we are temples of God, truly Christ's body, nourished by Christ's own flesh and blood in the new life we are called to live (Gal 4:6; Heb 13:15; Eph 1:23; Jn 6:56).

In the end, when death is swallowed up in victory, we will achieve the prize, the goal of supernatural vocation in Christ which is the Kingdom of God and his glory—God's heirs, co-heirs with Christ, our firstborn Brother (1 Cor 15:54; Rom 8:17).

Method and Message for the Catechist

It is not possible to speak of method in teaching religion un-less the catechist has first grasped the message. "How" we are to proclaim "this mystery relative to Christ" (Eph 3:4) follows from our knowing and living "what" it is we proclaim. For it is not a mere body of truth with which we are concerned but a message of life. The "viva voce" of the teacher, the heart in-flamed with a realization of what it is to be sharing divine life by grace so that he communicates this message by his very presence, is truly *the method* with which to be concerned.

However a more careful look at the message itself tells us how we are to proceed, for we must not only be *proclaimers* but *teachers* in contemporary terms of the mystery of salvation if it is to be relative to the modern student in the world.

Let us outline something of the "how" to teach. In so doing we will see that while our method is in the service of the mes-sage, it is not something wholly distinct from that message.

Biblical Catechesis

To proclaim Christ effectively we must see how God has presented him to us. This "how" is contained in a story (l'his-toire), a history of salvation. Not in abstract definition does God communicate his message through Christ, but in the con-

111

crete circumstance of "flesh and blood" reality. The Old Testament is not composed in the abstract. Nor is the New Testament any more abstract. Because of man's condition—nothing being in his mind which was not first in his senses—God adapts his message to the concrete stories, types, figures and events that speak of his saving actions among men.

Sacred scripture therefore should be our catechism because it is God's catechism. Our catechesis must be biblical: what we are to teach is drawn from the scripture, for all that God has made known to us is found in some way in the sacred book, as this in turn is found in the mouth of the Church.

To proceed by way of a concrete story is in fact God's own way of teaching. "In many fragmentary and various utterances, God spoke of old to our ancestors through the prophets; at the present time . . . he has spoken to us through his Son" (Heb 1:1). It is our Lord's way. "And now, beginning with Moses and going right through the prophets, he interpreted to them whatever is said about himself anywhere in the Scriptures" (Lk 24:27).

What are the results of his telling a story of salvation (for in fact he always taught in story form, through those unexcelled parables of his)? His listeners were struck with the flame of love, as they listened to the magnificent works of God, "magnalia Dei," recounted by his Son. " 'Were not our inmost hearts on fire,' they said to each other, 'as he spoke to us . . . explaining to us the Scriptures?' " (Lk 24:32).

In an economy of words and actions which comprise sacred history, centering always in him, our Lord recommends to the catechist that he "pore over Scriptures . . . they are my standing witnesses" (Jn 5:39–47). "The New Testament," says St. Augustine, "is hidden in the Old. The Old Testament is visible in the New." And there is the famous observation of St. Jerome: "To be ignorant of the Scriptures is to be ignorant of Christ."

On numerous occasions our Lord drew from the Old Testament either stories, persons or events to teach what he wanted

112

his followers to know. In John 8:12 he alludes to the presence of God in the pillar of fire (Ex 13:21) to make clear that he is "the light of the world. He who follows me will . . . have the light of life." The story of Jonas provides the opportunity to speak of his own resurrection (Mt 12:40). The brazen serpent of the desert gives him occasion to explain his salvific work, "And just as Moses lifted up the serpent in the desert, so the Son of Man must needs be lifted up, that everyone who believes in him may have eternal life" (Jn 3:14–15).

The manna of the desert is but a pale image of him, the bread of life. "Moses did not give you the bread from heaven: for only the bread that comes down from heaven for the purpose of giving life to the world is God's bread. . . . I am the bread of life" (Jn 6:31–35).

Because the mystery of Christ is framed in salvation history, St. Paul directs Timothy to make his study and catechesis biblical: ". . . the sacred writings . . . can instruct you for salvation through the faith which is in Christ Jesus. All Scripture is inspired by God and useful for teaching" (2 Tm 3:15–17).

Throughout the Acts of the Apostles we find that communicating the good news was always done in a biblical narrative way, the scripture itself or an adaptation of it to the understanding of their hearers being the apostles' method (Acts 2,3,10; 7:2–53).

This likewise is the method of the Fathers. In fact the concrete narrative of salvation is found in resume in every creed. Thus God's way or method of teaching divine truth, Christ's way, the way of the apostles (see Acts 2,5,10 as well as St. Stephen's magnificent salvation history in Acts 6–7) are always through the concreteness of the scriptures.

The distinction then of method from message is somewhat artificial. Modern catechetical procedure is really a renewal and updating of what has always been the case in our catechesis: what we teach we draw from scripture, replete with concrete images rather than abstract formulations of doctrine. We give great importance to the story of salvation centered in Christ, so that biblical catechesis "draws all the doctrines of Christianity to the central doctrine which gives meaning to the whole: God's call to a new life in Christ."[2]

The fact that there is a "built-in" method to proclaiming the message gives rise to a consideration of all the concrete elements —apart from historical events—which the catechist must always employ. The need of our time is to make clear and meaningful the changeless truths of faith in contemporary terms. Universal elements in God's way of making himself known provide the inventive for this aggiornamento in catechetics.

Among the concrete image God employs to make himself known are the storm, fire, lightning, the cloud—signs of his presence and creative action. Consider the word "storm." God creates, and the sacred author speaks of the *storm,* meaningful as a creation-life symbol to a semi-desert people, "and the spirit of God was found moving over the waters" (Gn 1:1). When he recreates a world made foul by sin, as described in the story of the flood, the storm again appears. When he recreates a new people in the New Testament the image of the storm again returns. "When the day of Pentecost had come, they were all together in one place. Suddenly there came a sound in the sky, as of a violent wind blowing, and it filled the whole house where they were staying. And there appeared to them tongues like fire which distributed themselves and settled on each one of them" (Acts 2:1–3).

Christ used visible signs of invisible grace, of divine life channeled to men through sacraments. As God gave water to the Israelites, Christ gives baptism, the living water of new life; as kings, priests and prophets were anointed with oil, it is with oil that we are "Christ-ened" and made sharers of those same three prerogatives; bread and wine, universal signs of the staple foods of life, are transformed into his body and blood. Christ's

[2] *The ABC's of Modern Catechetics,* Johannes Hofinger S.J. with William J. Reedy, New York 1962, 21.

words are always strengthened by concrete deeds: since he has come that we may have life he can say to a young man or woman: "I say to you arise" (Lk 7:14; Mk 5:41). Just as his words brought about concrete effects then, so now he acts in sacraments. His words are the words of a man who is God. The Word of God always brings about concrete effects: "He spoke, and the world was made" (Ps 32:9). So concrete is his Word that the "Word became man and lived among us" (Jn 1:14).

Liturgical Catechesis

If what we teach is drawn from the scripture, then God himself speaks to our students through us. But what we teach is re-presented in terms of the liturgy. The liturgy is dogma prayed. Our catechesis aims not only at imparting clear, correct knowledge but also at forming worshipers of the Father. It is a message for *living*. The Church thus re-presents the doctrine drawn from scripture in concrete, prayable, dramatic form in the liturgy.

The *events* of salvation history are in fact reviewed, renewed and, in mystery, relived in the liturgy. All the turning points in the history of God's intervention in human affairs to form a people (Israel of old; the baptized of the New Testament) are *celebrated* and *re-presented* by a liturgical feast or season, so that biblical-liturgical catechesis follows this principle: what we teach from the concrete presentation of scripture we live in the liturgy.

As the scripture gives us a total view of Christ, from creation to re-creation, from his first to his second coming, so too does each season of the liturgy. Thus Advent speaks to us not only of the first coming of Christ in history, but of his coming each day in mystery, and especially of his second coming on the Last Day. Each of the cycles—Christmas, commemorating the Person of Christ, and Easter, his redemptive work—point always to the living Christ who will come again. This is the Christian's

115

hope. As Advent cries out for the parousia: "Come Lord Jesus, come," so does the very last line of scripture, Maranatha: "Come, Lord Jesus" (Ap 22:21).

Thus what we draw from the scripture we re-present through the liturgy. The more biblical our teaching the more certain we are as catechists that our religion classes are also religious experiences—for the scripture gives life. This preparation in the classroom is to lead to the liturgy in which the Word, received in the classroom and again in the liturgical service at the epistle and gospel, is climaxed by the receiving of the Word-Made-Flesh, present in the holy Eucharist. We are twice nourished at Mass: with the lessons of the Word, with the Word-Made-Flesh. Our catechesis must be so structured as to parallel this living reality.

If the first two approaches to the one message are through scripture and liturgy we employ the sound pedagogical principle of moving from concrete to abstract, known to unknown. Abstractions are not for children of any age! And so God reveals in the concreteness of history, and we pray our doctrine in the sensible concreteness of the liturgy.

Systematic, Meaningful Catechesis

We employ a meaningful language in the systematic explanation of what we teach. All during our *catechizing* we should be *explaining,* using language comprehensible to the level of the students we have before us. We use a concrete life situation, events, people, things with which they are familiar, to go from the scripture to the reality of the doctrine we wish to explain. This means using hands, feet, eyes, voice, activities such as drawing, singing, gesturing, pantomime, tableaux and reading. Our students are not body and soul. They are in the Hebrew notion "soma"—soul-body. The whole child is to be educated religiously; he is saved or lost in his completeness as body-soul. Thus our appeal is to his senses as well as to his intellect, memory and will. Our language is his language and it is the instrument

116

by which we make real and meaningful to him God's life-giving language, his Word.

We arrive at careful formulations of what concisely, clearly and accurately he must know, for we train the intellect. These formulas are privileged ways of stating divine truth and should be fixed in the memory, once understanding has been inculcated by means of our words, the Word of God and the action of the liturgy. But such materials for memorization are always the point of arrival, never the point of departure.

So our first step in following sound educational psychology is to *prepare* the student for the doctrine or practice we are to teach, using a story or a picture from real life or within his experience. Then we *present* this doctrine or practice, again using the concrete story, figure or image *from scripture*. We *explain* the doctrine in clear contemporary language, and show how this doctrine is lived in the liturgy, which now becomes a form in which we *re-present* and *review* what was presented and explained. Fourthly we summarize in clear correct formulas (using scriptural and liturgical formulae as well as catechetical) what the child knows and understands. The final approach to the one message is through being ourselves witnesses to Christ and bringing our children to witness as well.

Witness to Christ

Most important, we apply what is taught to the child's level of living the faith. We suggest ways of responding to God's gift of love and do what we can to prepare the way for the Spirit to move where he wills. This response should take place in the classroom—in prayer, preferably a liturgical prayer which sums up the point taught.

Our ultimate objective is primary: it must be our daily meditation before we prepare, present, explain, summarize and apply. It must precede our plan to clearly draw from scripture and re-present through the liturgy what we teach. This objective is to bring our children to a total life commitment to Christ in faith. It is to bring them in their own lives to witness to God in a life of loving and prayerful action. Already committed to Christ in baptism, each of us makes compromises: "How can I choose this and still not abandon my choice for Christ." Our own commitment as catechists, our own life of faith, must shine forth to our students: "If I cannot have this and at the same time have Christ, I do not want this."

So important are we as a sign to the children, as a "method" of communicating the message, that in us they must see what we teach them to live. If the scripture gives life and the liturgy gives what it teaches, viz. an increase of divine life shared, we are the chosen instruments (not mere volunteers) to channel these twofold sources of grace to our youngsters. We cannot be worthy instruments unless we possess what we wish to give them.

Our apostolate catches us up in sacred mystery: we are involved in a life process as catechists. Through us, acting in us, the Spirit enters into our children. We are involved in a sacred historical action, generating Christ in others. Truly do we say with St. Paul of our ultimate aim: "My little children . . . even now, *I am in labor,* that Christ may be formed in you" (Gal 4:19).

PART TWO

MAN MEETS GOD IN FAITH

THE second major area of catechetics concentrates on man's faith-response to God's mysterious coming in the fourfold signs. Faith is considered here in its traditional fullness. More than the holding of certain truths, faith is that which takes the whole man and brings him past a new mentality and new behavior to a communion of life with God in Christ. This dynamic, personal conception of faith seems to be the meeting point for the best fruits of contemporary theology, and is the hinge which secures catechetics to the Church's present-day pastoral renewal.

Living Faith: Major Concern of Religious Education

ALFONSO M. NEBREDA S.J.

IN the epistle to the Romans we[1] read: "Whoever calls upon the name of the Lord shall be saved. But how are they to call upon him in whom they have not believed? And how are they to believe him whom they have not heard? And how are they to hear, if no one preaches? And how are men to preach unless they are sent? As it is written: How beautiful are the feet of those who preach the gospel of peace; of those who bring glad tidings of good things. It is true, all have not accepted the gospel. For Isaias says: Lord, who has believed our report? Faith then depends on hearing, and hearing on the word of Christ. But I ask, have they not heard? Yes, indeed: Their voices have gone forth all over the earth, and their words to the ends of the world" (10:13–18). The letter to the Hebrews states: "By faith we understand that the world was fashioned by the word of God" (11:3).

These passages hint at an intimate relation between words and faith. By words God comes to meet man; in faith man answers the call of God. Word and faith are inseparable twins. It was but natural that these two should come to the fore in an era

---

[1] This article has been developed from the first in a series of lectures given by the author at the Crossroad Study Week held at Grailville in August 1963 and which appeared in the Grail Council of Religious Education *Bulletin* 26. We are grateful to Miss Eva Fleischner of the Grail for preparing the lecture for the *Bulletin*. The author has expanded the article into its present form for a book to be published by Loyola University Press as part of its Pastoral Studies Program. Loyola University Press has graciously given permission to print the article in this symposium.

like ours, in which the Church feels herself more than ever in the state of mission. And this is exactly what is happening in theology and missiology and in the pastoral renewal, i.e. in liturgy, catechetics, etc.

It is interesting to observe the various associations that the word "missionary" evokes, not only in the minds of the faithful but often even in our priests. The missions seem to be something partial, a field among other fields in the Church, centering somehow on the exotic and catering to the fantasy of our people. No wonder then that even the best Christians, busy as they are working for the cause of Christ in their respective fields, are not inclined to give too much attention to the problem of the missions.

In contrast to this somehow geographical and juridical conception of the missions a new understanding in the Church, much more theological and spiritual, is growing. From foreign missions we pass to the "mission of the Church" which, in the words of Father Le Guillou, French Dominican specialist in ecumenical problems, can be defined as "the act by which the Church goes beyond the frontiers of her own life to bear witness to Christ among those who do not know him. The essential intention is to lead from nonbelief to belief."[2] The missionary approach concentrates on conversion. As is evident it is directed to faith or, better, to the organic process by which men rise from unbelief to faith, and by which believers advance from initial conversion to a deeper and more personal communion with God. Conversion remains the heart of the missionary concern of the Church. In terms of faith we realize immediately that we can no longer maintain a rigid distinction between missionary and Christian countries. Even in so-called Christian milieux we daily face people who do not believe, the pagan or neo-pagan whom we meet in growing numbers. There are the fallen-away Catholics and the "baptized non-Christians." The Church as a whole is in the state of mission. Over and above geographical

[2] M. J. Le Guillou, *Mission et unité,* Paris 1961, vol. I, 88.

frontiers and peculiar situations the basic pastoral concern of the Church seems to be everywhere the same: to lead men from unbelief to belief in Christ and then to baptism, and to lead from initial faith to a faith which is deeper and more personal.

Itinerary of the Adult Unbeliever to Faith

What is the proper setting for a study of the process of faith? It would be incorrect to set up as the standard those who were baptized as children, for at the time they could not have ratified personally the pledge and promises of the sacramental life. Although theologically justified and numerically normal in our Christian lands, the case of infant baptism cannot serve as the norm. The standard is and should be the adult who knowingly and willingly presents himself to the Church of God and asks for baptism which will turn him from a son of man into a son of God.

It might be well here to dispel a common misunderstanding. Some people seem to think that baptism gives faith since the ritual of baptism begins with the priest's question: "What do you ask of the Church of God?" and the answer: "Faith." They think that it is in baptism that one receives faith. If so then God would be acting in a most unlikely way, thrusting himself upon man, forcing his gifts on someone who does not want to receive them. This is precisely why faith must precede the sacrament of baptism if the sacrament is to have any meaning. The Church's entire tradition is most emphatic on this point.[3] We do not speak here of the *habit* of faith, which even infants receive at baptism; rather we are referring to faith as the psychological attitude which precedes baptism. A global initial faith is essential. The recent permission granted by Rome to use the separate

[3] See J. Mouroux, *The Christian Experience,* New York 1954, 48–60. I purposely limit myself to the baptism of adults. The infant baptism follows another line, well justified by sound theological principles; but for all its numerical normality it cannot be considered as the type when we study things from the angle of faith.

123

stages for the administration of baptism is a welcome and encouraging sign. In our actual baptismal ritual we have a formula that combines both the ritual of baptism proper and the ritual used in the first centuries for introduction to the catechumenate. One enters the catechumenate precisely with the understanding that he asks for faith and is already praying for faith.

The study week on mission catechetics held in Bangkok in November 1963 described, for the first time in the history of catechetics, the three stages which normally highlight the process of the adult journeying toward faith: *pre-evangelization,* that is, a stage of preparation for the kerygma which, taking man as he is and where he is, makes a human dialogue possible and awakens in man the sense of God—a sense indispensable for opening his heart to the message; *evangelization* or kerygma, that is, the dynamic heralding of the substance of the Christian message in view of the conversion or global acceptance of Christ as the Lord; *catechesis proper* which, leaning and banking on the conversion obtained through the kerygma, systematically develops the message in view of initiating man into Christian life and in view of building the Christian personality. Only at the end of these three stages can an adult be considered ready to receive baptism, which indeed will crown and seal the whole process.

Here precisely lurks the danger which threatens to spoil in its roots the pastoral activity of the Church in so-called Christian areas. As our children shortly after birth receive baptism, the crown and seal of the entire process of conversion, there is danger of assuming that the process is complete. For the adult this process often means a long and tiresome struggle.

Even if we are certain that our apparent securities will be shaken we should honestly ask ourselves: how many of our baptized people have been evangelized? How many have ratified with an adult conversion the commitment to Christ which others in their name made at the hour of their baptism? An authentic pastoral concern may not bypass this fact: as long as our Christians have not digested the content, fruits and activities of these three stages—above all conversion and real acceptance of Christ, which is the heart of the whole process—we cannot speak of Christian adults. We have somehow to journey through the three stages with our Christians, but in the reverse order: catechesis proper, evangelization, pre-evangelization. In the next article Father Hofinger develops this point in detail.

In the missions we confront many people who want to be baptized but who cannot be—for instance students whose parents will not permit baptism. These people although not baptized nonetheless believe. And because they believe they are Christian, in the sense in which St. Augustine called catechumens "Christian." As opposed to this category however we meet today in many Christian areas an enormous number of "baptized non-Christians." By these are meant not fallen-away Catholics but the many people who come regularly to Mass and receive the sacraments but who, in regard to their belief, are not yet convinced that Christian faith is something quite different from external observance and practice. Distinction must be made between the level of the sacraments and the level of personal faith. People can be validly baptized who have never made an adequate personal commitment. As soon as men can act in a personal way they should be led to make a commitment, by which faith becomes a human reality for them. To lead men to an adult conversion and true commitment to Christ is one of the greatest challenges facing religious education.

Even for fervent Catholics conversion must be a permanent dimension of Christian existence. Only in heaven will we rest. Until then we must try and try again, because what we conquer today we may lose tomorrow. A huge no-man's land always exists in us which must be subdued and subjected to the domain of faith.

For these reasons the missionary approach is not limited to so-called missionary countries, but pertains also to the very core of Christianity's apostolic dimension. If therefore our pastoral activity is to be realistic it must confront the education of faith as its primary task, but a faith which is beyond and above the holding of certain truths. It must lead to a faith which takes the whole man and brings him past a new mentality and new behavior to a communion of life with God in Christ. This is the meaning of living faith: personal encounter with God in Christ. This deeper, more dynamic and more personal concept of faith seems to be the meeting point for the best fruits of the theological renewal of the last decade. And it is also the hinge on which swings the most promising task of the Church's pastoral renewal. It is like a return to the Church's early history when emphasis was clearly on faith and on the Word.

Living Faith and God's Word

St. Paul says plainly: "Faith comes from hearing" (Rom 10:17). This is why, when we speak of faith, we implicitly include the transmitting of God's word. Word and faith remain central to the fresh discoveries, or better to the recoveries in contemporary theology. In our Lord's missionary command word and faith come first: "Go into the whole world and preach the gospel to every creature. He who believes and is baptized shall be saved, but he who does not believe shall be condemned" (Mk 16:15–16). Matthew's gospel implies the same thing: "Go, therefore, and make disciples of all nations, baptizing them in the name of the Father . . . (Mt 28:18). First faith, then baptism. St. Paul even says that he has not been sent to baptize but to evangelize, that is, to preach and confront his hearers with faith: "For Christ did not send me to baptize, but to preach the gospel, not with wisdom of words, lest the cross of Christ be made void. . . . It pleased God, by the foolishness of our preaching, to save those who believe" (1 Cor 1:17–21). When the apostles realized that they could not perform all the activities of the infant Church they decided to remain servants of the word. Other matters could be managed by deacons and others.

126

But this aspect of serving the faith—serving the word in order to provoke faith—was of paramount importance to the Church's first pastors:

> So the Twelve called together the multitude of the disciples and said: It is not desirable that we should forsake the word of God and serve at tables. Therefore, brethren, select from among you seven men of good reputation, full of the Spirit and of wisdom, that we may put them in charge of this work. But we will devote ourselves to prayer and to the ministry of the word (Acts 6:2–4).

A fuller understanding of the significance of words makes clearer the meaning of faith, and especially its personal, existential character. Words can be looked upon from a rather static viewpoint, merely as signs which manifest one's thought to another. Modern psychology however insists on the interpersonal, dynamic character of words. Words have *content* for they represent something. But they are also a *summons* for, as modern psychology insists, they are addressed to someone and tend to elicit a response from the other. Thirdly they are an *unfolding of personality* for they manifest the speaker's interior attitudes and dispositions. Words tend to set up a "summons-response circuit:" explanation-attention, command-obedience, promise-trust, testimony-faith. Words can be used merely for utilitarian purposes at a very impersonal level, as in newspapers, but on a higher level words can become self-expression. They reveal something of the speaker. For this to take place there must always be a mutual opening up, both the speaker and hearer respecting one another in the mysteriousness of their personalities. Mutual trust, availability and at least the beginnings of friendship are required.

When speech reaches this higher level, it is the sign of friendship and love; it is an overflow and expression of the freedom by which one opens himself to another and gives himself to him. Speaker and listener give and are given to each other. And where the word is not

127

equal to the expression of this giving, it is accompanied by a gesture or even a life commitment, as in conjugal love or in the apostolate.[4]

God's word is conceived at this higher level. Revelation is a dynamic word which involves a summons, an invitation to man to the obedience of faith with a view of sharing life. As Latourelle explains in "Faith: Personal Encounter with God," God's speech not only informs, it effects what it signifies, changing the status of man. It establishes bonds of love and friendship with man. In this sense revelation is more than the unfolding of certain truths: it is God's unveiling of his very personality under the motivation of an intense love. And it calls for a response of faith likewise accompanied by love so that there will be, on the part of man, a consecration and commitment. Word and faith thus go hand in hand to effect a living communion with the all-holy God.

Sacraments and Faith

A most difficult yet important problem concerning faith is how to draw a sufficiently accurate map of the spiritual topography of one's hearers. Certain outspoken questions of teenagers, or a peculiar reaction of penitents in the confessional, should open our eyes to the reality, be it a painful one, that many of our "Christians" do not in fact believe in the full sense of the word. They possess perhaps an academic appreciation of their faith, but a personal allegiance does not seem to be involved. Who is not acquainted with young Catholics who meet with serious doubts in their religious convictions or even "lose their faith" when they come in contact with certain secular environments? Most likely a survey of what many Christians think about the sacraments would reveal that many have lived only in a *notional* assent to the truths of faith without having

[4] Rene Latourelle S.J., "Faith: Personal Encounter with God," *Theology Digest* X, 4, Autumn 1962, 233.

128

made this assent something *real* in their lives—to use the well known distinction of Cardinal Newman. For these Christians the important thing in a sacrament is not the encounter with a person but the correct performance of a rite. It is here perhaps that the consequences of the polemic approach of post-tridentine catechetics have made themselves most strongly felt. The concern of safeguarding the importance and integrity of the sacramental order, which the Protestants had attacked, brought Catholics to stress the ex opere operato vigorously in the explanation of the sacraments. Justified in itself and even necessary this emphasis was nonetheless unfortunate in its one-sided belaboring of the efficacy of the sacraments.

Almost until the time of the Council of Trent the main emphasis was always on faith. After Trent however a significant trend developed which we may take as a warning against too close ties with local or temporal situations. Catechesis must be adapted to the needs of the times, yet must not reflect too exclusively the one-sided preoccupations of any given era.

Prior to Trent both the theology and the catechesis of the Counter-reformation concentrated on combating the Reformer's negation of the core of the Church's sacramental activity. Because Protestants denied the supernatural role of the sacraments Catholic theologians and later the catechists stressed their objective efficacy.[5] This aspect must be stressed. At the same time however we should remember that the sacraments are, as the Church's venerable tradition has beautifully explained, either *signs of faith* or they are nothing: even worse than nothing: they may be simply magical formulas which mislead people.[6]

Present-day theology and catechesis are doing much to recover the balance of seeing the sacraments within the context of

[5] See Matthew J. O'Connell, "The Sacraments in Theology Today," *Thought* 36 (1961), 40–58, and especially 41–44 for a brief exposition of the tridentine sacramentology as being too much determined by polemical concern.

[6] See P. Fransen S.J., *Faith and the Sacraments,* London 1958; also "Sacraments, Signs of Faith," *Worship* 37 (1962), 31–49.

faith. Still it must be admitted that many Christians continue to regard the sacraments solely as efficacious means of grace and fail to see the sacraments in their truly vital and meaningful context, that is to say, in faith.

As an example of this persistent attitude we might take the case of a young boy who is a very fervent Christian. He goes to confession every Saturday, receives communion every Sunday. It is now Monday, and unfortunately he has committed a serious sin. What, we might ask, as derived from our everyday observations, is the very common attitude of such a person? (It might be added parenthetically that we are not attempting to exaggerate or caricature the situation; very often, through inadequate understanding of the sacraments, many people often do forget that the sacrament of penance must be seen in the context of faith. We do not refer here to people who say to themselves: "Well, now I am in mortal sin. I might as well go on sinning since I am going to confession next Saturday. What difference does it make if I confess the sin once or many times!" Such a mentality we immediately recognize as outlandish. Rather we refer to the case of a typical Catholic who confesses regularly.)

The boy who has sinned is not going to confession until Saturday. He is uncomfortable in his sin, perhaps unaware that he could and should have the sin forgiven at once through an act of perfect contrition, and then as soon as possible afterward go to confession. No one has taught this boy that what is more important than the sacraments, from a psychological point of view, and therefore from the point of view of his attitude, is the way he looks at the sacraments.[7] If the sacraments mean to him that he meets Christ, all is well. But if Christ is met in the

[7] For an understanding of the reemphasis of the opus operantis in the reception of the sacraments, see E. Schillebeeckx O.P., *De Sacramentale Heilseconomie*, Antwerpen 1953; L. Villete, *Foi et Sacrement*, Paris 1959. See also K. Rahner, "Personale und sakramentale Frömmigkeit," *Schriften zur Theologie* II, Einsiedeln 1954, 115–41, summarized in *Theology Digest* (1955), 93–98.

sacraments, why is the youth not aware that Christ is someone living today? Why does he think he must wait until Saturday to apologize to this living Christ? Obviously he either disregards or misunderstands many elements here: the very concept of contrition, of grace, which is essentially restoration of a friendship that has been broken. To such a person the sacraments are static or purely material things.

When Saturday finally arrives the boy goes to church. He kneels down and starts to prepare for his confession. But is the boy's main concern to prepare for what is most important: to meet Christ and to tell him personally that he is sorry? This would be a real meeting. Or is he simply taking all precautions to perform a rite which emphasizes mainly the practice, the correct performance? If this latter is true then we should not be astonished when a mature professional man of fifty comes to us and confesses in the very same words a child uses—the same words he has used since he was seven, when his second grade teacher prepared him for his first confession.

Let us return to the boy. He comes out of church and someone remarks: "Wonderful, isn't it? You can almost see in his eyes the brightening effects of the grace of the sacrament." Nonsense! To what "grace of the sacrament" does the person refer? What he observed was exactly what any normal citizen feels when he has paid a fine or his income tax: "Now everything is in order. I have paid." Is it not true that, for many Christians, confession means going to church and being ready to work off a fine or receive a reprimand from the priest?

For a number of people the whole sacramental world is all but meaningless. Can we imagine two persons who consider themselves friends and who yet never speak to one another? We would have to conclude that either they are not friends or that something is wrong with them. There are Christians for whom confession is nothing more than an expression of "being in line." Thus they come to confession and say: "Against the first commandment, nothing. . . . Against the second commandment,

131

nothing. . . . Against the third commandment, nothing. . . ."
But is Christianity really so negative as all that? The main concern in Christian existence for such people apparently is security
—"being alright." We are not "alright"—we are sinners. The
first Christians had a wonderful awareness of the nothingness,
the sinfulness of man. And by man we here mean a Christian.
St. John even says: "If someone says that he is not a sinner he
is a liar, and he makes God a liar" (1 Jn 1:10). What is the
meaning of God sending his own Son to save us from our sins
if we have no sins and do not need salvation? A Christian is
not "in line." He is "in Christ." The idea of morality held by too
many Christians is that the commandments oblige us much like
a law-enforcing agent does. But this conception denies the very
essence of Christian morality, which is liberation from any law,
the replacing of law by the Spirit of Christ in the atmosphere of
faith.[8] For St. Paul "in Christ" is at the same time the realm
of faith and the realm of morality. Everything is perfectly uni-
fied there.[9]

Let us take another imaginary example. An old Virginian
of one hundred and fifty years ago comes back to life again. He
enters one of our offices and sees a young girl talking on the
phone. He stares at her in astonishment and finally says: "This
girl must be crazy. She's talking to herself!" What is the difference between talking to oneself like a madman and talking
over the phone? In the second case there is someone to answer
the call. This very thing happens when one performs a rite,
a sacrament; for instance when a priest baptizes a dying child
in front of a whole family which does not believe. The priest is
very much aware in such a situation that he appears most
strange to the onlookers. Everyone stares at him. He pours a few
drops of water on the child and believes that this has a wonder-

[8] See S. Lyonnet, "Saint Paul: Liberty and Law," *Theology Digest* XI
(1963) 12–18.
[9] I highly recommend the book of P. A. Liégé O.P., *What is Christian
Life?* New York 1961.

ful, literally a divine meaning. Everyone standing around him has seen the same reality, but they say: "What does this mean?" What is it, precisely, that makes us see this reality which the nonbeliever does not see? Faith of course! It is only in the context of faith that, for the first time, the whole sacramental reality of the Church—which is precisely salvation history prolonged and actualized for us—comes to life.[10] Faith remains the context of intelligibility which both gives meaning to the sacraments and is nurtured and deepened by them.

Recovery of a Richer Concept of Faith

Another important aspect from the missionary point of view is the recovery of a more global, all-embracing sense of faith. During the Reformation the Protestants attacked faith as *content* and faith as *profession.* So it was necessary to stress orthodoxy in content and to profess outwardly that one was a Catholic. It was normal for men like Bellarmine to stress these two points, faith as profession and faith as truths to be believed. If Catholics had kept the other elements along with these two, all would have been well. But they forgot, practically speaking, to stress the other equally necessary elements, such as commitment and trust. Protestants had stressed these one-sidedly, and Catholic theology and catechetics went to the other extreme. Consequently for at least the last two centuries, and still today, faith has meant simply "orthodoxy," that is, a correct statement and holding of certain truths.

Let us not forget that no one can nourish his spiritual life with orthodoxy alone.[11] "You believe that there is one God.

10 See Bernard Cooke S.J., "The Sacraments as the Continuing Acts of Christ," *Proceedings of the Catholic Theological Society of America* 16 (1961), 43–68.

11 F. X. Arnold has described in a masterly fashion both the historical deviation and the balanced Christian view of faith as fides quae and fides qua at the same time. See, among others: *Dienst am Glauben,* Freiburg i. Br. 1948, 24f; *Glaubensverkundigung und Glaubensgemeinschaft,* Dussel-

You do well. The devils also believe, and tremble" (Jas 2:19). The aim of catechesis can never be simply to transmit correct information. Our whole emphasis in teaching has been usually on correctness with the result that we seem to go even farther: instead of orthodoxy we venerate "orthology," the science of speaking correctly. We insist not only on thinking correctly but on speaking correctly! But there is more to Christianity than this. There must also and above all be correct practice, correct life, because faith *is* life.

This truth was practically forgotten for the last two centuries in catechetics. It is remarkable that in the last thirty years we seem to have changed roles with Protestant theologians. Originally they had stressed so much the aspect of trust and commitment that we went to the other extreme and insisted one-sidedly on objectivity, correctness, orthodoxy. Today Catholic theology stresses, even more forcefully than Protestant theology, the personal aspect of faith. Consider for example Jean Mouroux's books,[12] or the work of Father Alfaro of the Gregorian,[13] or Roger Aubert's very fundamental book.[14] These works insist so much on the personal, existential trust-sense of faith that we seem to have adopted the Protestant view. The Protestants on the other hand insist more than ever before on the objectivity of faith, without which one cannot distinguish true faith from superstition. This is a good, healthy sign, indicating greater balance. Yet we should heed this process because the same thing has been happening with catechesis for centuries. The danger always exists that one is too encircled in his own approach. Catechesis must of course always be expressed in categories that

dorf 1955, chs. 1–2; "The Act of Faith as Personal Commitment," *Lumen Vitae* 5 (1950), 251–256; "Faith as Assent and Commitment," *Lumen Vitae* 2 (1956), 571–82.

[12] *I Believe*, New York 1959; *From Baptism to the Act of Faith*, Boston 1963.

[13] *Adnotationes in tractatum de virtutibus, ad usum auditorum*, Romae 1959. See also his "Persona y Gracia," *Gregorianum* 41 (1960), 5–29, and "Fides in Terminologia Biblica," *Gregorianum* 42 (1961), 463–505.

[14] *Le probleme de l'acte de foi*, Louvain 1958.

can be understood by a particular age or milieu. But we should not emphasize things one-sidely as in the past.

Today we are returning to the best theological tradition of St. Augustine or even St. Thomas, to the traditional formula which explained faith as credere Deum, credere Deo and credere in Deum. Credere Deum means to believe God as the object, the target of our thinking, provided we do not forget that God is never an object but remains forever a Person. It is remarkable to note St. Thomas' emphasis on this point. He says: "Faith never stops at the statement but goes beyond the statement to the reality explained in it."[15] We find the same idea in Newman, who emphasizes the need to stress real assent above notional assent. This is an important point for all catechesis.

We often make wonderful statements; but do we ask ourselves what they mean to children? "I believe in the incarnation!" I do not believe in the incarnation. What is "incarnation?" It is a word. The author remembers one of his theology professors in Spain who said once, when discussing the incarnate Word—in Spanish Verbo encarnado: "If you talk like that in a village, they might think it is one of those gunmen, El Verbo, a bandit." Encarnado in Spanish also means "red"—so we have the Red Bandit. These terms are relics from medieval times when it was considered the finest achievement to choose the most abstract of abstractions. Today we no longer have this mentality. Why go on speaking about the Trinity, the incarnation, the redemption? These are words, abstractions that do not exist. I believe in the Father; I believe in Jesus; I believe in the Son; I believe in the Holy Spirit. These are personal realities. All this may seem like an external detail, but unless we attempt such purification, our children will at best be happily content with mere abstractions, mere words.

When we say credo Deum we mean that we believe God as someone. We mean not merely assent to a truth but essentially adherence to a person—an adherence from within. This is

15 "Fides non terminatur ad enuntiabile sed ad rem," II IIae 1, 2, 2m.

precisely faith, which implies the whole activity of the Holy Spirit leading us to a new knowledge.

The second aspect is credere Deo, which means to believe God. When we say to a person: "I believe you," it is different from saying: "I believe something about you" or "I believe a truth." The words "I believe you" imply a total context where the person as such is involved. This is the second aspect of faith which must be stressed. We tell God: "I believe you. I do not need extra reports or proofs—I believe you!" When a girl tells a boy: "I believe you," the deepest level of personal relations is involved. To say: "I believe you" to God means to accept God as the highest witness, who gives us the only type of certainty needed in Christianity. For the certainty of our faith comes not from the evidence of a truth but from the credibility of a person.[16]

When we say credere in Deum we refer to a new dynamism by which God is simultaneously the highest truth, the highest value and above all the highest happiness. We do not need to make distinctions. By committing myself and being involved as a whole person, I know that Christ—and God in Christ—is assuring me of my highest happiness and my highest truth.[17]

These ideas on relationships are gradually becoming normal background for the whole field of catechetics. If we study the evolution in catechetics over the last fifty years from the angle of faith, i.e. leading a man from nonbelief to belief, we recognize a shift of emphasis from the *object* of belief (a stress on information, instruction, teaching), to the *subject*: how does faith affect me as a believer, my mentality as well as my behavior? How do I become a Christian person? This is what Father van Caster in a remarkable article[18] calls the stage of formation, the

[16] See the two articles by F. X. Arnold published in *Lumen Vitae* and cited above.

[17] For the significative usage of "credere in" in Christian Latin, see Christine Mohrman, *Etudes sur le latin des Chretiens,* Rome 1958, 195–203.

[18] M. van Caster S.J., "Teaching, Formation and Initiation," *Lumen Vitae* 16 (1961), 607–16.

stage when Christian values begin to form and build up a Christian personality.

Finally, emphasis in recent years has shifted to *interpersonal relationships*. God's revelation is studied in a much more personal light, and man's answer in faith is also thoroughly personalized. Thus faith is stressed as a fully personal commitment. As Father van Caster says clearly in his article concerning instruction, formation and encounter, the correct order is usually assumed to be a chronological one. First inform our students, give them correct information about God. Then gradually this information will produce a sort of formation. The students will change their personalities, begin to think as Christians and behave somewhat like followers of Christ. Only then at the peak of this process will come the third state: initiation into the mystery of God, communion with God.[19]

The contrary can also be true however. Unless we start at the very beginning with the aspect of initiation—leading our students to meet God and to experience God as someone—even the level of formation will not be achieved nor will the information be transmitted correctly.

The Personalist Approach

Current developments in phenomenology and existential philosophy as well as psychology are helping to penetrate the reality of the person more deeply. These insights are aiding us to understand better the Christian reality. This personalistic concern seems to be the convergent trend in many different milieux today: Catholics like Gabriel Marcel, a man like Martin Buber who is a Jew, a Protestant like Paul Tillich, or a man like Shestov, a Russian Orthodox. All these men realize that we are entering an era in which, precisely because a depersonalizing process confronts us daily, a catastrophe will befall us unless we

---

[19] See the beautiful article of F. Taymans d'Eypernon S.J. "Faith, Man's Communion with God," *Lumen Vitae* 9 (1954), 182–93.

react and realize more deeply the uniqueness of our personal lives.

This trend provides wonderful background for a richer understanding of the meaning of faith. We ordinarily assume that "knowledge" is one simple reality in all cases. This is not correct however. To give an example: it is one process to know *something* and quite a different action to know *someone*. Unless we realize this we will continue day after day, even as good Catholics, to apply to persons the same categories we apply to objects—seeing in people not their personal features but only their functions. This person, who is he? Merely a professor at the university, or a policeman, or the postman. Professor, policeman, postman are titles which reduce him to a number, a figure. We are simply trying to satisfy our depersonalizing instinct. Rather this person is Mr. Jones—a unique, individual person.

We must begin by emphasizing strongly what is unique. In all nature we will not find two things exactly the same. Any scentist will admit that not even two leaves are alike. This uniqueness applies still more to persons. If we could only see into the hearts of two twins and their ways of reacting to things and persons, we would be astonished that people could confuse them. For each is remarkably different. This is the mark, the trademark of God! He seems to throw away his mold every time he creates anything—especially when he creates a human being.

The author is often asked: "How can you prove that God loves me personally?" The reply: "Either God loves you personally, or he does not love you at all." For the only reality that exists is you and you and you. We speak of men, women, boys, girls, etc. but these concepts are our inventions. We are proud of our so-called universal concepts and devote numerous philosophical theses to them. We are proud of these distinctions and rightly so—if we compare ourselves with a dog or other mere animal. But when God looks at us, at our way of reasoning and abstracting, he must be highly amused. We are forced to "kill" things in order to feed them into the pigeon holes of our brains. We speak about "the trees." What is "the trees"? In order to put an object at the level of our grasping and handling we build up a universal concept and apply it to everything; but it no longer fits anything adequately because, after all, this tree is this tree, and that tree is that tree. All reality is unique; persons especially are unique. For our comfort we have invented concepts that seem to work—much like a biologist who wants to analyze life by dissecting it. In order to analyze he kills the life. In this way we deal with things, and in this same way we find ourselves dealing with persons.

What then is the way to know a person? First of all we cannot fully express ourselves in words or concepts because each of us is unique. If our words did truly express us then we would be inventing words every day, until finally no one would understand us. We would have to invent our own individual vocabularies because our experiences, if sufficiently analyzed, are all unique. The fact is that great personalities in moments of deep personal consciousness actually do invent expressions—what we call poetry, inventiveness, creativity. When we feel deeply in sorrow or in joy we frequently realize that our words cannot express what we feel, and we retreat into silence. This is a normal human experience because words, which are a common expression applicable to and used by all, become worn out. They do not express accurately what we sense is unique in ourselves. The same thing applies to our concepts which, as we saw, are built up by abstractions that siphon out, so to speak, the common features of uniquely existing reality.

How then is a person known? Only through the revelation of himself. What is the meaning of revelation? It means that a person comes out of himself, makes himself understood, shows himself. We cannot know someone unless he agrees to manifest his intimacy to us. If a boy goes to some place where no one knows him and decides not to talk to anyone or make a single gesture, no one will know him. They may know something about him—that he is very strange. But they will not really know him. They can look at a hundred pictures of him but will not know him as a person unless he goes out of himself, unless by words and actions he reveals something of what he is really like.

Another very important point, which applies also to God, is that we are known much more by indirect means—the tone of our voice, the look in our eyes, a gesture, silence—than simply by words alone. This is true because, as we said above, words alone somehow kill the very uniqueness of our self-expression. What then is the way to know a person? Not through words on an impersonal level, but through a sort of sixth sense, an intuition,[20] a kind of sympathy, a feeling with the other. Max Scheler in his classic work *Nature of Sympathy* provides a wealth of insights into this important problem.[21]

Imagine that we have heard many things about a person but have never met him. Do we know that person? No. We know *about* him. Unless we meet him we will not know *him*. By meeting a person we do not of course mean being merely physically present with him. We can meet him as if he were a tree, and our impression will be a wrong one. Rather we mean personal meeting—what is called intuition, sympathy, a sort of connatural knowledge which is already understanding and, therefore, love.

P. de Letter[22] offers an excellent analysis of the point discussed here. Encounter is the meeting of persons in an I-thou relationship on the level of mutual understanding and love. Not

---

[20] Gerald A. McCool, "The Primacy of Intuition," *Thought* 37 (1962), 57–73, reviews in a penetrating way new trends in Catholic thought concerning intuition. He has in mind works of A. Brunner, Balthasar, K. Rahner, but especially the important thesis of C. Cirne-Lima, *Der personale Glaube,* Innsbruck 1959.

[21] New Haven 1954.

[22] See "The Encounter with God," *Thought* 36 (Spring 1961).

purely conceptual knowledge however; rather a sort of general *synthetic* intuition which results not by reasoning but by "seeing" from the ensemble of many partial experiences and ideas. Knowledge of a person cannot be expressed in a concept which, of its very nature, refers to a quality or form and does not of itself represent a *subject*. Person involves relation and opposition to the other. Only by intuition do we know a relation. The intuition reaches the person from the light of this synthetic view. Meeting is essentially the conscious living of the I-thou relationship.

From Love to Knowledge

Of the personal realm it is not true to say that knowledge produces understanding and love. The contrary is correct. Only love produces understanding, and therefore true knowledge. This point is essential for the whole of catechetics. Unless we approach a person with a well disposed attitude we will miss the point. Consider for example the mother of someone considered a criminal. Do we not say that she is blind because she is convinced that her son is at heart truly good? But the blindness is really ours. Only she has the eyes to see who her son really is. We approach him with cold objectivity—actually the very opposite of true objectivity. We are so objective that we have killed the very feature of personal knowledge and have reduced the person to a thing. We must realize that people agree to reveal themselves out of love. The moment we enter into contact with another person in an attitude which is not creating, permeating, breathing love in a sort of radiation, the other person instinctively feels ill at ease. He will instinctively react by putting on a mask, so that we will be unable to know him. We will go home and say: "Of course I know that person." But all who know him will say that we have missed the point. We have seen a caricature of him because we have seen only the façade

141

and imagined that that was the person. Almost without realizing it this person had decided to retreat into himself, refusing to open and reveal himself, so that even with the best intentions we were not able to see and hence know him as he is.

To know a person is to meet him fully at that point where not only our mind but especially our heart decides. Father de la Taille, one of the greatest theologians of this century, could write: "The light of faith, although residing in the mind, does not enter man through the mind, but through the heart. There is its door of entry, the passage through which God pours this light more or less abundantly, more or less alive, according as love itself lives in us beyond any other affection, or, on the contrary, as self-love dominates over or oppresses love of God."[23]

Newman possessed the wonderful intuition that the problem of the approach to faith is not intellectual but essentially moral, a problem therefore of the heart. He highlighted the moral aspect, not in the sense in which the classical apologist stressed that sinners who refuse to leave their sinful state will not see God—following our Lord's words that only "the clean of heart will see God." Not in this obvious, often superficially understood sense, but in the very true sense that we can never understand a value unless we are already connaturally open to it. This is a very practical point for us today. Many Catholics do not have the proper attitude toward peace, precisely because they are breathing an atmosphere where real peace is mere theory. They have a hierarchy of values in which peace is secondary. All that applies to values applies much more directly to persons.

Unless the approach of faith begins with a global meeting with God, not only will formation as such not be achieved in a true Catholic sense but even the process of information, which we call instruction, will never be truly Christian. We can therefore say that the missionary stimulus forcefully centers the

[23] M. de la Taille S.J., "L'oraison contemplative," *Recherches de Science Religieuse* 9 (1919), 279.

Church's entire research on and practical concern about faith as the core of her mission. Hence she focuses the attention of our catechetical movement where it belongs, on the essentials. For "this is life everlasting, that we may know you, the only true God, and Jesus Christ whom he has sent."

Stages Leading to Faith and their Role
in the Catechesis of the Faithful

JOHANNES HOFINGER S. J.

ONE great hope for the spread of the catechetical renewal has been the growing desire for cooperation manifested in countries throughout the world. In mission territories for example the prejudice against modern catechetics as something strictly European, of little or no value for the missions, is gradually receding. Happily, while the catechetical mistakes of former times are no longer being welcomed, borders are opening to the first results of a promising rebirth. The pastoral reform of the ecumenical council promises to end any remaining isolationism of yesterday.

Leaders of the contemporary catechetical movement are convinced that the basic principles of the renewal are valid and applicable everywhere. This was perhaps most solemnly expressed in the international Study Week of Eichstatt in July 1960 and in the "Program of the Catechetical Apostolate" which resulted from this convention.[1] The universal value of modern catechetics was also stressed in the international Study Week for the Far East held at Bangkok in November 1962.[2]

This firm stand for the universal validity of the principles of

[1] About the international character of this meeting and its program, see the report of Gerard S. Sloyan in *Worship,* December 1960, 48–52.

[2] A. Nebreda S.J., "East Asian Study Week on Mission Catechetics," *Lumen Vitae* 17 (1962), 717.

modern catechetics is not a denial of the need for differentiation according to various situations in the catechetical apostolate. The Bangkok Conference precisely stated: "Although the basic principles of Modern Catechetics are equally valid for mission lands as well as Christian countries, the missionary catechesis has its special problems, particularly insofar as it constitutes a first evangelization and leads to conversion."[3] In this process of leading to faith three stages are apparent: pre-evangelization, evangelization and catechesis proper. Admittedly, these stages belong to mission catechetics in its strict meaning of gradual guidance of the unbeliever to faith and conversion which is crowned by the sacrament of baptism. But does this necessarily mean that the three stages are restricted to mission catechetics? Are they not applicable in other situations? As a matter of fact, close similarities with the three stages in missionary catechesis are evident in any well arranged instruction of converts or in the regaining of fallen-away Catholics. For both entail a gradual guidance to a Catholic faith never possessed or unfortunately lost. In both a real conversion is required. But over and above all this, are their equivalents never found in the religious formation of the faithful? The answer to this question will indicate some important tasks in the religious formation and guidance of the faithful, and at the same time show how our own catechetical apostolate can profit from comparison with other situations.

1. THE PROBLEM

In this article we will consider the three stages of missionary catechesis in relation to the religious instruction of those who possess the faith. The three stages of prebaptismal catechesis have no strict application in the religious instruction of believers, since their goals—faith and baptism—have already been achieved, and there is no need of conversion in the usual sense

---

[3] A. Nebreda, S.J., op. cit.

of the word. Nevertheless a little reflection will show that much can be learned from the process of missionary initiation.

Does the mere fact of baptism received conclusively prove that the goals set for the processes of pre-evangelization, evangelization and catechesis proper have been sufficiently achieved? To answer this question a distinction must be made betweeen what may be called the ontological or sacramental level and the religious-ethical level of personal commitment to God. The first means God's free gift, our ontological union with God through the grace of baptism and the other sacraments. The second refers to man's personal and definitive commitment to God, which is called faith. Faith here is clearly not the infused virtue of faith but the free act and personal attitude of faith, the word being taken in its full meaning as it is used in the New Testament and in the writing of the Fathers. Consequently it includes all the other necessary dispositions required, according to the Council of Trent, for the conversion and justification of an "adult." (Denz., 797f) This level then may simply be called the level of faith.

According to God's plan of salvation, which requires man's free cooperation with God's redemptive action, the level of faith should correspond to the sacramental level. For this very reason the unbeliever is prepared for baptism. Prebaptismal catechesis aims primarily at provoking and stimulating genuine faith in the catechumen, so that at the moment of baptism the level of his personal commitment may correspond to the sacramental level to which God will elevate him. Should not the catechesis of the faithful be viewed under a similar aspect? In baptism the faithful have received God's gift. They have been made children of God. From then on they must "walk in the newness of life" (Rom 6:4). They are expected to live a life of faith. In the sacrament of confirmation they have been deputed to strive for maturity in Christian life, which supposes maturity in Christian faith. Often they have received the Eucharist, the sacrament of spiritual growth. Each holy communion has resulted in an in-

146

crease in their sacramental level. Who would dare say that their growth in personal commitment to God always keeps pace with the growth made possible by the sacraments? It is the special aim of religious formation to make them realize and acknowledge the great task awaiting them. As catechists our responsibility is to help them attain to the perfection of both levels.

The same conclusion will be arrived at if catechesis is considered in its function of guiding the catechumen to a sincere, heart-felt conversion. Are all the faithful we catechize truly *converted?* Have they in their hearts broken with Satan and the world as they solemnly promised to do before baptism? For those who have never done so, or who have unfortunately turned back to the "flesh pots of Egypt" after a sincere and complete surrender to God, religious formation after baptism must of necessity possess a function similar to that of prebaptismal catechesis. It must discover and remove obstacles and prepare the way for a sincere and complete conversion.

The catechesis of innocent, baptized children seems at first sight to be completely different from missionary catechesis. In fact however it is not. These children were baptized when they were still infants, powerless to prepare themselves for the sacrament and to acknowledge God's gift. But at this time when we teach them religion they are becoming increasingly more able to make their own personal and definitive commitment to God, which is required for the fully voluntary reception of his gifts. Our catechetical instruction therefore replaces the preparation for baptism characteristic of missionary catechesis. In both cases the aim of religious instruction is effectual guidance to a Christian life that is in full accord with our dedication to God in baptism.

If such a relationship exists between the prebaptismal preparation in missionary catechesis and the catechesis of the faithful, the three stages of missionary catechesis must have their analogues in the religious formation of the faithful. What precisely are these analogues and what are their special functions?

2. The Nature and Special Function of the Three Stages

It is of significance for our subject that the initial studies on the process of conversion and the catechetical problems involved had in view, not the evangelization proper to mission countries, but the pastoral care of unbelievers in modern Europe. Starting from their experiences with unbelievers in France, leading authors such as Fathers P. A. Liégé O.P. and Fra Coudreau P.S.S. were the first to inquire into the problem of conversion. Since then these studies have been more specifically applied to mission catechetics by professors in the missiological faculty at the Gregorian University in Rome, especially by Fathers Domenico Grasso S.J. and Alfonso Nebreda S.J. It was only recently that the findings of the European experts were widely publicized in the missions, mainly through the Study Week on mission catechetics held at Bangkok in November 1962, when the problems of pre-baptismal catechesis were thoroughly studied and the leading principles formulated. In this article we closely follow the official report of the convention as published in *Lumen Vitae*.[4]

The participants of the Study Week distinguished three stages in the catechesis of the unbeliever: 1) pre-evangelization; 2) evangelization; 3) catechesis proper.

1) Pre-evangelization

Of a mere preparatory character, this stage provides the necessary psychological preparation for an initial presentation of the Christian message. It aims to establish the first religious contact with the unbeliever, to arouse his interest and to dispose him to appreciate and accept God's message with an open heart. A more

---

[4] A. Nebreda S.J., op. cit., 717–730. Father Nebreda has integrated this report, which is set off in italics, into his article. See also Father Theodore Stone's reports on the Bangkok Study Week in *Worship*, February 1963, 184–189, and *Good Tidings*, January–February 1963, 3–8. These articles point out the importance of the problems discussed in the Study Week for the catechetical apostolate in nonmission countries.

complete explanation of its aim was given by the Bangkok convention: pre-evangelization must shake off the apparent security of a life entirely "insured" by the familiar life-surroundings, by the possession of material riches or techniques which transform the world. Men must experience a "break" within themselves if they are to be "reawakened" to the invisible and thus be ready to welcome the gift of God.

"The pre-evangelization prepares such a 'break' by making men consider the mystery of death, of life, of human thought and love, spiritual responsibility, etc. . . ."[5]

Pre-evangelization therefore has a twofold function, one negative and the other positive. It must clear the way to a right understanding and appreciation of the Christian message, and make the nonbeliever long for the fulfillment of his highest aspirations.

The guiding principle for this first contact with the unbeliever is what the Study Week calls an "anthropocentrical" approach, by which the catechist must take the man as he is, with his thought patterns, opinions and the influences of his environment and culture. The catechist must find out what his current interests and pressing personal problems are.[6]

In dealing with would-be catechumens the catechist must be armed with understanding, love, patience and respect for their legitimate views.

There is no definite subject matter for this preparatory stage. The catechist should use whatever will help best in preparing the way for the *kerygma*. This includes what the Study Week has labeled "positive apologetics," which "proceeds from a true understanding and appreciation of whatever is good and acceptable in a man's culture. It consists in taking due consideration of the man with whom we speak, and in removing the personal concrete obstacles which prevent his ready acceptance of the kerygma."

[5] A. Nebreda S.J., op. cit., 724.
[6] See the article by Father Stone, op. cit., 5.

149

2) EVANGELIZATION

In the stage of evangelization the unbeliever is presented for the first time with the core of God's message—the kerygma—the joyful tidings of our salvation through Christ. Here the catechist must exert every effort to expose in a winning and convincing manner God's plan of salvation as the invention of his infinite love. In this condensed proclamation of the Christian message, the compelling fact of Christ as the Lord must be revealed with striking clarity. "In a technical world where man feels himself lost 'in a lonely crowd,' stressing such facts as God coming to us in Christ, Christ living among us as our friend and personally loving each of us, helps to awaken man to hope, and helps to evoke conversion."[7]

The main goal of evangelization is conversion. "Conversion" refers to that decisive change of mind by which man admits the basic insufficiency and error of his accustomed view of the world and of life, and willingly accepts God's message as the basis for the new life he is determined to start. His acknowledgment of Christ as the Lord implies a decision on his part to rearrange his whole life according to Christ's law. But at this point the convert will not as yet possess a detailed knowledge of all the implications his acceptance of Christ as the Lord will have for his way of living. His conversion as of now is by no means complete, but there is no conversion without this inner change.

Not all converts have to change much when they turn to Christ. Yet the greater the alteration of their life and the faster the inner change develops, the more will the convert experience a "break" with the past.

The stages of pre-evangelization and evangelization constitute the so-called pre-catechumenate. The purpose of evangelization is to lead the unbeliever to conversion. In this stage he comes to faith and surrenders to Christ, and delivers himself to the Church to be prepared for baptism. At this point the catechumenate begins.

[7] Bangkok Study Week.

150

3) CATECHESIS PROPER

In this stage the candidate is further acquainted with God's magnificent plan for his life, and with what a truly Christian life requires of his generosity. This more detailed exposition of Christian doctrine seeks to deepen his faith, complete his conversion and make firm his resolution to adhere to Christ. Evangelization and catechesis proper do not differ in their basic approach—for in both stages the Christian message must be presented as the joyful tidings "of the unfathomable riches of Christ" (Eph 3:8)—but rather in the completeness with which they present the doctrine of salvation. Both transmit Christ's message, but evangelization aims at a reorientation of life while catechesis brings out the implications of this reorientation and prepares the convert for the sacrament of baptism, and for a genuine Christian life thereafter. While still a catechumen, the convert must become accustomed to the kind of life to which he is called as a member of Christ.

3. THE ANALOGUES IN THE CATECHESIS OF THE FAITHFUL

The title of this section is a clear indication that no slavish imitation of missionary catechesis is here intended. Although in the ordinary catechesis of the faithful there is no need to follow the sequence of the three steps that lead to baptism, certain elements of the three stages proper to mission catechesis are present. Here they will be considered in the same order as in the preceding section.

1) PRE-EVANGELIZATION

Pre-evangelization in missionary catechesis aims to awaken the religious interest of the unbeliever, and to prepare him for his surrender to God in faith. Similarly, he who catechizes the

151

faithful must stimulate their religious interest or awaken it if it has been lost, and he must confirm and protect their faith against the dangers of a secularized environment.

To be fruitful, religious instruction must encounter sufficient religious interest on the part of the student. Catechists in public schools may find a lack of interest a more pressing problem than those in Catholic schools or pastors in the midst of their loyal congregations. A lack of interest among students in public schools is often expressed by not attending religion class. While disinterested students in a Catholic school may not stay away, their lack of interest will hinder them from profiting fully from religious instruction. This disinterestedness will foster routine in religious matters and will finally lead to tepidity. If genuine interest is habitually lacking, religious instruction ceases to be a help: it becomes a burden and a danger to the life of faith. This is particularly true of very frequent, perhaps daily religion classes, especially with adolescents.

As in the stage of pre-evangelization in missionary catechesis, the solution is not to make the catechism class merely amusing or interesting. The lesson must awaken and nourish "religious" interest; it must arouse an efficacious desire for closer union with God. Are we not in danger of overestimating the value of entertaining activities and audiovisual helps and consequently of aiming at a profane or merely intellectual interest? Entertainment may help to maintain discipline but it does not dispose the student for an encounter with God.

Pre-evangelization must make the unbeliever aware that something most important is still lacking in his life; it must undermine his state of apparent security, self-satisfaction and religious saturation. As it is not enough for the would-be convert to admit the beauty of the truth of the Christian religion without any personal commitment, so too, in the religious formation of the faithful, the message remains insufficiently transmitted unless the people realize their need for closer union with God. Self-satisfied religious saturation would render them incapable of

152

receiving God's Word with ready hearts. The best spiritual food is of no value if not received by those "who hunger and thirst after justice." In preparing a given subject for an audience on all levels of catechetical instruction, attention should be paid to the religious dispositions of the recipients, and to that special aspect under which the material ought to be presented in order to arouse genuine religious interest.

A remarkable study of the characteristics, religious needs and problems of different age levels is found in *Modern Catechetics* by Gerard S. Sloyan.[8] This book shows how to approach students and secure their favorable response.

The typical pre-evangelization themes by which the unbeliever is challenged to an initial spiritual "awakening" are not confined to this stage. If properly used and adapted to the conditions of the audience, they retain their place throughout the whole process of religious formation, especially when a re-awakening of religious interest is required. Some examples of these themes are the significance of life and death of man, of human thought and love, and of spiritual responsibility. With students of higher grades the catechist may begin with an analysis of basic human aspirations and attitudes, such as true happiness, autonomy, freedom, sincerity and uprightness, showing how all these lead to God and make necessary a religious orientation of our whole lives.

If the task of arousing religious interest and keeping it awake is understood in this way, it is closely related to the other task of substantiating and protecting faith. To the believer who has been baptized as a child in a Christian family, faith came as his parents' most precious heritage without his realizing it.

How then can he be expected to appreciate it adequately? A Christian family and a Christian environment beyond the narrow limits of the individual family can transmit the fundamentals of faith, but they can never supply the indispensable

[8] New York 1963.

personal contribution of the believer himself, who must grow to the maturity of faith.

The process of maturing in faith comprises a threefold element. In blind confidence the child accepted Christian faith from his parents. At the start there was no assent of faith in the theological sense of the word. As the child grows he must learn that faith comes from God and that it requires on his part a personal commitment to God, who has called him and claims him as his very own. Here exists a close analogy with the task of the missionary in pre-evangelization. The catechist must plant genuine faith in the heart of his pupil. "I have planted" (1 Cor 3:67), the apostle says of this, his basic apostolate.

Since the most important requirement in the whole process of "Christianization" is here involved, the catechist must never "suppose" that the parents have already sufficiently taken care of it. Without his assistance the faith of countless students will remain in the embryonic stage, a "childish" faith without any personal commitment to God. The catechist, like the missionary, must bring about this maturity in faith before beginning a more detailed exposition of Christian doctrine. But this has to be done—again as in missionary pre-evangelization—in perfect accord with the psychological disposition of the pupil. He should be taken as he is, with the limitations of his age and level of education.[9]

The education to mature faith necessarily includes a second element. The believer, according to his personal situation, must be led to realize the motives of his surrender to God in faith. The prevailing incredulity of today makes this explicit knowledge even more necessary. A starting point for guidance to such realization may be found, in accord with the apologetics described in section two, in the good and acceptable features of the cultural ambient. No separate course in apologetics pre-

[9] The On Our Way Series by Sister Maria de la Cruz H.H.S., grades 1–6, and grades 7–12, now in preparation, shows how education to faith is an organically maturing personal commitment to God. A high catechetical standard is found in all the volumes of this series that have already appeared.

ceding the positive explanation of the Christian message seems necessary or desirable in this case.

The third element in maturity in faith is a factual harmony of the believer's religious belief with his whole view of the world and of life. Lack of such harmony, if it does not create obstacles to faith, will at least prevent faith from penetrating the whole life of the individual and from supernaturalizing his thinking and planning. How often do we find people who, in their devotions, cultivate Catholic forms of piety but whose business life and social views openly contradict their Catholic faith! A good catechist must know that his pupils are greatly influenced by powerful mass media, such as radio, television, movies, newspapers and comic books. In preparing a lesson he must always keep this fact in mind, and discern how this influence may have made his audience disposed, or indisposed, for the message of this particular lesson. Quite often he will do well to set aside some time for bringing about a proper disposition at the beginning of his class. In good teacher manuals, a note to the teacher in each lesson reminds him of the main difficulties his students may have with this particular lesson, and suggests the methods of overcoming them.[10]

2) EVANGELIZATION

From the stage of pre-evangelization we learn methods of catechesis for those baptized who for one reason or another are not sufficiently prepared to accept the message of salvation in its fullness. With evangelization there is a difference. The leading principles of this stage have important applications for the religious formation of all kinds of faithful. Evangelization consists in a forceful presentation for the first time of the core of Christian message as the joyful tidings of our salvation through Jesus Christ. In mission catechesis it precedes the more detailed

[10] Models of such notes for the teacher are found in all volumes of the On Our Way Series, and in *Christian Action*, Father Stone's teacher's manual for Grade 12, Chicago 1963.

explanation of Christian doctrine. It brings the unbeliever to realize for the first time the transcendence of the Christian religion. Together with divine grace evangelization makes him turn joyfully to God who calls. The unbeliever decides to answer this gracious call generously by a new orientation of his life. This we speak of as "conversion."

In the catechesis of the faithful, instruction does not start with an evangelization exactly like that just described. But every Christian should be given the great external grace of being presented with the core of the Christian message at the crossroads of his life, in a manner similar to the evangelization of mission catechesis. This is the special way of presenting the joyful tidings in good spiritual retreats or in parish missions. In the process of religious formation, this introduction to the Christian message in its depth is important when one must prepare for an important decision which will give his life a definitive direction, for example when one is about to graduate from high school or college.

Apart from cases in which some reorientation of life or some peculiar awareness of the Christian calling is needed, evangelization has a place in the normal process of religious formation. Let us take a child who grows up in a good Christian family, and is sent to an excellent Catholic school where the work of the family is continued and gradually completed. Everything is done well; the student loves his religion and steadily progresses in the knowledge and love of God. Yet something may still be lacking, even in such circumstances. Despite his willing response the student may not yet have realized the greatness and depth of his Christian vocation. He knows his religion, but he has never experienced its full challenge: he has never been "shocked."

Whoever is acquainted with the pastoral situation of today will agree that we have picked an exceptionally favored example. In countless more "normal" cases the students know enough about their religion to pass the tests, but a more thorough analysis of their religious knowledge will show that they do not know God. They have never been initiated into the mystery. In the long years of their religious instruction catechesis has not achieved its primary aim, that of fostering personal faith. These students need not be taught many more details of Christian doctrine; what they need is faith: they need evangelization. With divine grace evangelization will make them realize, for the first time in their lives, what a real Christian is, how the Christian religion is a happy destiny and at the same time an unparalleled challenge. In short, evangelization will give them a wholesome "shock."

Shock in this connection is a word widely used in contemporary mission catechetics. It refers to the profound and intense spiritual change that takes place in the convert when he awakens from paganism and accepts Christ as the Lord. He finds himself confronted with a different view of life and of the world. Shock here is not used in its strict medical meaning; it merely emphasizes that the first encounter with Christ by personal faith is usually experienced by the convert as a sudden agitation of mind, when he realizes the undeserved gift and happiness of his Christian vocation, and is led to break with his past. A similar result will take place in the catechesis of the faithful whenever anyone through evangelization awakens for the first time in his life to a full consciousness of his Christian existence.

We spoke above of average students. Cannot the same be said of countless adult Christians too? Obviously they need the same remedy. The consequences for priestly preaching in the church are self-evident.

3) CATECHESIS PROPER

Instruction, in the catechesis of the faithful, is now a preparation for the other sacraments. This sacramental catechesis should always show clearly how our sacramental life is the unfolding of our baptismal life.

157

Independent of the preparation for a particular sacrament, post-baptismal catechesis has by its nature a sacramental function, as does the instruction of the catechumenate. It aims at an ever fuller understanding, appreciation and joyful acceptance of God's plan for us. ". . . Joyfully rendering thanks to the Father, who has made us worthy to share the lot of the saints in light. He has rescued us from the power of darkness and transferred us into the kingdom of his beloved Son, in whom we have our redemption, the remission of sins" (Col 1:12–14).

The catechesis of the faithful who have been baptized while children is by its nature a subsequent initiation into the new life which starts with baptism, for as St. Paul says, "all who have been baptized into Christ have put on Christ" (Gal 3:28). It therefore aims at forming Christians who are worthy of their name. Through his spokesmen Christ must reach maturity in his members. This is the special task of the pastors and teachers whom Christ gave his Church, "in order to perfect the saints for a work of ministry, for building up the body of Christ, until we all attain the unity of faith and of the deep knowledge of the Son of God, to perfect manhood, to the mature measure of the fullness of Christ" (Eph 4:15). St. Paul experienced the difficulty of this great task: "My dear children," he addressed the Galatians, "with whom I am in labor again, until Christ is formed in you" (4:19). The apostle realized how much help the Galatians still needed after baptism to reach the goal of religious formation.

Since the faithful who are baptized while infants cannot appreciate the "unfathomable riches of Christ" (Eph 3:8) conferred in the moment of baptism, the catechetical instruction of later years must lead them to realize the "newness of life" (Rom 6:4) which started with baptism and is to be developed by means of the other sacraments, and which finds its most sublime expression in the participation in the holy sacrifice of the Mass. At Mass our Lord reenacts with his mystical members his sacrifice on calvary. Thus the catechesis of the baptized has to draw from the "mystagogical" catechesis of the Fathers, as we find it for example in the catechetical instruction of St. Cyril of Jerusalem. It means more than just "teaching" the mystery of Christ. It means "guidance" to an ever more perfect participation in that mystery. It is only by this kind of religious formation that the liturgy obtains the central place due to it in genuine catechesis.

What has been said here may show that the science of catechetics finds itself today in a situation similar to that of liturgical studies. Like the renewal in liturgy the catechetical revival is not a product of the missions. Even after each of these disciplines had reached an advanced stage of development in the west, it was a long time before either took root in the missions. During recent years however this situation has greatly changed. An enormous interest in the catechetical and liturgical renewal has developed almost everywhere. But it has quickly become evident that the missions cannot merely copy western models. Intelligent use of such models requires a discernment of essentials and accidentals as well as creative thinking and an insight into the special conditions of the missionary apostolate. With these supposed, the missions will not only learn much from the progress made elsewhere; they will even be able to make valuable contributions to the further development of catechetics and liturgy in nonmission countries. The fact that European students have been quick to acknowledge the great advances which the pastoral renewal is making today in the missions is a token of the open-minded cooperation which at present prevails in the fields of liturgy and catechetics.

PART THREE

TRANSMISSION OF GOD'S MESSAGE

The art of communicating God's message is integrally related to the first two areas of catechetics. This implies that the goal of living faith, the characteristics of the three stages in the process of faith, mentalities and milieux, be kept in the foreground in determining techniques and methods best suited to transmit God's message. In this area of catechetics psychological and sociological factors are considered, teaching techniques and methods, programs for training catechists, catechetical structures, but always in harmony with catechetic's core: personal communion between God and man in Christ.

Values: Religious and Secular

JOHN J. O'SULLIVAN

PERHAPS no other subject causes as much controversy among sociologists as the study of values. Despite this fact values may have their place in a text for the teacher of religious education; awareness of values will guide a teacher in the making of any study plan. If a teacher would understand students, whether as individuals or as classes, he must identify values and know how they may conflict. Everything that is useful, desirable or admirable to the person and group has a value.

There is value in looking at values. Expect the study to be trying. Whatever we look at reflects back some distortion because of our culture. The one we have in mind is the American Catholic (whether student or teacher) who wants very much to be a member of the society around him while remaining a loyal believer in the kingdom of God. The integration is more difficult to achieve than is generally supposed.

Our teachers know that there is one Church: they may be taken aback to read that there are many catholicisms. Yet why should one register surprise at anything so obvious? We, in this country, are not Spanish Catholics nor do we conduct ourselves like our brethren in northern Europe.

What examples will help us to understand the problem a teacher faces? However we answer that question care must be taken in choosing examples. Otherwise we risk being misled.

Certainly the teacher (and later the students) will have difficulty in uncovering the opposition between the values of this

163

society and the values of the Church. Americans are proud of their country: they take their values for granted. They almost resent any challenge of what they prize and preserve.

As Catholics we have a problem arising because we have been a minority. Our "success" has been startling. To suggest that we can (and must) do our teaching in a more basic way, and in a more Christian way too, seems, in some senses, almost disloyal.

Here is a good question with which to wrestle at the very beginning: do we know what must be done in order to be more Christian?

Do we even know exactly in what Christianity consists? The first Christians knew it because Christianity then was very near in its beginnings, and the adversary against which it fought could not be unknown or misconceived by anyone; it was paganism . . . ignorance at once of sin which damns, and the grace of Jesus Christ which saves. As for the Church, not only then but throughout the ages, it has especially recalled to men the corruption of nature by sin, the weakness of the human mind without revelation, the impotence of the will to do good when it is not aided by grace. . . . We are still today in a world which believes itself naturally healthy, just, and good, because having forgotten sin and grace, it takes its corruption for granted.[1]

So wrote Gilson.

When we think about it, this has always been the problem. How does one make Christ incarnate in this society? Our Lord said, speaking of values: ". . . and your light must shine so brightly before men that they can see your good works and glorify your Father who is in heaven" (Mt. 5:16).

If there are changes around the students, a good teacher will want to teach realistically. This is the reason for saying that each generation must be taught differently.

Cardinal Suhard wrote from Paris: "The first duty of man is to live in the truth, to live in the truth of our relationship with God. . . . We must create a new order . . . restore our spiritual values." Religion cannot be taught by the rattle-off method.

---

[1] *A Gilson Reader,* Anton C. Pegis (ed.), Garden City 1957, 35.

Our students need more; teachers must know how to give more. A current novel explains why the Church is not as successful as it had been in an earlier period: "The world is educating itself faster than the Church."

We can agree then that the life of our people and their children is changing. Mass media of propaganda "distort" truth and everything presented. In 1950 one of our most discerning secular educators spoke of his problem in this culture:

> I do not see how any educational system can be expected to cope with the comic book, the radio, the motion picture, the slick-paper magazine, television, and the sensational press. The tremendous skill and the enormous resources available to these moral and cultural agencies make them more influential in molding the lives of our people than the whole educational system.[2]

His anxiety would surely not be greater than that of the religious educator.

Our culture and its secular values must always have importance for good religious educators. It is very easy to speak of "living in the truth" and to envision a classroom with questions and answers. It is an easier thing when only one person is involved. But this is not the same problem at all. Students do not live single, solitary lives.

Millions and millions of persons react unthinkingly and without question to anything around them which is popular. A Christian student must learn—and be convinced—that a thing is not necessarily true just because a great many persons think it is, nor is conduct correct because many persons act in a certain way. Not many southern Catholics knew that they were to oppose racial injustice.

There is corruption in the markets of business, in the halls of governments, in athletic stadia for games; scandals still reverberate in that "wasteland of the trivial." Bribes are given and taken in county courthouses, in the state house, even in the

---

[2] The quotation is from a broadcast by Dr. Robert Hutchins on the Town Hall of the Air. Date of the broadcast is not available.

nation's capitol. The press gives publicity to good people and even more to the bad. Who can point to a strong insistent demand for a sweeping renewal on all levels?

For the sincere believer religion is the most important reality in his life. As a study it is the cardinal subject in the Catholic school system. In the student's experience (as in his teacher's) it must be a hub around which all else revolves. But usually it is a rare student who thinks of his religious education in any of these ways.

One student, speaking for many, was devastating when he said: "All I ever learn in religion is religion. It has nothing to do with my life." He is arguing that his values are not examined. Moreover this student comes from a large family: he was more accurate than he knew in laying a finger on what had been, at every level, the limitations of our religious education.

In Father Sloyan's view, "the high school hooligan is lacking in God's wisdom. He is poor, not rich in Christ. Much remains to be made up to the Lord's fullness while this twisted set of values roams abroad in the school's corridors. The problem[3] must be faced as the anguish of *this* Christian community which it is. For the moment, Christ's splendor is dimmed in His brothers. He is not the perfect image of the invisible God in this school." The early Christians had a sense of privilege as the "people of God." Our young people lack that experience and conviction, almost to a person. Yet it is the same God who loves and protects his people. This generation must learn its privileges from its teachers if they would deserve their role or act out their part.

The questions to which we must pay attention (and for which religion has answers) are as basic as these:

Do I know the word of God?

Do I love the Mass?

Do I have respect for God's truth?

[3] Gerard S. Sloyan, "Catechetical Renewal," *Worship* II (January 1963), 96.

What is the *life* that becomes a Christian?

How can I escape being a "phoney?"

Will I be a price-fixer in business or a "boss" in politics?

Will I join the Peace Corps?

How can I have a good family in this society?

Can I assign any better reason for my living than "having fun?"

Chapters like this are necessary for many reasons. A review of what we have been doing can be revealing. We have been giving answers to people who did not understand or ask questions. Teachers are realizing that this Christian must have an *ideology*. His whole way of life must be related to God and his Son. This is the reason for repeating that each generation must be taught differently. Good teachers know this and react to it.

It is not enough to learn *about* religion. "Other-directed" students are converted: this is what the phrase means. Hence students must be *converted* in this course. To see the meaning of this statement teachers might contrast our practices with those at the beginning of the Church's history.

First of all the apostles, commissioned by Christ, preached his gospel. On hearing it those who believed were *converted*. Then came the asking of questions and the receiving of answers, a time of *instruction*. Then *baptism*. (On Pentecost the whole process was acted out in a single day, but soon more time was required.) Later it became more clear what it was to be a Christian.

Our problem is to identify what has happened to us who live hundreds of years after Christ. As would be expected, there have been many changes. The conversion, the instruction and the baptism of the early Church have not been inverted. We have baptism; we have many years of instruction; but our problem centers on conversion: does it always follow? Do teachers know that they should seek this objective?

Every person lives in a culture. And culture makes it easier

167

for him to act, with a minimum of thinking, about his decisions and actions. Monogamy, chastity, justice in dealing with others, loving care in rearing one's children, have been values in some cultures. There are "half-values" for us because some values have not been completely accepted in our society at this time.

Good teachers will weigh what Joseph Fichter S.J. writes of this culture and they will judge how it affects the mind and the heart of its members:

> A person can be socialized to accept as normal both ends of the contradiction. If the child is accustomed from his early years to the compromised patterns in his elders, he tends to accept them without questions. This is a prime example of the culture molding the individual. The culture overcomes logic since everybody is thinking and acting in these ways, the individual is inhibited from questioning the obviously approved system of behaviour, contradictory as it may be. . . . Most persons are constantly subject to cultural influences without being fully aware of them."[4]

Thus we see that instinct moves the person in preserving his individual life, but intellect, and even a *Christian* mind, must guide one in his loyalty to Christ and in his service of neighbor.

Every person has both a personal and a social life. As teachers we do; and so do our students. One may examine himself on his relationships with other people. But the social sciences are one's help in measuring the effect of interactions between the Catholic faithful and their many neighbors.

Whoever would conduct such a survey must face directly the confusion of our young people and the resulting problems for teachers that flow from it.

There is a consensus on this point between a secular authority and one of the popes. David Mace, sometimes called a marriage counselor to the world, shared this view of what is happening to our young people:

> We have produced today something which I think is unique in the history of a complex civilization and human culture. We have pro-

4 Joseph H. Fichter, *Sociology,* Chicago 1957, 39.

duced a generation of young people who have taken upon themselves
to decide, among themselves and for themselves, very largely what
their patterns of behaviour, what their standards and values, are going
to be. This has never happened before. Always previously, the young
people of the rising generation have been told by the members of the
former generation how they are to act, what they are to do, and what
their values have to be. These patterns of action, behaviour, standards
and values have been required of them under intimidation and compulsion.[5]

Pope Pius XII affirmed this view in what he said to the
"modern young woman." It would be a bold teacher, or a daring
priest or religious, who would speak so bluntly to young people
without disclosing the sources of these lines:

She takes for personality and vigor what is only basically care-
lessness, imprudence or even shamelessness.

She lets herself be caught in a trap, even when she does not throw
herself into it head first.

She has the illusion of experience and thinks herself on this account superior to young girls of past generations.

She believes she can with impunity read everything, see everything,
try everything, taste everything.[6]

One does not quote such lines merely for the pleasure of in-
dicting our young. Teachers must understand their subject,
their students and their times. The study cannot be effortless.

The analysis of Harold Taylor seems to account for one
source of the problem:

The present generation of parents in America has grown up to believe that children should have the maximum of freedom at an early age.
Parents of this generation have learnt well the lessons of the liberal
child-rearing in the twentieth century. But in learning these lessons,
they have encountered another set of problems. If the child emancipates

[5] From an address given to the Minnesota Family Life Council in Minne-
apolis, Minn. on October 7, 1960.

[6] Pope Pius XII, "Moral Dangers to the Girl of Today," quoted in *The
Popes on Youth,* compiled and edited by Raymond B. Fullam S.J., Buffalo
1956, 228.

himself from parental authority at the age of twelve or fourteen, and is free to make many of his own personal and social decisions, then he throws himself upon the values of his society and must sacrifice the mediating effect of his parents' judgment about the quality of the decisions he is making.

Formerly, when the family did make such judgments, the younger generation had to deal with a set of ideas and values that served as a standard from which it could deviate if it were so inclined. But with livelier emancipation there is nothing to deviate from, since the young person is already adrift with his own age group, adapting himself to group values and attitudes that determine his place in life. . . .

Young people have, in a sense, been told to be emancipated. They therefore take emancipation as a value, but often have no where to go with it.[7]

To these facts there are two reactions. How odd that believing Christians should be caught in such a process of compounded confusion! And yet how natural it is that this should be the state of a Christian who has neglected to identify his own values system and contrast it with the dominant different one which is the more widely accepted in this society.

The Catholic Church is now a formidable force in the American community. And that community is constantly changing. By contrast almost all societies and cultures in which our Church has been present have been stable, if not static. Where changes did occur they took place gradually over a period of time.

In consequence of the American involvement, no teacher dares to treat any student as though he were a kind of "guided missile" for whom teachers are to predetermine certain responses. To use the language of the time, the young Christian must be a functioning, responsible adult.

The American community and the Catholic Church both have a deep respect for human liberty. Christians can agree with Americans on this value. For a number of reasons this harmony is not always understood by those in the Church who exercise

[7] "What the Family Isn't Teaching," *Saturday Review of Literature,* May 18, 1963.

authority or do the teaching. After all, "the glorious liberty of the Sons of God" is a thought rooted in scripture.

Democracy (as Pope Pius XII pointed out) is the most difficult form of government, along with being the best form of government. It emphasizes personal responsibility; so did Christ. From the family we receive our life; from the state we receive our social and civil life; from the Church we receive our eternal life in Christ. These several societies, in return, demand for their dues that each person act out his several different (and often conflicting) roles.

Our society is becoming more complicated. School is the place for learning what one is to be and to do. Education is a process whereby one acquires the skill for thinking, deciding and acting. One immediate effect of this developing society is that the fully functioning members in it will need *more* education. One proves his humanity by thinking clearly and acting decisively.

When things go badly for us it may be because we have thought poorly, or reasoned inadequately. "One does not sabotage the Holy Spirit if he uses the mind God gave him."

The Christian of course has virtues which enable him to approach problems in a way different from other peoples'. They also affect the response he makes to life and its experiences.

Ideally each Christian who is worthy of the name must identify his talents; he then develops them as his responsibility; after that he dedicates them to his Father in heaven; finally he devotes them to the service of his neighbor. There is some reason for thinking this practice is not widespread.

As an experiment or as a tentative theory, the Catholic who is a teacher of religious education might accept the theory that the Church has never existed in a cultural situation quite like the one in this country.

In our early history we were a persecuted and despised minority. Centuries later the Catholic faith had converted Europe and given it its distinctive nature as Christendom. About four centuries ago, there was a revolt in Europe, and a Reformation both within and without the Church. Fifty years ago atheistic Communism became a decisive force in the history of our time.

Teachers must weigh the effects of revolutions and crises on their own era in history. Here, in the United States, we do not suffer overt persecution either from our government or from the majority of our fellow citizens who do not share our values. On the other hand, we receive no direct help from this culture in protecting our religious values and in witnessing to Christ as he has asked us.

Our study of these young people, up to this point, suggests the analogy of watching the flow of a river. While the volume of water is moving downstream, wind may cause ripples or waves which may lead an observer to judge that the water is actually flowing upstream. The teacher's problem, if he would be adequately effective, is to identify the direction in which the generation is moving, and judge the extent to which his students can join in that movement.

A liberal writer, Harvey Swados, passes judgment on the college crowd:

In Fort Lauderdale, Florida, in Galveston, Texas, in Santa Monica, California, thousands of college students have battled police, not for the dignity of their fellow men or the inviolability of human life, but for their own inalienable right to invade these beach areas during their vacations. . . . As long as it is possible for thousands of young people to call themselves college students, and to demonstrate to the world that they have nothing more important to do with their time, nothing more important to do with their lives, than to foregather for weeks on end at public playgrounds in order to commit a public nuisance—for just that long our society will stand condemned as one which, as I said above, gives American youth everything except a reason for living and for building a socially useful life.[8]

If it is disturbing, or even dismaying, to secular writers that college students can conduct themselves in this fashion, those who engage in religious education will be even more reflective and critical.

[8] *A Radical's America,* Boston 1956, 256–57.

172

The Person and Thought

It is useful for a teacher to construct a profile of his student—of that abstraction called "modern man." What do we *know* about them as opposed to what we may *think* is true about them? C. G. Jung has said that "the meaninglessness of life is the neurosis of our age." His experience was chiefly if not exclusively European; before we can reject him for this reason we must reckon with Dr. Karl A. Menninger of Topeka, Kansas, an American. His version goes like this: "Most Americans today exist without purpose, without significance. They have no articulate philosophy of life. They do not live within any frame of reference." These facts are significant for all who teach our young Christians.

"Modern man" has always been disturbing. What is our response to the oratory of a lenten preacher at Notre Dame Cathedral in Paris: "The modern man *wants* nothing and *needs* no one!"

Back to our own environment again. A popular novelist, John Marquand, once predicted that many Americans will end their lives with a stationwagon and an annuity, vaguely suspecting there may be some other reason for living.

During Mental Health Week one thoughtful columnist expressed this observation: "Too many people are sick of living. . . . There is a lack of moral and intellectual discipline. The child believes himself the center of the universe, and receives a rude shock when he finds out he is not."[9]

Our absorption with the soft life has provided a cause of concern for others. Some people have said: "America has become a tinny carnival of comfort, empty of purpose, giving no thought to the morrow." It is not hard to provide data for this indictment. "TV scandals, juvenile delinquency, soft education, things like meat and fuel oil, consumer-gouging rackets, are symptoms of the American defect." There is a certain uneasiness and dis-

9 *Newsweek,* October 24, 1955, 66.

quiet that comes to anyone who surveys American life in so critical a fashion.

The Person and the Economy

This is an economic society. Economics is the dominant *institution* and "the value of a dollar" can become the supreme value for many unthinking people.

Fortune magazine reported in one of its articles about our business activity:

If American business men are right in the way most of them now live, then all the wise men of the ages, all the prophets and the saints were fools. If the saints were not fools, the business men must be.[10]

This is not a popular line of thought. It is not a position around which many will rally. We should encourage young people to ask how this work or profession will affect the man who enters them: how will it affect him and his wife who honestly wants a Christian family?

One novelist wrote of what was happening to us in the late 1950s:

This was the era, domestically, when everything was half done; this was the time when the job on the car was always half finished, the suit came back from the cleaners half dirty, the yard work was overpriced and underdone. The great "Age of the Shoddy" came upon America after the war, and "everybody wants his" became the guiding principle for far too many. With it came the "Age of the Shrug," the time when it was too hard and too difficult and too bothersome to worry about tomorrow, or even very much about today.[11]

A population of 180 million people may enable us to prove almost anything about almost everything. However the difficulty of the problem does not dispense us from trying to solve it. One of our most trying exertions is to collect and relate our facts.

---

[10] "The Moral Failure of the American Business Man," September 1957.
[11] Allen Drury in *Advise and Consent*.

But here is a fair example of the conflict between the Christian and the American value systems.

These are almost harsh criticisms of a society and its economy which we have socialized against judging unfavorably. We might recall what Pope John XXIII said: "Unfortunately, an outlook (which) is widely prevalent today . . . reduces the whole meaning of life to a panting search after pleasure and the gratification of all desires. It unquestionably involves great harm to body and soul alike."

Pope John knew the simplicity of the good life. So did Christ who, in his lifetime, was a laborer. The Lord could be (and was) identified by Joseph's craft. Christ was not classified as a "priest" in the Jewish society of which he was a member.

The religious life to be found in the New Testament involves a distinctive value system. This system demands a concept of nature, origin and destiny in man which is not generally accepted in the American community.

Whoever will remain faithful to these Christian ideals must, as a condition for his fidelity, in some way receive help from other believers.

Since there are many categories of people in every society, teachers must know what is the dominant value system widely accepted. For it will be this larger segment of the society which imposes its philosophy and its patterns of unreflective conduct on almost all persons.

In a society like ours, which is undergoing rapid change, there will be disorganization and conflict—families, schools, parishes will all suffer from a "cultural lag." And these are due to the failure of an individual (or of an institution) to keep up with the changes. It is hard to excuse teachers who are lacking this knowledge of their times.

Christians are to love temporal things as servants. If it is a matter of material values such as money, abundance, technical progress, the Christian will use them as long as he judges them aids in doing the work of God.

There is a problem arising for Catholics when they live among people who have lost the balance between what is human and divine. To the temporal, the neighbors we have might have given, not their love, but their preference. What could have been lawful has now become idolatry. This is the most typical and terrible of the errors of our time because through it the temporal world is divorced from God.

Christians are to realize religious aspirations within the framework of all life. Spirituality, as every good teacher must realize, refers to the way in which the mystery of faith is lived. There are not two kinds of sanctity or two kinds of faith. There is only one divine life that the Father communicates to all through his Son, through the outpouring of the Holy Spirit.

What will be the response of the Church through her teachers to the challenge of our time? The last ninety years has seen the growth of the human race at an unprecedented rate. It has almost trebled. We have witnessed technological progress the full implications of which not even the foremost men of science can guess. Nation has opposed nation in aggressive and defensive war.

Again, by reading history (which Pope John XXIII said is the teacher of life) we discover the changes in value. And as late as World War I a man wrote to a former teacher of his:

> There's no feeling of romance in the job, nor on the contrary, any feeling of self-sacrifice. We're going into it with everything we have, sure of eventual victory, careless about the personal outcome. . . . If we come back, all right. If we do not, well, we might have loved some woman. We could have done the work of our choosing. But to have died honorably, were better than women and work; above all else, the cause will triumph.[12]

A quick check with those now in service, or those who had been in service earlier, will indicate how rare a reaction this would be now.

The apostle to the Gentiles was clear in his objectives and

[12] William H. Whyte, Jr., *The Organization Man,* New York 1956, 17.

176

definite about his values. St. Paul expressed his hopes for his fellow Christians in this way: "And this is my prayer for you: may your love grow richer yet in the fullness of its knowledge and the depth of its perfection so that you may learn to prize what is of value; may nothing cloud your conscience or hinder your progress 'till the day when Christ comes. . . ."

Perhaps we can sum up some of the things we would like to write about values and our responses to them by adding a long quotation from Gustave Weigel S.J.:

> Today, more than ever, the man in our society must make great efforts to form and strengthen his personality. This calls for the development of asceticism which means the exercise of man's power to say "no" to spontaneous urges of instinct. The fruit of asceticism need not be rigor or stubborn inflexibility. The ascetic does not necessarily turn down the suggestion of instinct, but he will never be swept away by it. He refuses to say "yes" to unjudged impulse. After judgment he may well say "yes" not because it is instinctive but because it is reasonable. Instinct, as such, is indifferent to the reasonability of its action, but is not so structured that every instinctive desire is necessarily irrational. Man's intelligence must judge in every case and asceticism makes him fit to judge. . . .[13]

This is a Christian value. It is the life of moderation which Pope John said was to identify the Christian.

However "no man is an island." We are not solitary; we are social. John L. Thomas S.J., noted family sociologist, has set forth on many occasions what he calls the basic prerequisites for forming a family program, which is essential for the preservation of the Catholic minority in this country. His thought is essential to a teacher of religion, and helpful in understanding this problem of values. What follows is an adaptation[14] from Father Thomas' program:

    1) Catholic ideals constitute a distinctive set of values based

---

[13] *The Modern God*, New York 1963, 143.
[14] Based on "A Program for the Catholic Family," *Theology Digest* IV (Spring 1956), 124.

on a clearly defined concept of the nature, origin and destiny of man.

2) These ideals have functional requisites: that is, their realization in a given society requires the support of related institutions and practices.

3) The dominant group regulates the changes which take place in institutions and cultural practices. (In the United States Catholics are not dominant.)

4) In a society like ours, undergoing rapid change, disorganization and conflict may arise.

5) A Catholic minority can maintain its ideals intact either by isolating itself (which it cannot do) or attempting limited integration with the dominant group.

The point to be stressed is this: Catholics must maintain a clear distinction between essential values and their concrete implementation. Those who blindly "follow the crowd" and still attempt to maintain Catholic standards demonstrate a distressing lack of logic.

On the educational level, the teacher must regularly make a careful restatement of the meaning of life in terms of Catholic values and contemporary living conditions. Much of the religious teaching in this country has been the joyful activity of priests and nuns. They have brought to their roles as teachers an admirable dedication. Unfortunately their own experiences, in novitiate and seminary, have not always helped them as much as they might in understanding the society in which lay people live, and the social pressures by which students are moved and shaped.

This is surely the reason why the Sacred Congregation of Seminaries and Universities has insisted that sociology must be a requisite in all the seminaries of the world.

Man is a social animal. He receives influences from others and to some degree has the capacity of effecting their lives too.

The United States of America, of which we are justly proud, is not a Catholic country. Catholics cannot endorse wholeheartedly its institutions and its values. Whoever teaches must know this, and whoever would teach well must see the adaptations which must be presented in teaching lay people for an active, responsible membership in this secular community.

Pope John XXIII may be remembered as one of the best Christians and the most successful teachers in our times. In 1961 he wrote of the Christian performance in what some have judged to be an autobiographical note: "Every believer in this world of ours must be a spark of light, a center of love, a vivifying leaven amidst his fellowmen. And he will be this all the more perfectly the more closely he lives in communion with God in the intimacy of his own soul." This is an acceptable statement of our basic value.

The Catholic Message and the American Intellectual

ANDREW M. GREELEY

It would be appropriate, I suppose, to begin this paper with a definition of the two terms contained in the title. However, at the risk of obscuring the issues involved, I am going to do something very typical of American intellectuals and refuse to define my terms. Other papers in this volume attempt to describe the Christian message and the controversy over what an intellectual is would detain us too long. It suffices to describe an intellectual as one whose primary concern is the manipulation of ideas (or "symbols" as some of them would say) and the discovery of new ideas; he very likely will be found in the university, though by no means all university professors can claim the title of intellectual except as a matter of courtesy. Increasingly, however, he may also be found in the corporation or in government and some of his breed manage to serve all three at different times in their careers—or even simultaneously.

The basic assumption of this paper is that to date the American intellectual has been impervious to the Christian kerygma as it is propounded by the Catholic Church. It is immediately evident that this assumption is unfair to a good number of people who have no trouble reconciling their intellectual interests with their faith. It also tends to overlook the many believers of other religions who are to be found in the intellectual world. However it is still fair to argue that the basic thrust of American intellectualism in our century has been nonbelieving. The "typical" intellectual (in the sense of the one who best embodies the ideas

180

and ideals of the intellectual community) is not likely to be a man of religious faith—at least in any orthodox definition of faith.

When one speaks of "obstacles" standing in the way of contact between the Catholic message and the American intellectual, one is speaking of obstacles to a dialogue. It must be recognized that faith is a gift which is not in our power to give. There is no question of our attempting a sales pitch to "convert" the intelligentsia of the republic. The problem is rather that the Catholic and the secular intellectual are both concerned with ideas and both possessed with some reason for conversation. However the conversation is not occurring. The Catholic is unable to explain who and what he is to the intellectual and to discover why the intellectual cannot accept his position. The intellectual, on the other hand, is unable to find out what makes the important phenomenon of American Catholicism operate and to discover if perchance it might have any relevance in his search for truth. The Catholic because of his faith is forced to want to clear away obstacles to faith and the intellectual because of his honesty is forced to admit at least the abstract possibility of faith.

There are many different kinds of obstacles to dialogue between Catholicism and the American intellectual and there is strong reason to suspect that the ultimate reason why Catholicism is unacceptable as a philosophy and a way of life is not dissimilar from the reason why all traditional religions are unacceptable. However, in addition to the standard objections that the intellectual has to all religions (at least for himself), there are some special objecions which apply paricularly to Catholicism. In this paper we will consider three kinds of barriers which separate the intellectual from the Church—those which have nothing to do with the Church, those which apply to existing and changeable aspects of the Church, and finally those which seem to pertain to the essence of Catholicism—and indeed of all orthodox religious faith.

The first set of obstacles—one might almost call them the

irrelevant ones—have to do with ignorance and prejudice. There is a good strong strain of nativism still to be found in the white anglosaxon element of the American intelligentsia. The Protestant religion of their ancestors may not have survived (except in a very vague fashion) but abiding distrust for the Church of Rome is about the only remnant of ancestral religion. When an American bishop makes a statement the WASP intellectual hears from the dim memory of his childhood the voice of Innocent III or Cardinal Torquemada. Since he is considerably more sophisticated than the fundamentalist preacher, the intellectual does not permit his bigotry to become violent or even loud. Indeed it is likely to be very rational and even accompanied by footnotes. Nevertheless he cannot help but feel, semi-consciously, that Catholics are ignorant, lazy, superstitious foreigners and that neither they nor their Church are to be trusted. The truth of the matter is that the WASP intellectual knows less about Catholicism than he does about Islam and that his view of the Church is a compound of ignorance and stereotype which keeps rising to the surface of his personality no matter how sophisticated he appears to be.

The Jewish intellectual views Catholicism from a different historical perspective than the anglosaxon though one that is hardly likely to dispose him favorably to the Church of Rome. Memories of pogroms in Poland are not far removed from his mind and experiences with the Catholics in his neighborhood as he grew up do not reassure him. Nor does his fear of ecclesiastical power grow any less when he reads of the long centuries of persecution of Jews by Catholics. The American Church may not be notably anti-semitic in 1963, but the scars of two millennia of conflict are not erased in a few decades. Even though he may not accept much of the content of the Jewish religion, the Jewish intellectual remembers that the Catholic Church has been the traditional enemy of his people, and he is not prepared to trust it, much less listen to it. It is not especially surprising

182

that he sees threats and plots in every new move of the bishops. He is afraid of the Church—and finds it difficult not to hate it.

The massive monolith myth of the Church has not yet died. An image of Catholicism as a tightly organized and rigidly disciplined, quasi-military organization with a central policy-making body whose orders are followed accurately and unquestioningly by a blindly obedient membership is still part of the intellectual's world view. The Catholic hierarchy wants power and the Catholic laity is out to get it for them.

(Thus even such rigorously honest journals of the Intellectual Establishment as *The New Republic* and *The New York Times* occasionally let some anti-Catholic bias slip into their comments. The classic example is the subject of federal aid to public schools. Even though more Catholic congressmen consistently vote for such measures than against them, both journals seem convinced that the defeat of the bills is the single-handed work of the cardinal archbishop of New York. Such a claim would concede to His Eminence a control over Protestant congressmen from the Democratic south and the Republican middle west which it is highly improbable that he exercises. The truth of the matter is that the conservative tone of the first two Kennedy congresses was such that aid to public schools on the primary and secondary levels would have been unlikely no matter what the Catholic Church said or did not say.)

Nor do the Catholics they encounter reassure them. Clergy and laity alike seem loud, pugnacious, anti-intellectual and authoritarian. It often does not take too much imagination to see potential fascists in many Catholics—and after all, look how active they are in the John Birch Society. Since the Catholic Church is so well organized and disciplined, it follows that practically all Catholics are like that. It does not seem to occur to the intellectuals that much of what they dislike about American Catholics is part of the immigrant group experience and has nothing to do with religion and that the Church is a dynamic and pluralistic organization with perhaps more members (both lay and clerical) committed to the principles of the ADA than to those of the John Birch Society.

Obviously the anti-Catholicism of the intellectual described in the last few paragraphs is something of an exaggeration. A good many intellectuals are completely free of it and others do not give it a very important place on their list of concerns. The problem is not one of massive dislike but rather of ignorance mixed with misconceptions which get in the way at those few times when the intellectual even bothers to think about the Church.

It must be noted in all fairness that the situation is changing rapidly and that dislike is being replaced by a friendly and sympathetic curiosity, partly because of the intellectual's honesty which forces him to reexamine his stereotypes and partly because of the change in the image of the Church brought about by the two Johns—one on the banks of the Potomac and the other on the banks of the Tiber. Even though the American bishops had said it often, the intellectuals apparently never believed in the Church's acceptance of the separation of church and state until John Kennedy proclaimed it and was not contradicted by a single member of the hierarchy. (One cleric claims that this was enough to earn for the late president the title of Ecclesiae Doctor.) The late Holy Father captured the imagination and the affection of the intellectual perhaps to a greater extent than he did of the ordinary American Catholic for whom popes come and popes go. The freedom of discussion at the Vatican Council and the dramatic changes going on as a result have also persuaded the intellectual that the monolyth myth was just that. One does not intend to argue that the Church has suddenly become popular in the intellectual community; however it is safe to say that it has never been less unpopular.

Still, there is more to the intellectual's disinclination to listen to the Catholic message than his ignorance of the message or his prejudice against the organization. There are a good number of aspects of contemporary Catholicism which are very real and very much opposed to the values of the intellectual. The man of faith may understand that these elements are not part of the essence of his faith and indeed may to some extent represent a human corruption which has crept into the Church considered as a human organization. However the man who does not have faith finds this distinction hard to make.

First of all the intellectual is a "liberal:" he believes in freedom of thought, in the right of every man to follow his own conscience and to make his own decisions. There is an orthodox Catholic interpretation of freedom (of the kind propounded by Father Murray and more recently by Cardinal Bea) which the intellectual would not find hard to accept. However the administration of the Church which he encounters is still that of the post-tridentine Garrison Church in which, for many reasons, the emphasis has been on authority and order rather than on freedom. Tight central control, censorship, the Index, secret denunciations, the harsh language of some ecclesiastical documents and the stern authoritarianism of some ecclesiastical figures are historical accidents which are in the process of undergoing profound change; but these accidents seriously disturb the "liberal piety" of the intellectual and he does not see how he personally could accept them and still keep his self-respect. He is told that there is nothing in the essence of Catholicism which would not permit more "democracy" in the administration of the Church; but he does not see much evidence of this possibility as yet.

Secondly the intellectual is a moral relativist and finds the Catholic natural law approach to ethics intolerable. To say that he is a relativist does not mean that he does not have firm moral principles; he most assuredly does. Indeed in some respects he is likely to be more puritanical than a Catholic casuist and more concerned with the moral implications of his actions than the average Catholic. His relativism consists not in a rejection of morality but rather in a rejection of a morality which seems to be dogmatic, apriori and insensitive to human happiness. In

185

practice his differences with Catholics often are limited to matters of sex and marriage where he feels the rigid and unbending Catholic natural law position does not take into account the complexities of the human condition and the sufferings that rigorism inevitably causes. The Catholic could reply that in reality natural law ethics are also based on the quest for the happy life and that the modification in sexual morality which the intellectual desires will ultimately lead to more unhappiness than happiness. He could also argue that the intellectual does not understand what natural law really is (and neither do most Catholics), that recent developments in moral theology have made it much less casuistic and much more humanistic, and that in some non-Catholic circles the value of an authentic natural law position is being reexamined. However, even if granted that part of the difficulty is semantic and that there has been some closure in ethical systems in recent years, the fact remains that the intellectual can hardly subscribe to an ethical system which is based ultimately not on natural law but on claimed divine revelation. In other words the question of moral systems may not be insoluble in itself if the underlying question of revelation could be resolved; but as we will note later, this is the truly insoluble problem.

Thirdly the American intellectual is an empiricist. He arrives at truth by investigation, by ascertaining the facts, by working experiments, by testing hypotheses and ultimately by counting. He cannot be comfortable with a religious system that proceeds in apriori fashion, that claims to have dogmas that cannot be verified by empirical observation. This is not to say that he does not have his own dogmas, but he chooses to call them "assumptions" which somehow or the other make them less harmful. He assures us that he does not know whether his assumptions are true but that, in fine Kantian fashion, he had decided to act as though they were true. Unfortunately when you call a dogma (such as the proposition: "Truth must be empirically verifiable") an assumption you thereby remove it from the area where it can be discussed. If believers would be willing to concede that their dogmas were assumptions, the intellectual would have no trouble coexisting with him.

Again the conflict is to some extent more verbal than real; many Catholics will admit that in recent centuries there has been a tendency on the part of Catholics to let the certainty which applies to a rather limited body of propositions in dogmatic theology be transferred to other areas of human endeavor where dogma has no relevance and that this tendency has obscured the basically empiricist nature of Thomism. The intellectual will reply that indeed the rationalism of the schoolmen made possible the development of the human mind which was required for the scientific revolution, but that this revolution occurred only when the intellect had broken with traditional religion. He will further observe that if there is no opposition between religious orthodoxy and science there ought to be more practicing Catholics in the physical and social sciences. The point is well taken and the Catholic is reduced to arguing once again about historical accidents.

Fourthly the intellectual is by training and taste a critic. His keenness of mind enables him to see what is wrong with established institutions and to demand change. He is possessed by a certain playfulness of mind which inclines him to be less than impressed with arguments from tradition. He likes to experiment with ideas, to turn them over and examine them from all sides, to juxtapose them in previously untried positions. He is always questioning the worth of the existing order and its sacred canons and would rather like to know what the world would be like if these canons were dropped. Now such an attitude is clearly necessary in the empirical sciences if any progress is to be made. Nor is it to be ruled out in religion either as the revolution of Pope John has demonstrated. Nevertheless the temptation of the intellectual is to act in the domain of religion as he does in his own field and to risk rejecting the unchangeable (from the religious viewpoint) with the changeable. There is the contrary problem that the ecclesiastic is strongly tempted to put the mantle of unchangeability over what in reality are merely traditional ways of administration or personal or cultural prejudices. It is thus by no means always clear to either the intellectual or the churchman what is indeed essential and what is not. (Half a decade ago the change which has occurred in the Catholic position on ecumenism would have been unthinkable to many churchmen—and still is to some.) However, even if this were clear, the intellectual would still find himself wondering why certain elements of religion are to be exempt from the critical examination to which he wishes to submit all propositions. Once again one comes up against the bedrock question of revelation.

Finally the intellectual is personalist in his approach to social problems. Suffering and injustice upset him and he believes in social reform (drastic if necessary) to correct situations which prevent the development of the human personality. Even though the Church's social teaching clearly sympathizes with such a stand, the intellectual often feels that Catholics—especially those in positions of ecclesiastical authority—are so concerned with social order and stability that in practice they adopt positions of extreme conservatism in the face of social problems. While he is willing to concede that the American Church has produced a fair number of reform oriented priests and people (especially in the labor movement), he suspects that the situation in the Latin countries is more typical of Catholicism. Once again the two social encyclicals of Pope John (and the involvement of the Church in the Negro protest movement) have weakened his criticism, but he is far from convinced that these encyclicals have got to the grass roots.

In the past several paragraphs we have pointed out that there is much in the style of the American intellectual that makes him skeptical of Catholicism before he even hears its message. He is liberal, pragmatic, empiricist, critical and personalist while the Church seems to him to be authoritarian, dogmatic, deductive, conservative and often less than human. If he has made a careful study of the Church he may be willing to admit that much of the difference is the result of historical accidents, though until very recently he would have said that the historical accidents were proving remarkably durable. However, even though much of the difference can be explained away, there are residual differences which are not historical accidents but which come from the fact that the Church claims to possess special truth communicated to it by God. Even though most intellectuals have not cut through the first two categories of obstacles to a dialogue and hence are not too concerned about revelation, it would nevertheless seem that here is to be found the core problem.

It is not merely a question of revelation. Indeed if there is a God the intellectual would certainly not mind it if he would communicate with men. Unlike his deistic ancestor he would not presume to limit God's freedom (no decent liberal would). Indeed he is enough of a personalist to much prefer the God of Abraham, Isaac and Jacob to the God of Aristotle. The problem is not revelation but the existence of a revealer. The essential question is whether there is a supernatural (as he would put it) or a transcendental (as a Catholic would put it). Is there a God, a life after death, a reality which in any sense goes beyond the worldly? The intellectual rather thinks not.

He may say he is an atheist; but this is inaccurate. Surely he is not a "militant atheist" because he would take it as terribly poor taste to attempt to convert anyone to his unbelief. In fact he's quite interested in believers and just fascinated by believers who apparently share many of his values. He would be equally fascinated, one fears, by someone who plays the bassoon. Nor does he oppose religion which is a "good thing" for a lot of people since it plays some important "social functions." (O marvelous sociology which discovered functionalism!) He may think it is a good thing for children to be raised in some kind of religious tradition and finds religious services esthetically satisfying. Indeed if he can find a religion which is satisfied with serving as an integrator of culture and a purveyor of esthetic experience, he may cheerfully embrace it. His atheism is not that of one who is firmly persuaded that there is no God. He admits he cannot disprove the existence of God; but also claims that neither can God's existence be proven. In the strict sense of the word he is not an atheist but an agnostic. He is not sure whether there is a God or not, though he is inclined to suspect that there isn't. God has become an unverifiable hypothesis.

It is perhaps not unfair to say that from the viewpoint of human history this is a rather curious position. One wonders how such a crucial question came to be unanswerable. Part of the reason is that modern science could only come to be by desacralizing the world, by breaking with the sacred, by revealing the man-made nature of all symbols. Only when science was able to suggest that God was a symbol which man had created in his own image and likeness was science able to be free of the bonds within which religion had held it. Even though the Christian would argue that this process was the result of tragic blunders and by no means necessary, the scientist realizes that in actual fact modern science came into being only when God had been made a hypothesis. He does not see how science can afford to concede the existence of God unless he becomes empirically verifiable or unless science proves false to its own traditions. Positive science cannot answer the God question and the positive scientist would rather not like to try. If forced to it he will admit that there are other modes of human knowledge, but he is not especially inclined to try them on this question.

The conclusion we are faced with seems quite pessimistic. If the intellectual's philosophical position makes it impossible for him to give any definite answer to the hypothesis of the transcendental, is there any possibility of a dialogue between him and the Church. Granted that the Catholic and the intellectual share many common values (perhaps more than either of them realize), granted that many of the obstacles to dialogue can be cleared away (especially as the freedom and humanism of the Church become more obvious in the current reform), it still seems almost inevitable that dialogue on the ultimate question is not possible as long as the intellectual is forced to say: "I do not know whether the subjects which you want to discuss can be the subject of discussion, because I do not think we can determine whether they really exist or not." In the face of this shrug of the shoulders the Catholic is perforce reduced to silence. It is not even a question of whether the intellectual would be willing to listen to the arguments of traditional natural theology because they would, after all, bring one only to the God of Aristotle. It is rather a question of whether there would be any form of legitimate human knowing by which he could determine whether there is Someone who transcends. The agnostic intellectual can do nothing more than say that he is not sure whether faith is possible. In practice therefore he usually acts as though it were not possible.

The situation is not however quite this pessimistic. The questions of value and meaning are becoming central for an increasing number of American intellectuals. While it seems safe to say that most of them are not convinced that a solution cannot be found within a closed positive system, nevertheless there are a few who are beginning to wonder whether an existence from which the question of transcendence is systematically excluded can be said to have meaning in any final sense of the word. The collapse of the Marxist dream and the destruction of faith in progress at Buchenwald and Hiroshima have made these questions more insistent. In Europe, where for obvious reasons the question has been faced more rigorously, existentialist philosophy of one kind or another has been called upon to provide an answer. In the United States, partly because life has been so much more comfortable, intellectuals have not been so eager to make the existentialist leap. If they begin to do so however it is possible that the new existentialist dimensions of Catholic theology will open the way to a common ground where dialogue will become possible. One must honestly say that the possibility does not seem imminent, though it is less distant than it was a quarter of a century ago.

Moreover there does not seem to be any reason why Catholics and secularist intellectuals need not begin discussion on levels lower than the "God" hypothesis, just as infallibility of the pope is not the first item on the agenda of discussion with Protestants. It seems that there has never been a time when intellectuals were more fascinated by the Church or more eager to learn about it. Until they learn more about the Church and until the Johannine reform makes the Church a much brighter "light to the nations" than it has been, it does not seem likely that the question of transcendence is even going to be raised. Nor will the intellectual believe that Catholics can be competent scientists until he meets great numbers of them; he will be persuaded that Catholics can philosophize about the meaning of science without looking over their shoulders at an ecclesiastical inquisitor when he encounters a Catholic who indeed does so. (And let it be noted that a philosophy of science does not consist of juxtaposing paragraphs from the *Summa* with quotations from John Dewey.) Nor will he be convinced that freedom is quite possible and even necessary in the Church until it becomes clear that Catholics do in fact enjoy this freedom. Lastly he will admit that Catholic social teaching is more than just theory when he observes large numbers of Catholics who are interested in rights or in people who are not Catholics and who are willing to work with all men of good faith in securing those rights.

Finally it would be too much to insist on the basic philosophical difference which separates the believer from the secularist intellectual in such a way as to obscure the fact that the preludes of faith involve more than the philosophical. The intellectual would be more inclined to believe that there is something to be said for the Catholic interpretation of the world if he saw that this interpretation produced people who loved more. The power of Christian love is the most effective means of eliminating the obstacles of faith for all humans, be they illiterates or Ph.D.s. The problem is the same as it has always been: there is so little Christian love. We are terribly ordinary people making terribly extraordinary claims. Small wonder that intellectuals—or anyone else—see no point in listening to us.

A Pastoral Theology Program for Seminaries
JOSÉ CALLE S.J. AND PAUL BRUNNER S.J.

Introduction

IT already sounds rather commonplace today to speak of a crisis in the teaching of theology. At present there is an immense bulk of literature striving to analyze the problem's causes and suggest possible solutions.

It seems that in the teaching of theology we have borrowed too much speculation from scholasticism, while almost entirely losing the vital dynamism both of scriptural and of patristic theology in the great tradition of the Church.

The awareness of this fact has been at the root of a renewal of theology, preeminently ecclesiological, biblical and liturgical, that began to take shape more than half a century ago. What is important for us to realize at the present moment is that such a renewal has made, in quite a short time, a remarkable impact in the life of the faithful.

If we compare the present renewal in theology with nineteenth century neo-scholasticism, we will immediately observe some striking differences.

Neo-scholasticism was an effort to readjust our "theologia et philosophia perennis" with the notions and concepts of modern philosophy. It almost exclusively operated in the field of theological speculation, and consequently had little influence in the life of the faithful.

The present theological renewal is rather an effort to bring about closer cooperation of men with the work of Christ in the actual economy of salvation. It is focused on the ever-actual activity of the risen Christ, who since the day of Easter and Pentecost, as Head of his mystical body, works in the world the conversion and sanctification of men.

Thus current theology, without overlooking the speculative values of dogmatic truths, is in itself a movement thoroughly pastoral. And therefore it offers some very solid grounds for the scientifical elaboration of a genuine pastoral theology.

A Problem of Terminology

By pastoral theology we are accustomed to understand something which in reality should rather be called pastoral technology, in the form of certain practical advices for the administration of the sacraments, the application of moral principles in the confessional, the observance of rubrics. We have no objections to any of these techniques. On the contrary it will be very imprudent to send a young priest to his parish without a necessary knowledge of these practical aspects.

But pastoral technology can never substitute for pastoral theology. The former absolutely depends on the latter to perpetually maintain the significance and efficacy of pastoral action. Just as there are dogmatic heresies because of the individualistic choice of some theologians regarding dogmatic truths, so also pastoral heresies exist because of the personal choice made by some pastors with regard to the functioning of the Church. It is the task of pastoral theology to preserve pastoral action from any sort of didactic, juridical or ritualistic pragmatism that does not originate from the inner vitality of the mystical body of Christ.

Definition and Division of Pastoral Theology

If we analyze these two words "pastoral" and "theology," we realize that theology means first of all that we are to deal with a

195

science, and then with a science that is theological, nourished by the Word of God and based upon the Word of God. On the other hand pastoral determines the object of this theological science. This object is nothing else but the vital functioning of this living organism: the mystical body of Christ.

Thus pastoral theology may be defined as the "theological science of ecclesial actions." The vital functioning of the Church, that is to say, ecclesial actions, is in reality the work of Christ himself, who through the instrumentality of his members, and according to the hierarchical structure of his body, continuously exercises his threefold mission: as prophet, king and priest. Thus the threefold mission of Christ communicated to the Church determines not only the object but also the essential and natural *division* of any genuine pastoral theology.

The prophetical mission of Christ in the Church implies a *prophetical* pastoral theology, with all the problems encountered in the proclamation of God's word. The sacerdotal mission of Christ in the Church implies a *liturgical* pastoral theology, with all the problems in the sacramental and sacrificial life of the faithful. Christ's royal mission in the Church implies a *guiding* pastoral theology leading to the promotion, protection and expansion of the life of charity, which is the law of God's kingdom.

From what has been said it is easy to see where to integrate the questions of pastoral theology into the total synthesis of systematic theology. Pastoral theology has its place in ecclesiology as an autonomous part of the tractatus de Ecclesiae.

Here arise two practical questions that bother many a prefect of studies: First: how to find the necessary time for the study of pastoral theology without increasing any further the *total* number of classes in the theological course. As of now there is but one solution: to eliminate from other subjects questions and theses that are of less importance today. The council will most probably make things easier. Second: *what* questions should be treated in a course of true pastoral theology, and *how* to develop them with organic unity and dogmatic basis. The present syllabus is an attempt toward the solution of this problem. It is limited to prophetical and liturgical pastoral theology, because in dealing with their topics, we usually do encounter greater doctrinal as well as practical difficulties.

1

Prophetical Pastoral Theology

By José Calle S.J.

1) Notion of the prophetical mission of the Church: the vital function of the mystical body, "actus vitalis Ecclesiae," by which God reveals himself in the fullness of his Word, Jesus Christ, who lives, acts and speaks in the Church and through the Church.

2) Ministry and mystery of the Word of God: The ministry and the mystery of the Word contain the whole economy and pedagogy of the history of salvation, from the eternal Word of God in the Trinity to the Word made flesh in the incarnation. From the Word that created the world, and the history of Israel to the fullness of the Word revealed in Christ and by Christ, building up his body, prolonged in his preaching (Word), which by faith (fides ex auditu—Rom 10) commands its growth and expansion century after century since the day of Pentecost (Omnia per ipsum facta sunt—Jn 1).

3) Prophetical mission and theology of preaching: the prophetical mission of the Church demands from the preacher a necessary knowledge, not only of some rhetorical techniques, but of a genuine theology of preaching. The theology of preaching is the theological reflection upon the mystery and the ministry of the Word of God that gave a right understanding of the meaning, content, guiding principle, aim, pedagogy and efficacy of the act of preaching.

197

a) Meaning. In the act of preaching God intends to reveal himself as the Father who in his Son, through the Holy Spirit, calls us to share in his divine life (Fili in Filio—Gregory of Nyssa).

b) Content. Nothing else but the mystery of Christ.

c) Guiding principle. The principle commanding the whole economy of salvation is the reality of Christ, seen by the Father as the head of his mystical body: "Christus totus," through the mystery of the incarnation. Then, since preaching is the prolongation of the mystery of the Word made flesh, the guiding principle is also the "law of the incarnation." As the Son of God became true man, wholly accepting human condition, so God, by deciding to convey his message through human words (Fides ex auditu), has implicitly accepted the dynamism and conditions of human words. Consequently only when the words of the preacher are meaningful for the man as he is and where he is will the word of God incarnate itself in the heart of man.

d) Aim and Pedagogy. The aim of preaching is as we have seen to provoke in man a personal response to the Word of God. This response (living faith), over and above a mere acceptance of certain statements as true (information-instruction) or even a building up of a new behavior and mentality (formation), is a communion of life with the Word incarnate: Christ living in the Church (initiation into the mystery of the Person). It means therefore a true Christian conversion and a progressive transformation in Christ, "conformes fieri imagini Filii sui."

e) Efficacy. The act of preaching has in itself a supernatural efficacy, not ex opere operato as in the sacraments, or ex opere operantis Ecclesiae as in the sacramentals, but "sui generis." Its efficacy comes first of all from the fact that in the act of preaching Christ himself continues his prophetic mission through the instrumentality of the preacher; and second from the Word of God itself which, according to constant Catholic tradition, has an inherent supernatural efficacy.

4) Through the prophetical mission of the Church, man meets God in faith. Awareness of the problems of man meeting God in personal communion of faith; theological justification of the need of anthropological, sociological and psychological data to understand the problems of man's approach to God; and the "law of incarnation" make it imperative that we take into consideration man as he is and where he is. Therefore:

a) Religious anthropology should provide: basic orientation to the problem; analysis of mentalities; prevalent contemporary trends of thought; old roots of modern prejudice against Christianity and its implications, etc.

b) Religious sociology should provide some notions on social structure and religion; religious mentality in different milieux; trends in contemporary mentalities and their relation to religion; group dynamics, etc.

c) Religious psychology should provide: a basic understanding of psychic structure and religion; religious psychological development; psychological ages, psychological types; their dispositions to accept or to reject various realities of the Christian message; the psychology of Christians in pagan or dechristianized societies, etc.

5) The prophetical mission of the Church and the problems of transmission of the message.

a) Historical survey of the transmission of the message across the centuries; justifications and rectifications; the transmission of the message in the symbols of the apostles; patristic era; medieval era; post-reformation; enlightenment; modern era; methodological crisis; kerygmatic renewal; recovery of the dynamic aspect of the message and awareness of the human dispositions conditioning the transmission of the message.

b) Fundamental methodology in the problem of transmission: through the transmission of the message God meets man and man meets God in the personal encounter of faith. This "personal" character of faith demands that the manner of approach and the ways of transmitting the message to different classes of men be conditioned by the "law of incarnation" that takes into account the human conditioning for the entry, the message and the concrete situation of man in his response to God. Thus the fundamental methodology in the transmission of the message respects the four possible stages where a man can be with regard to God, namely: 1) pre-evangelization, 2) evangelization, 3) catechesis proper, 4) advanced catechesis.

1) Pre-evangelization: *addresses* those baptized or unbaptized who consciously or unconsciously live a life of practical rejection of Christ. *Aims* at awakening spiritual readiness to accept God's message. Guiding principle: imperative need of religious psychosociological data at this stage. Procedure: dialogue leading to a gradual discovery of man, of God and of Christ.

2) Evangelization: *addresses* those who are already prepared to accept God's message. *Aims* at provoking an initial conversion wherein faith begins. Procedure: a dynamic heralding of the core of God's message.

3) Catechesis proper: *addresses* those who are initially converted through a global but personal faith. *Aims* at a sincere commitment to Christ. The main laws of the catechetical apostolate:

a) Basic idea: catechetics considers the catechetical apostolate as a mission imparted by the Church to participate in Christ's proclamation of the good news of salvation to men. The whole of catechetics is to be inspired and regulated by this basic idea.

b) Aim: the aim of the catechetical apostolate is not knowledge as such, but living faith—a faith which responds to God's call (message).

c) Message: the emphasis is on content more than on method. With regard to content, the catechetical apostolate emphasizes concentration on the central theme of God's love accomplished in Jesus Christ (dead, risen and living

200

in his Church) and presented as a gospel (good news) oriented to life.

d) Method: the main lines of method are to follow the dynamics of faith: to present the religious facts (God's saving deeds), unfold their religious meaning, to stimulate a personal response to this call of God in Christian living. As such, method is a handmaid, but an indispensable one. In all its phases it needs thorough adaptation to those who are catechized.

e) Fourfold presentation of the faith: genuine catechetics requires the sound equilibrium of a fourfold presentation of the faith; through liturgy, bible, systematic teaching and the testimony of Christian living. Systematic teaching is not to be begun before the age of 10 or 12, and even then needs to be completed by and thoroughly informed with biblical and liturgical catechesis.

f) The catechist: because the teacher of religion is Christ's spokesman and witness, the teacher is more important than the textbook. He must first assimilate the message personally. He must build up his religious life from the message in harmony with professional training.

g) Textbooks: textbooks are in the service of the teacher and the pupils. Good texts are required which take into account the development of present-day theology. Outdated texts cannot be modernized by mere modification and revisions.

4) Advanced catechesis: *addresses* Catholics living a normal life of faith, hope and charity corresponding to their age and spiritual growth. *Aims* to develop the personality of a Christian in the threefold dimensions: as a *child of God, member of the Church* and *witness of Christ.* Content: whatever is needed, first, for the normal growth of the life of grace as a child of God, namely spiritual and moral guidance. Secondly whatever is needed for a greater consciousness of his

dignity and social responsibility as a member of the Church, namely more biblical and liturgical formation for greater personal participation in the sacramental and sacrificial life of the Church, i.e. mistagogical catechesis. Thirdly whatever is necessary for the fulfillment of his missionary task as a witness of Christ, namely more didactic knowledge of the message, and psychological and apologetical training.

Result: a fervent and apostolic witness of Christ in the world today.

Public speaking principles.

2

LITURGICAL PASTORAL THEOLOGY

By Paul Brunner S.J.

THE liturgical constitution of Vatican Council II, in chapter 1, paragraph 16, states: "The study of sacred liturgy is to be ranked among the compulsory and major courses in seminaries and religious houses of study. In theological faculties it is to rank among the principal courses. It is to be taught under its theological, historical, spiritual, pastoral and juridical aspects."

The principles and program below have been inspired by what is actually being done in several seminaries, especially in the theological faculty of Trier, Germany.

Preliminary Considerations

Aim: liturgical studies in the seminary aim at making future priests conscious of the fundamental importance of worship in the life of the Church (worship is the center and source of all

202

her activities), and so enable them to participate in it for their personal lives and for their apostolate.

Approach: the aim determines the approach. No erudition for its own sake, but only as far as it disposes seminarians for their priestly life. The approach must therefore be thoroughly pastoral.

Method: in studying the forms of Catholic worship (Mass, sacraments, feasts, divine office) the following questions should be developed:

Questions	*Aspect*
1) How did it come about?	Historical
2) What does it mean?	Theological and spiritual
3) How is it carried out:	
rightly?	Rubrical (juridical)
fruitfully?	Pastoral
4) How should it be explained to the faithful?	Catechetical (homiletical)

All these aspects are placed in the service of the pastoral approach. What finally matters is that priest and faithful live from the liturgy. Happily the liturgical reform of the ecumenical council is bringing the juridical and the pastoral aspect closer together.

It is essential that principles explained in the classroom be actually applied in the life of the seminarians in such a way that they carry out in the seminary whatever they will have to apply later in their parishes.

The students must learn to combine loyal observance of the rubrics with sound appreciation of their objective pastoral value. Prescribed rubrics are obligatory, but not all are of the same importance, and not all contribute in the same degree to the aim of liturgy. The teaching of rubrics must be completed by the study of episcopal directives and pastoral comments of liturgists engaged in parish life. To hide defects of those rubrics which need to be reformed would betray a wrong concept of obedience to the Church, and greatly hinder the liturgical renewal.

"Preview" for Philosophers

A liturgical initiation should be given at the very start of seminary life to enable the students to participate fruitfully in the intense liturgical life of the community, especially in the Mass and divine office.[1] Concerning the eucharistic celebration at this stage it seems recommendable to emphasize those parts pertaining to the faithful. This will help the seminarians participate in the Mass with spiritual profit during the long years of preparation for priesthood. It will also directly provide material which will be useful to them later as priests in developing the active participation of the faithful.[2]

Some seminaries have the laudable custom of daily reciting a canonical hour in common, and in such a way that within one week all the hours are recited. A short initiation into the meaning of each hour, and of the "opus Dei" in general, is necessary if this recitation is to be fruitful and loved by the seminarians. Time allotted for spiritual conferences and preparation for meditation may be used once in a while for this purpose. Short breviaries in the vernacular are useful tools for future priests.[3] By using them for common recitation, future priests not only become more acquainted with the riches of the psalms, hymns and prayers, but also learn how to use them later on in their parishes. Only by using vernacular, it seems, can Lauds and Vespers again become prayers of the parish community, as the Church wishes them to be.

[1] The scope of this article is limited to major seminaries. It is clear that liturgical formation ought to begin in the minor seminary. A useful teacher's guide is Rudolf Peil's *A Handbook of the Liturgy,* New York 1960.

[2] A model of such catechesis is to be found in Balthasar Fischer's *God's People Around the Altar* (twenty homilies, 58 pp.).

[3] Among the best known are W. G. Heidt O.S.B., *A Short Breviary for Religious and Laity,* Collegeville 1954, complete edition 1194 pp., abridged edition 758 pp. Hildebrand Fleischmann O.S.B., *The Divine Office,* New York 1959, 661. pp.

Program for Liturgical Study for Theologians

The following syllabus[4] complements the one on prophetical pastoral theology. It offers an outline for the course in liturgical pastoral theology. Its major divisions will be: 1) the fundamentals; 2) the Mass; 3) the ritual; 4) the divine office; 5) the liturgical year; 6) additional liturgical study.

I. THE FUNDAMENTALS

A) What Is Liturgy?

1) *The Liturgy in the Economy of Salvation:*

"downward" aspect (God comes to man)—divine revelation has taken the form of the history of salvation. The liturgy carried out in our midst is God's salvific intervention in the history of mankind. These actions of God were initiated in the figures (types) of the Old Testament, fulfilled in Christ through the paschal mystery and continued in the liturgy of the Church. "Thus the liturgy appears as the exercise of the priesthood of Christ, in Whom, by means of outward signs, the sanctification of man is communicated, and in the role proper to each, realized (Vat. II, Lit. Const. I, 7). "Upward" aspect (man goes to God)—"At the same time, the Mystical Body of Christ, Head and members, offers the entire public worship" (ibid.).

2) *Explanation of the Definition.*

a) The liturgy is the exercise of the priesthood of Christ,

---

4 In this program of liturgical study for theologians, we do not include the treatises on the Mass and the sacraments which are to be given by the dogma professor. However it is evident that the professor of dogma should make use of liturgy, just as the professor of liturgy should draw from dogma. The Constitution on the Sacred Liturgy confirms this point: "Other professors, while striving to expound the mystery of Christ and the history of salvation from the angle proper to each of their own subjects, must nevertheless do so in a way which will clearly bring out the connection between their subjects and the liturgy. This consideration is especially important for professors of dogmatic, spiritual and pastoral theology and for those of Holy Scripture (I, 16).

the invisible high priest; the priest as representative of Christ and the Church; the members of Christ's mystical body, sharers in his priesthood through baptism. These are therefore the three partial subjects of liturgy.

b) The liturgy is a complex of efficacious signs. The Word incarnate is the "primordial sacrament" of the economy of salvation. The "law of incarnation" applies also to the liturgy: the invisible God comes to us through visible signs, and through visible signs we go to him.

3) *Pastoral Consequences*

a) If the liturgy is the exercise of the priesthood of the whole mystical Christ, active participation of his members is provided for in the definition itself. It is the right and duty of the faithful.

b) If the liturgy is a complex of signs by which God comes into personal contact with man and man expresses his commitment to God, these signs are necessarily relative to epochs and cultures. They are to signify, that is, to teach and communicate invisibilia per visibilia. If the signs (words, gestures, music, architecture, painting) cannot be easily understood, they lose the function for which the Church has created them, and therefore should be altered.

c) From the above two considerations we draw the conclusions formulated by the liturgical constitution of Vatican II: since the liturgy is, according to its etymology, by the people and for the people:

1) We must bring the people to the liturgy (liturgical formation), i.e. teach them the meaning of the sacred signs, and the parts they have to carry out.

2) We must bring the liturgy to the people (liturgical reformation). This means:

a) The liturgy should be simple so as to be easily understood.

b) More vernacular should be used.

c) The rites should be adapted to various cultures.

d) Provision for community celebration should be made in the rubrics.

e) More power of adapting the liturgy should be given to the bishops.

Note: In these lessons it is essential to show that the liturgy, as the life of the Church, cannot be fixed once and for all places, but needs to be periodically readapted to various epochs and cultures. The power of making such adaptations reposes in the hierarchy (holy see and bishops) alone. But the suggestions have to come from—and the experimenting done by—pastors engaged in the care of souls. Mere fidelity in keeping the letter of the rubrics does not correspond to the expectations of the Church.

B) Spirit of the Liturgy.

The liturgy is the great school of Christian prayer. Liturgical prayer is:

Christ-centered: mainly through, in and with Christ to the Father.

Dogmatic: echo to God's revelation centered on the mystery of Christ.

Eucharistic: emphasis on praise and thanks.

Biblical: nourished from God's own words.

Communal: corporative worship of the mystical body.

Sincere: free from all kinds of falsehood (exaggeration, sentimentality).

C) Elements of the Liturgical Celebration.

1) The "Ecclesia" or assembly, derived from the Jewish "Qehal."

2) Its hierarchical structure: celebrant, ministers, schola, faithful.

3) The dialogue between God and his people.

   —God's Word in the assembly

   —The people's response:

      Singing: Psalms and canticles, hymns

      Prayer: Doxologies and acclamations; the people's prayer;

the "presidential" prayers.
—Structure of the liturgical celebration:
    Reading (homily).
    Chant.
    Prayer of the people.
    Prayer of the celebrant.
4) The Signs.
    Theology of the liturgical signs.
    Postures, gestures, actions (the prayer of the body).
    Sacred things and places (house of God, altar).

II. THE MASS

As the center and climax of Christian worship and spiritual life, the Mass should be given the prominent place in the program of liturgy. After the first initiation of philosophers from the viewpoint of their daily participation, the future priest has to become even more thoroughly acquainted with this most sacred of all his priestly functions.

Father Jungmann's *Mass of the Roman Rite* seems to offer the method best adapted to our pastoral purposes. After a brief survey of its development across the ages, the Mass is studied part by part in its present-day form, which is explained by the evolution of previous forms. The recourse to history is necessary if priests are to understand the meaning of the actual forms, carry out pastoral directives intelligently and guard themselves from initiatives foreign to the genuine liturgical tradition. It also provides the future priests with solid background material for preaching the central mystery of Christian life.

The seminarians must also be taught the pastoral directives which command the active participation of the community, together with the rubrics which govern the celebration of holy Mass. They must learn to say the orations and the Preface in a loud voice, to dialogue with the people in an inviting manner that arouses dignified and joyful answers, to coordinate their actions with the interventions of the commentator, to pace their rhythm of recitation with that of the faithful. They must be made to understand that to the laymen's sacred right to active participation corresponds the duty of the priest to make this participation possible and meaningful.

III. THE RITUAL

The same "genetic" method as indicated for the Mass seems to be fitting for the pastoral study of the sacraments, the divine office and the liturgical year.

The sacraments are studied in their present forms, but they must be explained by the previous forms which they have undergone. Only then do the actual forms yield their genuine meaning.

Here again the study of the rubrics must be completed by the study of pastoral directives suggested by pastoral centers and approved by the ordinaries. The students must learn to make the administration of sacraments, especially baptism, catechetically effective; to conduct meaningfully and beautifully the celebrations of first communion, confirmation, marriage, burial; to take pastoral advantage of the anointing of the sick, visitation of the sick, blessing of a new house. They should also study the radiations of the sacraments in family life: baptismal and first communion customs, family rites in connection with marriage or death. Inquiries in this field should be encouraged.

IV. THE DIVINE OFFICE

To ensure a joyful and fruitful performance of the "opus Dei" during the whole priestly life, a study of the divine office is absolutely necessary. The seminarians must learn the "parochial" origin of the breviary; its monastic development; the "mystic" of the divine office as the sanctification of the day's hours gravitating around the eucharistic celebration; the structural laws

209

of the Church's official prayer; the various elements of liturgical prayer: readings, chant, prayers of the people, prayers of the celebrant. The psalms especially have to be explained as Christian prayer, as do the particular structure and spirit of each canonical hour. Helps for praying the breviary and remedies in "breviary crises" should be given the future priests.

Seminarians should also be taught how to organize "celebrations of the Word of God" as recommended by Vatican Council II. The structural laws of these celebrations should be explained. The future priests must be provided with the material they will use afterward in their parishes. Such celebrations must also be a part of the liturgical life in the seminary.

Here also belongs the pastoral utilization of the benedictions of the blessed sacrament, novenas, first Friday devotions, marian devotions, processions, etc. Future priests must learn how to integrate these into the liturgical life of the parish and fill them with its spirit.

V. THE LITURGICAL YEAR

The main aspects to be emphasized are the Sunday celebration and the pastoral problems connected with it; the triduum sacrum with its preparation: Lent, Christmas and Advent; and the "theology" of the celebration of Christian feasts. The atmosphere of the seminary should reflect the liturgical spirit of the day and of the season, not only in the chapel but also in the refectory, classroom and recreation hall (decorations, posters, Advent wreaths).

VI. ADDITIONAL LITURGICAL STUDY

Since the material described above is very abundant, it might perhaps be necessary to let seminarians complete their liturgical formation by personal reading. However at least a short introduction giving the correct orientation should guide the students on the following points:

A. Varia.

1) The house of God and its furnishing—their meaning and consequences for the architect.

2) Christian art: its aim and means.

3) Liturgical and religious music.

4) Adaptation of the liturgy to the genius of the people.

5) Symbols in Christian worship.

6) Oriental liturgies.

7) How to train altar boys, etc.

B. Brief History of Liturgy.

1) Pope Gregory the Great: creative origins, community celebration.

2) From Gregory the Great to Gregory VII: Franco-Germanic developments.

3) From Gregory VII to Trent: multiformity and progressive clericalization.

4) From Trent to Vatican II: rubrical uniformity and people's passivity.

5) *The Liturgical Renewal:*

a) Restoration of the monastic liturgy: love for medieval forms (Solesmes), return to patristic forms (Maria Laach).

b) Extension of the monastic liturgy to parishes (Pius X).

c) Popular Liturgy: Dom Lambert Beauduin: the missal and the dialogue Mass; Pius Parsch: the "Bet-sing-Messe."

d) Scientific justification of the liturgical movement: Jungmann: liturgy is essentially pastoral.

e) The hierarchical Church takes the lead in the movement: Pius XII and John XXIII.

f) Vatican Council II: substantial conformity instead of strict uniformity; the people's active participation.

These topics could be fruitfully developed in workshops or

seminars, or in conferences given by the seminarians themselves under the guidance of the professor.[5]

Editor's note: This article has outlined a program for two divisions of pastoral theology: prophetical and liturgical. It has not touched on the third division which derives from Christ's royal mission in the Church. Christ continuously exercises his kingly mission through the instrumentality of his members and according to the hierarchical structure of his body. Thus guiding pastoral theology treats of that which leads to the promotion, preservation and expansion of the life of charity, which is the law of God's kingdom. The purpose of guiding pastoral theology is to offer a theology of parish life, study parish and diocesan structure, principles and technique forming parish leaders, etc. One of the practical phases of guiding pastoral theology is a study of the goals, purposes and techniques of parochial organizations: CCD, CFM, Legion of Mary, Vincent de Paul, Holy Name Society, Altar and Rosary Sodality, CYO, YCW, parish school, ushers, Mass commentators and lectors. It should include a detailed examination of the division of the parish CCD: parent-educators, schools of religion, apostolate of good will, fishers, discussion clubs; and of the parish CCD board. In addition it should offer direction in the formation and structure of a parish council which aims at coordinating, under the guidance of the pastor, work of sanctification of all the elements of parish life: CCD, parish school, parish societies. The course should also help clarify the functions, operation and services of diocesan and deanery service organizations, such as the chancery office, DCCM, DCCW, diocesan CCD, school board, Cana, Conservation Council.

[5] The author is indebted to Father Graef S.V.D., professor of liturgy in Christ the King Seminary, Quezon City, Philippines, for his valuable suggestions.

The Catechetics Course in the Major Seminary

FRANK B. NORRIS S.S.

As recently as twenty-five years ago many, if not most major seminaries in this country did not offer a course in catechetics as a part of the official curriculum. The reason is not hard to discover. A "course" in catechetics simply wasn't thought to be necessary. If a seminarian was mastering *theology* what earthly need had he to learn how "to teach *catechism*"? The old Latin adage: "Qui plus valet minus valet" (he who can do the greater thing can do the lesser) seemed to apply here with all its rigor. Furthermore the very structure and the overall spirit of the catechism were basically those of the manuals of theology over which the young candidate for the priesthood had pored during four long and arduous years of study. Surely if anyone was prepared to teach catechism it was the priest or the major seminarian.

Here we have touched, I believe, on the heart of the problem. In the past it was all too often unconsciously assumed that the content of theology courses was itself an excellent summation of the full Christian message and, consequently, an admirable guide for "instructing the people." No doubt many, even then, saw the necessity, in popular presentations, for simpler and more attractive language, for sound psychological and pedagogical techniques. But only a few—certainly in this country—were critical of the basic content or approach either of manuals of theology or of their paler reflections, the popular catechisms.

We have gained some deeper understanding of the problem over the years. What we have come to realize—though by no

213

means universally even at this date—is that we can no longer entertain unquestioning and uncritical notions of "traditional" theological texts. We see now, with ever increasing clarity, just how much these works are the product of a polemical age in which highly defensive and apologetical attitudes affected the approach to theology as a whole and to its separate parts. In a standard theological textbook pride of place is given to the "theses"—those assertions concerning Christian doctrine which are judged to be of major importance. Affirmations of lesser moment are placed under the heading of "corollaries" or of "scholia." A careful examination of the assertions that are given the rank of thesis within a given tract of theology will show that it is above all conciliar definitions that are accorded this lofty distinction. This is perfectly understandable. But what is frequently amiss is that equally important truths, which were never directly under attack and therefore did not require conciliar definition, are not given the attention that is intrinsically due them. An imbalance in the total view of a given section of theology inevitably follows.

Let us take as an example the tract on the holy Eucharist. In the typical manual of theology the "theses" center above all on those truths concerning the Eucharist which were directly challenged at the time of the Protestant Reformation. Greatest attention is given to three major assertions: first that Jesus Christ is really, truly and substantially present beneath the outward appearances of bread and wine; second that the "real presence" comes about because of the "transubstantiation" of the bread and wine; and third that the celebration of the holy Eucharist—the Mass—is a genuine and indeed a propitiatory sacrifice. Each one of these truths was explicitly and bitterly denied during the embattled years of the sixteenth century. Clearly the Council of Trent had no choice but to define all three in solemn fashion. Since, too, these articles of our faith continue to be the object of dispute even today, it is perfectly in order that they would merit "thesis importance" in a theological treatise. But what is most

214

unfortunate is that other equally important aspects of the full mystery of the Eucharist are not always given "equal time." They are frequently mentioned in passing, to be sure, but they just do not command sufficient space and attention to make their proper impact upon the mind of the young student struggling to master the elements of scientific theology. Such crucially important but neglected aspects of the mystery of the Eucharist would be: the place of the Eucharist in the whole economy of salvation; the relation between the Eucharist and the Church; the Eucharist and our resurrection; the Eucharist as the communal act of praise and thanksgiving of the entire Christian community. These are not considerations of minor moment. On the contrary they are at the very heart of the Church's teaching on the sacrament-sacrifice which is the deepest and fullest expression of what she has become in Christ.

Traditional texts in theology therefore do at times reflect an imbalanced attitude toward the full Christian message. This is simply another way of saying that they are not kerygmatic in their orientation. For the essence of a kerygmatic approach to any area of theology is *fidelity to the objective content of the message.* If proper stress and emphasis is given where objectively they belong, then the orientation is basically kerygmatic, no matter how technical or abstract the language of the text may be. For what is being insisted upon in this case—whether it be in biblical or scholastic terms—is the full and rich "good news" that must ever be the theme of the Church's preaching (kerygma). Primarily it is the lack of proper emphasis upon objectively important truths—and not scholastic terminology as such—that is at fault in so many theology manuals to date.

The "traditional" catechism is the theological textbook writ small. The emphases of the one are faithfully reproduced in the other. The silences of the one are the silences of the other. It is the immense and challenging task of contemporary catechetics to provide religion texts free of defensive imbalances and filled with the positive content of the integral Christian message. Important steps have been taken in this direction in recent years both in this country and abroad.

What then of the catechetics course in a major seminary? Its importance should be apparent to all. The seminarian of today must be able to assume his proper catechetical role as the priest of tomorrow. This means that he must have the clearest possible grasp of the Christian message in all its fullness and that he must be able to communicate that message to the men, women and children of his day. In other words he must know *what* to teach and *how* to teach it. Content and method therefore will be the great concerns of a catechetics course.

We are not yet ready however to consider immediately and directly the catechetics course itself. The reason is that the knowledge proper to Christian catechesis is not purely academic and "objective" in nature. It is knowledge that is acquired by *an experience of the thing known* even more than by a scientific study of it. Christianity, after all, is not a set of truths about God, Christ and us (no matter how attractively these truths are presented), but a personal relationship that we are invited to live with God our Father, with Christ our brother and with all men as brothers in Christ. Study by itself can give us only a highly imperfect "knowledge" of these interpersonal relationships. A "real" knowledge of them can come only *through experience.* Consequently if the catechetics course in a seminary (or anywhere, for that matter) is going to achieve its full effects, the total life of the seminary must be an experience of the full Christian life. Primarily this means that the seminary must be a true Christian community, a reflection of the total living unity-in-love for which the Son of God died.

We are not indulging in heady, unrealistic dreams. Christ intended an experience of genuine community-in-love to be shared by each of his disciples *even here on this earth.* Without it our "knowledge" of the Christian mystery is almost necessarily truncated and fragmentary. The Mass offers us a clear case in point. A man may have studied the finest contemporary works on the Mass and, from a certain viewpoint, may have "understood" what he has read. But until he has personally had the opportunity of assisting at a truly joyful and communal celebration of the Lord's supper he will not acquire the "appreciation" of the Mass that normally only such a celebration can make possible.

True, when we speak of the total life of a seminary being an experience of community-in-love we are speaking of an ideal. Admittedly in practice the ideal is not always perfectly attained (and this is true not only of seminaries but also of other communities—families, convents, rectories, etc.—within the Church). Still this imperfection should not blind us to the reality of the ideal or deter us from its pursuit. The Christian life in all of its aspects is not something we ever achieve, once and for all, at any moment of our lives. It is something toward which we strive.

Again, in an ideal situation the catechetics course in a seminary would be in complete harmony with the courses in scripture, dogmatic and moral theology, and liturgy—and, for that matter, with all the courses in the seminary curriculum. Such cannot possibly be the case however unless the professors of the major ecclesiastical sciences have a genuinely pastoral approach to their teaching. This does not mean that "standards" must be lowered to accommodate the lazy and the dim of wit or that constant reference must necessarily be made to "practical" applications of theory to the concrete circumstances of the parochial ministry. A pastorally orientated course in dogmatic theology for example should not be reduced to the level of a series of sermon outlines. What must be understood is that we are training men to be intelligent, dedicated, first-rate "heralds of the Word." That they must also be men who can "think straight" and who have a solid fund of technical professional information in their grasp goes without saying. But this necessary professional lore—which will have its place in their ministry—must not be thought of as somehow sufficient or nearly sufficient in itself. The seminarian and the priest need, before all else, an unerring and articulate understanding of the full Christian message, of the gospel, or as St. Paul would put it, of the "mystery of Christ." The seminary professor, of whatever discipline, must keep clearly in mind the precise purpose of seminary training: to prepare men, under God's grace, to be the finest possible priest-servants of the body of Christ, which they will nourish with the *full* power of the Word and the sacraments entrusted to their care.

Professors of dogmatic and moral theology and of scripture have a particular obligation in this regard. For they normally exercise the greatest influence in the formation of the attitude of the seminarian toward the Christian message as a whole. If dogmatic theology is viewed as the science of orthodox propositions concerning Catholic belief, if moral theology is studied almost exclusively as the science of casuistry, and if scripture is presented chiefly as an attempt to solve a number of thorny and vexing "biblical problems," then the great object of each of these sciences—the "mystery of Christ" and our personal response to it—can easily be lost in the midst of specific questions and details. If on the other hand the seminary professor has a keen sense of the primacy of the central themes of the Christian message then he will know, in practice, how to arrange his course, so that a happy balance will be achieved between a heightened appreciation of the kerygmatic value of the matter under consideration and a competent grasp of the technical points that is necessary for a "professional" in the field. Choices will obviously have to be made concerning the amount of time and the degree of emphasis to be attached to specific questions within a particular tract. But deep convictions about the pastoral and kerygmatic purpose of seminary formation should make those choices relatively easy ones.

How, we finally ask, should the catechetics course itself be arranged? On the assumption that it has a recognized place

218

of importance in the official curriculum (a one semester course of three hours weekly would seem to be minimally necessary) the course, I believe, should concentrate on three major areas: 1) the history of Christian catechesis; 2) the content of the Christian message kerygmatically viewed; and 3) the methodology of Christian catechisis. To each of these areas we must now turn our attention.

The History of Catechesis

American Catholics seldom have any real understanding or intuitive sense of the great "tradition" of the Church. Left to themselves American seminarians are no exception to the rule. Living as we do in a relatively young country—where even now one can still talk of a "New Frontier"—we understandably have a limited interest in and appreciation of the past. "Tradition," for us, is what has been said or done for the past forty or fifty years. When such an attitude is transferred to the life of the Church however the result can be disastrous. Many religious practices which by our national standards would be truly "traditional" are, when measured by the yardstick of the Church's life, as of yesterday and have no automatic claim of admittance to the Church's authentic tradition.

A knowledge therefore of the long and varied history of Christian catechisis can, when properly presented, be an immense help in understanding and evaluating what is happening in catechetical circles today. What appears to the uninformed as an "innovation" will often be seen in the light of the history of catechesis to be a healthy return to an ancient and truly traditional approach. For example the contemporary insistence on the necessity of giving religious instruction solidly grounded in the history of salvation will appear not as an exaggerated interest in "bible stories" but, as it truly is, a return to a basic approach to catechesis that was championed by no less a theological luminary than Augustine of Hippo in his renowned *De Catechizandis Rudibus*.

Sheer number of years is of course no guarantee that a practice or a mentality is authentically traditional. For over a thousand years in some parts of the Church it was customary for the laity to receive the holy Eucharist no oftener than three or four times a year, at most. Yet this age-old practice could not have been more opposed to the real tradition of the Church. It is not enough therefore for a professor of catechetics to chronicle the vicissitudes of religious instruction over the centuries. He must prepare his students to judge the catechetical practices of any age in the light of the practice of that altogether unique period in the life of the Church, the apostolic age.

The seminarian must be given a keen appreciation of the fundamental "kerygma" of the nascent Church and of the positive, central religious themes that preoccupied the minds and hearts of the first disciples. An analysis of the primitive sermons of St. Peter as found in the Acts of the Apostles and at least a sketch of the key concepts of St. Paul would seem to be necessary in any significant study of the development in Christian catechesis. In a word the student must see that the touchstone of what is truly traditional in Catholicism is harmony with what St. Paul called "the mystery of Christ," namely the plan of the Father to bring all creation into a unity under the headship of the incarnate Son of God. Fidelity to all that is implied in the mystery of the redemptive incarnation is the standard by which to measure any catechetical (or sacramental or disciplinary) practice in the life of the Church.

A study of the history of catechesis therefore is not the pursuit of history for its own sake. It is rather an attempt to give the seminarian and priest of tomorrow a sure basis for evaluating the catechetical movement of our day. Although the sketch will be necessarily brief and concerned only with the highlights of the history of religious instruction, it would appear to be an essential part of an adequate seminary course in catechetics.

220

The Content of the Christian Message

We have gained many excellent insights in the past half century or so concerning the methodology of religious education. An appreciation of the importance of good audiovisual aids, of the necessity for student reaction and response during the period of instruction, of the value of variety and "change of pace" as an essential component of intelligent pedagogy, all of these insights are sheer gain to the serious and dedicated religion teacher today. Ignorance of or indifference to the valid findings of experts in religious pedagogy cannot be excused in catechists, clerical or lay—though no amount of methodology can ever begin to compensate for weakness in the *content* of religion courses. Let us know how to teach, by all means; but first of all let us know what we must teach.

As we suggested earlier, we cannot assume that a seminarian automatically has a clear grasp of the essentials of the full Christian message. He, like the rest of us, has grown up in a religious atmosphere highly colored by the defensive and apologetic concerns of the post-Reformation period. If the total life of the seminary is geared toward providing a genuine experience of true Christian community, and if the courses in the ecclesiastical sciences are consistently pastoral and kerygmatic in orientation, then the professor of catechetics may rightly presume, on the part of his students, a considerable understanding of the "content" of religious instruction. In reality such may well not be the case. If so then the catechetics course itself must provide as thorough a survey of the Christian message as is possible. I have personally found that the thirty brief instructions given by Father Johannes Hofinger S.J. in *The Art of Teaching Christian Doctrine* provide a sound basis for a kerygmatic presentation of the core of the Christian message. But whatever source a professor would choose, he must see to it that his students have a firm hold on the "good news" that they are to proclaim at every opportunity for the rest of their lives. The content of the Christian message must hold an unquestioned priority in any course in catechetics. Should a sacrifice of content matter become necessary, say because of a shortage of classes, let it be made in this area of the course only with the greatest reluctance. Our first duty is to the Word itself. This duty we must be conscious of before all else.

The Methodology of Christian Catechesis

Although its role is subordinate to that of content, methodology is nevertheless crucially important in the *art* of teaching Christian doctrine. We must know *how* to teach. While some few instinctively know how to present matter in a clear and appealing fashion (they are the "born teachers"), the majority of men must be trained in the art of religious pedagogy. Here we can and should benefit from the valuable findings of acknowledged experts in the field of religious education. The seminarian should for example be taught a psychologically and pedagogically sound method for organizing a course as a whole and for preparing individual instructions. Fortunately such invaluable teachers' guides as those accompanying the religion texts of the widely used On Our Way Series offer the seminarian an excellent source for an intelligent and up-to-date use of methodology in religious instruction. There are a growing number of catechetics texts, too, that treat the question of teaching methods quite adequately. Carter's *The Modern Challenge to Religious Education* and Jungmann's *Handing on the Faith* are examples of such contemporary texts.

One point concerning methodology that needs to be underscored in a special way is the necessity of making the religion class itself a genuine religious experience. Although there are marked differences between the two, nevertheless there are striking similarities between the "methodology" of the eucharistic liturgy and that of the kerygmatically orientated religious instruction. The Mass begins with a proclamation of the Word

222

of God (the scripture lessons) which, ideally at least, is followed by a relevant exposition of the meaning of the sacred text (the homily or sermon). The purpose of the Word and homily is to call forth a response of faith on the part of the worshipers so that *as individuals and as a holy people* they may go on to celebrate worthily the supper of the Lord (eucharistic liturgy proper).

The religion class too begins with a proclamation of the Word. For what is the "presentation" step in the widely used Munich method but a confronting of the students with an aspect of God's saving plan and, above all, with his great love for us in the Person and work of his Son? The "explanation" that follows does not consist in doctrinal points brought in to give the lesson substance and content. Rather—like the true homily at Mass—it is a real opening up of the riches that are contained within the proclaimed Word. True, the explanation given in a religion class will be more formally didactic than the familiar "instruction" of the Mass homily. Still the two serve fundamentally the same purpose. For both should issue in a response of faith *then and there:* in the Mass, so that the community may go on to celebrate together the eucharistic feast; in the religion class, so that the students may respond to the grace to live worthy of the calling they have received. Much has been written in recent years about the importance and necessity of creating a religious experience within the instruction itself and about the concrete ways this can be achieved. Catechists who have consistently worked toward eliciting a response of faith during the period of instruction—by a moment of silent prayer or a group recitation of a litany, for example—report that a true religious experience can be achieved on the part of the students in a way that is both natural and sincere.

A final word of caution. It often happens that the seminary professor of catechetics himself has had little or no recent experience in the instruction of the young. While he is perfectly capable of reading and assimilating what experts have to say on

223

the subject and of passing on their findings to his students, still his personal lack of firsthand experience suggests, it would seem, a measure of humility on his part. Rather than pontificate on all manner of methodological problems he would be well advised if from time to time he brought in experienced teachers, whether they be clerical, religious or lay, who can speak competently and confidently of the specific details of methodology. It not infrequently happens that there are excellent catechists among the seminarians themselves. They can be used to great advantage in adding a note of reality to the study of catechetical methods.

Some concluding remarks. It has not been the purpose of this chapter to spell out in detail the content and method that should form the basis of a course in catechetics in a major seminary. Rather it was to suggest the overall attitude that should prevail if the course is to achieve its purpose of preparing men to be enthusiastic and competent "heralds of the Word." We can perhaps best sum up our observations under three headings: the life of the seminary, the role of the catechetics professor, and the attitude and response of the seminarian.

The life of the seminary. At the risk of needless repetition we must again insist upon the importance of the overall spirit and attitude of the seminary. The seminary that is a true family in Christ provides the best possible atmosphere in which a candidate for the priesthood may acquire a full and rich understanding of the "good news" of salvation. Without such an atmosphere the task of the catechetics program will be made immeasurably more difficult.

The professor of catechetics. While he need not, absolutely speaking, have received graduate training in theology, the catechetics professor in a major seminary must certainly be at ease in the world of the theological and scriptural renewal of our day. He must himself be a "man of the Church," one who is vitally and personally committed to all that the age of Vatican Council II stands for. In proportion too as the catechetics program in the major seminary grows in stature and importance, the value of giving men a specialized training in the field of religious instruction will, it is hoped, begin to be acknowledged. Is it asking too much to suggest that a professor of catechetics be allowed to receive the formal training in his field that such an institute as the Lumen Vitae Center in Belgium can provide?

The seminarian. It has been my constant experience that the vast majority of seminarians today are eager to become excellent catechists. Where they have the opportunity to give religious instruction during the school year or vacation they almost uniformly manifest an interest and industry in the preparation and teaching of their classes that reflects admirably their whole attitude toward their Christian and priestly apostolate. It is to be hoped that some of the more pedagogically gifted among them will be given the chance to receive the more detailed and extended formation in the whole area of Christian catechesis that would so splendidly equip them for the general and specialized catechetical tasks of their ministry. It will be pure gain for the Church if, in the years to come, there is built up a body of priests in this country with the technical proficiency and the personal dedication of true experts in imparting the good news of our salvation in Jesus Christ.

Catechetical Formation of Religious

SISTER MARY CAROL FRANCES B.V.M.

A FRUITFUL consideration of the catechetical formation of religious must begin with the question of the role of religious in the Church today. As the Church herself is growing in an awareness of her organic nature in union with Christ, each member of the Church can come to a fuller realization of his particular vocation in the mystical body. Perhaps one of the most significant achievements of Vatican Council II will be its clarification of the nature of the Church, because such a clarification could have great pastoral implications.

Several of the encyclicals in our times have continually highlighted the Church as the mystical body of Christ. Relying heavily on the theology of St. Paul and the early Fathers, these modern papal documents, particularly *Mystici Corporis* and *Mediator Dei* of Pius XII, have stressed the supernatural oneness of the members of the body with their Head and with one another. In the words of our present Holy Father, Paul VI, who as archbishop of Milan spoke to the Second World Congress of the Lay Apostolate in 1957:

The Church's mission consists in continuing the life of Christ in the world, and bringing mankind to share in His mysteries: the Incarnation and the Redemption. It is thus the Church's mission to effect a living communion with Christ, and, as a result, a communion between brothers.[1]

[1] Most Rev. Giovanni Battista Montini, "The Mission of the Church," tr. of the Italian text of the address given to the Second World Congress of the Lay Apostolate, taken from *Unity Studies* 21, 12.

Of particular importance in our present study of the catechetical formation of religious is the divinely revealed fact that Christ, the Head of the mystical body, is the *Word incarnate.* As the Father's Word Christ bears witness to the fullness of truth. The communication of revealed truth is an integral part of his work as redeemer. The very life to which he is redeeming man, a share in the trinitarian life of the Godhead, of necessity involves knowing and loving, because it is a personal life of the highest order. Without the revelation of Christ man would not even know the existence of this life, to say nothing of the fact that he would not know how to enjoy the riches of this supernatural life even here on earth.

Clearer insight into the work of Christ the Word incarnate has been gained through the work of modern scripture scholars. All of the riches contained in the Hebrew concept of Yahweh's word are found in a transcendent way in Christ. Whether we consider the dynamic impact of the word of Yahweh touching man's world in the days of creation—"He spoke, and they were made" (Gn 1)—or the active power of his word as it came through the instrumentality of his spokesmen, the prophets, Yahweh's word was an essential part of his saving activity.[2]

In continuing the redeeming work of Christ the Church continues his work of communicating revealed truth. By means of her action God's saving word resounds throughout the world. Such a process is possible only in view of the mysterious union with Christ which the members of the Church possess. It is this particular aspect of the process of communicating Christ's revelation, namely a *real union* with him, that is pertinent to our present consideration of the function of religious teachers. The work of the magisterium proper also depends primarily on its union with Christ, but this essential aspect of the Church's teaching mission is not our direct concern here.

One of the most striking ways that the Church continues to

[2] John L. McKenzie S.J., "The Word of God in the Old Testament," *Theological Studies* XXI, 2 (1960), 183f.

227

communicate God's revealed truth is her witness to that truth in her very life. Her worship centering on the Eucharist; her concern with every need of man, great or small; her involvement in all of human life; her governmental structure—all depend on her faith in Christ and all he has revealed. Today it may seem trite to say that actions speak louder than words. Such a statement is true nonetheless, and mankind has never questioned it. Yahweh himself followed this pedagogical principle in the Old Testament revelation. His great saving acts bore witness to his love for his people and gave power and meaning to his words. In his greatest saving action, the sending of his only-begotten Son, he revealed his love in an unsurpassable way. The totality of Christ's revelation culminates on the cross because there is no more forceful way of revealing God's love to man— "Greater love than this no man has, than to lay down his life for his friends" (Jn 15:13).

But the cross apart from the resurrection is incomplete, not only in the fulfillment of the sacrificial action but also in the full manifestation of the Father's love. It is in the mystery of the resurrection that the Father's love is manifested in the glorified humanity of Christ. It is in the mystery of the resurrection completed in Pentecost that the Holy Spirit comes to renew the face of the earth through love.

The various facets of revelation as understood by man are all aspects of the great truth that God is love. It is his own life of love as Father, Son and Holy Spirit which he wishes to communicate to all mankind through Christ, that is, through the whole Christ, Head and members. Above all else the members must witness to the love of the Head, just as he bore witness to the love of the Father in the Holy Spirit. The witness to divine charity manifest on earth is the very core of the Church's life. Such a witness involves a *community of love* because its source is the perfect communion of love enjoyed by the three divine Persons.

This community witness to the charity of Christ is of prime

228

importance for the meaningful communication of the truths of faith. Without the living witness of God's people united in charity any attempt at explaining the Christian mystery is bound to be sterile and lifeless. Where is such witness to be found?

The living communal witness to the saving love of God is found first and foremost in the eucharistic assembly where it is actually caused. Its continued expression is seen more or less clearly in the fullness of parish life. But one of the most perfect expressions of witness to the communal aspects of Christian charity is the religious community. The community by its very nature bears a unique witness to the Christian mystery. Whether a religious is directly engaged in the teaching apostolate or not, it is very important for him to be aware of the fact that his religious life in a community plays a significant part in the life of the Church revealing God's love to man. For a religious involved in the catechetical apostolate the community aspects of witness take on even greater significance.

Contemporary theological developments in the Church can be very instrumental in enriching the understanding of religious vocation as a particular form of witness to Christ. The precious insights regarding the meaning of election and vocation of the people of God can have special import for the members of the Church called to religious life. All of God's great designs for Israel are brought to fulfillment in Christ. Now these designs are continued in the lives of his members in greater or lesser degree according to their precise union with him in his body, the Church. Above all it should be said of his religious: "I live, now not I, but Christ lives in me" (Gal 2:20).

Sacred scripture is the written record of the faith-life of the people of God responding to his revelation of himself. The extensive use of scripture which is such an integral part of the modern catechetical renewal demands of necessity that the teacher, the catechist, is a living witness to this faith, a person whose life is lived in faith. Religious life has neither intelligibility nor significance apart from faith. Its very structure is designed to nourish a faith-life bearing a direct witness to Christ in all its expressions. The more a religious understands and lives his consecrated life in faith, the deeper his insight should be into the faith-life of the people of God and, consequently, the more effective and meaningful will be his teaching.

It is not our purpose here to develop biblical themes at length, but merely to indicate that contemporary scripture studies can enable a religious to understand and appreciate his vocation to witness ever more fully. Such a deepening of understanding will have many repercussions on his religious life and consequently on the power of influence he exerts in communicating the Christian message. In fact any attempt to teach the Christian mystery without living it is doomed to the failure described by St. Paul as "sounding brass and tinkling cymbal." The Old Testament prophets were great spokesmen for God primarily in the way their lives bore witness to his covenant.

The more deeply we penetrate into the mystery of Christ as suffering servant, for example, the more clearly can we understand an essential aspect of the role of the members of the Church—the continuing of Christ's redeeming action in proportion to their union with him. In this mystery we find exemplified the profound truth that every loving acceptance of suffering bears fruit in the kingdom of God. Or we might consider the saving function of the remnant and the anawim, the little people of God, because this study throws great light on the significance of poverty and humble faithfulness in the working out of God's saving designs.[3]

The frequently quoted term "salvation history" contains a richness and significance which, if understood, can give new impetus to every aspect of apostolic action in the Church, including the communication of the *good news*. It is in this concept that we find the reason for the courage animating a Moses, an Isaiah, a

[3] Barnabas Mary Ahern C.P., *New Horizons,* Notre Dame 1963, ch. 10, "Mary, Prototype of the Church." An excellent description of the anawim is found on pages 202–05.

Paul and a John XXIII. God was truly with these men as he had promised, guiding, directing, using their human talents to accomplish the work of salvation. He was with his people in the old covenant, but how much more wonderfully is he with us in the new and everlasting covenant through the action of the risen Christ continually sending his Spirit. Salvation history means God is acting now in the lives of his people, directing every event according to his own design for man's happiness. Union with God means oneness in a dynamism infinitely active because it is a union with him who is Love.

When a religious ponders the meaning of salvation history (and how important it is that he ponder it deeply), along with the awareness of God's ever active presence with his people there comes a greater appreciation of each person's unique role in God's plan of salvation. A religious begins to understand more thoroughly the wonder of divine Love saying constantly to him, and in a different way to every man: "You have not chosen me, but I have chosen you, and have appointed you that you should go and bear fruit, and that your fruit should remain" (Jn 15:16).

Contemporary emphasis on the use of sacred scripture in catechetics is intrinsically related to the growing awareness of the indispensable role of the liturgy in Christian education. Conversely the role education plays in developing active liturgical participation will become ever more apparent as the liturgical renewal permeates the life of the Church, bringing to full fruition what may well be the greatest document of Vatican Council II, namely the Constitution on the Sacred Liturgy.

Here again our consideration is limited to certain aspects of the liturgy in relation to religious life in order to explain why a religious will be greatly helped in his teaching about the liturgy in proportion to the way he understands his own vocation in its liturgical significance.

The act of worship is the climactic act of all Christian life. It alone gives full meaning and purpose to every other act of

231

human life, great or small. Each human act is somehow caught up into the act of worship because it is in this act that man gives himself completely to his heavenly Father through, with and in Christ. In giving himself man gives all that he *does* since all that he does largely determines all that he *is* at any given moment.

No other vocation in the Church bears such complete witness to the total gift of self to God as does religious life. This gift of self is given as a response, a response in love to God's complete gift of himself which is at the very heart of the eucharistic action. It is above all in the Mass that a religious finds the meaning of his vocation.[4] The complete giving of self to God accomplished through religious vows is essentially a sacrificial action.[5] In the action of sacrifice God's acceptance of the sacrificial gift, the victim, can have only one result, a transformation of the victim into something sacred, something holy.[6] But in Christian life it is not a thing that is offered but a person. In religious life the person is offered in a most complete way. Because of God's transforming action a consecrated religious is brought to a degree of union with God that involves intense apostolic repercussions in the life of the Church because of our organic oneness in Christ.

All Christians must be brought to understand the meaning of their lives in relation to the Mass. It is not an exaggeration to say that insofar as we understand the Mass we understand Christianity, including its revelation and relevancy in human life. The very life of a religious should help give him a depth of insight into the meaning of the Eucharist, and such an insight cannot help but influence his teaching profoundly.

One aspect of the mystery of the Eucharist that is of major im-

[4] Further developments on the theme of the religious life in relation to the Eucharist may be found on tape recordings of lectures given by Bernard Cooke S.J. at Mundelein College in 1960.

[5] The following recommendation in section 80 of the Constitution on the Sacred Liturgy highlights this fact: "Religious profession should preferably be made within the Mass."

[6] Lucien Legrand M.E.P., *The Biblical Doctrine of Virginity*, New York 1963, 82f.

232

portance in understanding the religious life is its eschatological dimension. Our Lord's first miraculous *sign* performed at the wedding feast of Cana pointed to the Eucharist. In the gospels and in the Apocalypse the kingdom of heaven is referred to in terms of a wedding banquet, the wedding banquet of the Lamb. Every religious is a visible reminder of the invisible kingdom of glory which has already begun to renew the face of the earth because his very life points, like the Eucharist, to eternity. Every religious is meant to manifest the triumphant joy of the kingdom because our Lord is also speaking to those united to him by religious vows when he says: "I have come that your joy may be full" (Jn 17:13).

Joy is meant to be a keynote of Christian life, therefore it has a key role in the modern catechetical renewal. The good news, the joyful tidings, can never be communicated by a joyless messenger. Like the Queen of Prophets who was chosen to give the Word to the world, every bearer of good tidings must continually reecho her song: "My spirit *rejoices* in God my Savior" (Lk 1:47).

But joy may be missing to a large extent in Christian life, even in religious life, if faith is not strong, if hope is not constant and if love is not growing. And it is in this context that we may be able to understand more readily the place of theological study in nourishing the supernatural life from without and the place of prayerful recollection in nourishing this life from within.

Because of the oneness of revelation culminating in Christ, any and every aspect of that divine message makes the Christian life more meaningful. This revelation must be studied and studied prayerfully in order for its riches to penetrate a human mind and heart deeply enough to be communicated intelligently and lovingly. But it is also clear in the history of Christian spirituality that this prayerful recollection bears fruit according to the way it is nourished on God's revealed truth, both in its sources and in its explanations as found in the growing thought-life of the

Church. The catechetical challenges facing religious today make this whole question of theological formation more urgent than ever before. Let us now consider some specific recommendations for the catechetical formation of religious.

In returning to our first point—namely that a religious vocation is a vocation in the Church and must be understood as such —we come to the focal point in the formation of a religious. Every aspect of his life finds its meaning in this great fact of his very identity in the Church, a person dedicated to no one but Christ and therefore to his redeeming work in the world. Consequently every phase of his formation as a religious—instruction, reading, study, prayer, involvement in community life— should strengthen his awareness of his oneness with Christ in the work of redemption. However, as we have already indicated, this awareness depends in no small way on theological understanding.

In the beginning years of religious life scriptural and liturgical studies can be incorporated into the formation program. When the theology of the Old Testament and then the New is followed by a study of the liturgy, a student can acquire a penetrating realization into the fact of God's saving acts in history culminating in Christ's death and resurrection and continued in the liturgical life of his body, the Church. Without this type of concentrated biblical and liturgical study there is bound to be a certain shallowness in the use of scripture and liturgy in catechetics. There is really no substitute for or shortcut to acquiring a depth of understanding in the mind of a teacher, even a religious teacher.

The place of speculative theology in the catechetical formation of religious has been the subject of considerable discussion in recent years. The varied opinions put forth usually revolve around three factors: the type of speculative theology, the philosophical background needed for such study, the apostolic work for which the religious is being formed. Perhaps we can resolve some of the difficulties in this area by discussing the third point first.

Because our present study is concerned primarily with the religious of the United States, most of whom will be working in their native land, the American milieu is of prime importance in this question. Although our own missionary areas are numerous and varied and are increasing with great rapidity right in our large cities, nevertheless the general educational level of our laity is very high in comparison with laity in most other nations of the world. The impact of mass media on our people is almost inestimable. Modern thought currents, Christian and secular, find their way into most American homes through TV, radio, newspapers, magazines and paperbacks. Catechesis in America today means much more than a simple communication of the good news, especially to our adolescent and adult populations. It involves a direct confrontation with opposing ideologies often too subtly interwoven into the fabric of daily living to be clearly discernible. In order to meet this challenge, to discover and appreciate the honest searchings of modern man for meaning in life, to engage intelligently in the dialogue of our pluralistic society truly to Christianize American culture, most American catechists need speculative theology, not to mention the philosophical and liberal arts background that such study implies. And we might add in passing that the American catechist, religious or lay, who will be spending most of his life in another culture can be far more effective if his educational background is wide enough to make him a true Christian humanist, one whose charity can be warm, sincere and humble because of his genuine appreciation of other thought patterns and cultural expressions. As a matter of fact our ecumenical age calls for nothing less in its catechists.

The speculative theology designed to equip the catechist for these various aspects of the apostolate obviously cannot be limited to memorized propositions, theses and formulas. Rather it must be vibrant with meaning, concentrating on the essential aspects of Christian revelation. In this area of study as in no other can a student acquire a synthesis in his own mind of the wondrous plan of God for man—the enjoyment of trinitarian life through Christ in time and eternity. The speculative theology in question here is permeated with the main concepts of sacred scripture. It is keenly attuned to the liturgy, wherein its various truths are highlighted. It is excited about the developing thought-life of the Church. It is constantly aware of its relevance to contemporary life. It is a Christocentric theology.

What philosophical background is needed for this type of speculative theology? Experience indicates that basic courses on the meaning of being, the universe, man, God can be most helpful, if not essential, for the kind of speculative theology in question. On this question of philosophy another point to be considered is that of a liberal arts background sufficient to make philosophy meaningful. This is not to say that the liberal arts are studied in order to make philosophy meaningful, philosophy which then in turn is studied solely for the sake of making theology meaningful. Each area of truth has its own autonomy and must be respected on its own merits. But it is true that a person's grasp of truth in all areas of human thought and life enables him to understand ever more fully the significance of God's revelation as it touches all of human living. The catechist's area of apostolic activity will determine to a large extent how penetrating his vision must be of our universe with its supernatural implications.

For a religious catechist the study of speculative theology can begin after the necessary foundation has been established as indicated. This study need not comprise an entire semester on each treatise but rather involve an integrated study of the various areas of dogma centering on the mystery of Christ.

The study of our divinization in Christ through the life of grace can lead into a study of Christian morality as an expression of charity in modern life with all its complexity in personal and social life. An exaggerated legalistic, individualistic and negative morality has plagued the Church for too long, causing untold harm in the lives of our people and creating a most unfavorable image of the Church in the minds of far too many persons. It is not a haphazard coincidence that the same Holy Father who called an ecumenical council primarily for the purpose of renewal within the Church gave the world two of its greatest social encyclicals, *Mater et Magistra* and *Pacem in terris*. The modern catechist must understand Christian life in terms of the social apostolate if he is going to communicate this essential aspect of the Church's teaching.

Such an ordered theological sequence is perfectly attuned to the ordered presentation of Christian truths encouraged in modern catechetics, wherein God's saving love is portrayed and explained in such a way that man's loving response of Christian living should be joyfully forthcoming. A theological sequence of this nature leads quite easily into a study of modern catechetics; this study should come near the end of the period of formation as the religious makes ready to enter fully into the apostolic work of the community. Prior to this final theological course professional study of educational theory and method should be undertaken.

Guided experience in apostolic work should be an integral part of the formation period, provided these experiences are well timed and intelligently balanced with all the other aspects of religious life. As far as practical experience in catechetics is concerned, it is strongly recommended that it be incorporated into a formation program only after the necessary professional training has been given.

Finally it seems imperative that our young religious be alerted to the rapidly changing structural forms in the apostolate. In fact they must be ready to shape new structures whenever and wherever needed for the fruitful communication of the Christian message. What religious will be doing in the catechetical apostolate of today and tomorrow can merely be indicated here: establishing excellent religion departments in our Catholic schools;

developing more effective CCD programs; directing catechetical centers for research; supervising religious education programs in parishes; participating in adult education work; utilizing all avenues of communication arts; furthering the interfaith dialogue; forming lay catechists for every country of the world.

No other age in the history of the Church has offered wider catechetical opportunities to its religious than our own. This challenge of our times can and will be met by religious who understand and live their vocation in the Church, the people of God. Every advance in today's theological resurgence can be instrumental in helping religious witness Christ more effectively in the catechetical apostolate. The interaction of truth and love in their lives can lead them on to an ever deeper union with him "in whom are hidden all the treasurers of wisdom and knowledge" (Col 2:3). As their union with the Word incarnate becomes more intense he will use their minds and hearts—their entire beings—more effectively to continue his salvific work of communicating the truth that shall make man free. The catechetical apostolate needs the unique witness of religious as it never has before. Insofar as it finds this witness will it be drawn to accept him to whom the witness points—the Way, the Truth and the Life living on in his Church.

Formation and Training of Lay Catechists

RAYMOND LUCKER AND THEODORE C. STONE

THE training of lay catechists is one of the most pressing problems facing the American catechetical apostolate. The dream of "every Catholic child in a Catholic school" is as far from a reality today as it has been for the last fifty years.

A speaker at the twelfth annual convention of the National Catholic Educational Association in 1915 said that "over half of our Catholic children, perhaps fifty-five per cent, are outside the Catholic schools."[1] Today official estimates indicate that about 55 per cent of Catholic children of grade school age and more than 75 per cent of all Catholic students of high school age attend public schools. Every indication points to the fact that the situation will become more critical as the years go on. This despite the truly magnificent efforts and sacrificing devotion of the Catholic people to build, staff, maintain and develop Catholic schools throughout the country.

With the widespread development of Confraternity of Christian Doctrine elementary and high schools of religion, a veritable army of dedicated lay people is now involved in the catechetical apostolate. This was not always so. Until the last decade or two most of the religious instruction was given by priests and religious.

From all over the country we hear pleas for new courses of study, texts and materials, and for a restatement of the aims of

[1] William M. Costello, "Teaching Christian Doctrine to Public School Pupils," *Catholic Educational Association Bulletin* 12 (November 1915), 244.

239

lay teacher formation according to the encouraging developments of the modern catechetical renewal. Confraternity directors and others charged with the responsibility of forming lay catechists are experimenting with training programs which will adequately prepare the lay catechist to be a witness of Christ and to foster a personal encounter and commitment between the student and Christ.

Our purpose in this chapter is to present some guidelines for the formation of lay catechists. How should the lay teacher be trained, not only in terms of doctrinal and pedagogical instruction but in terms of his own personal meeting and commitment to Christ?

Our concern here is not that of recruitment of teachers. Undoubtedly this is an important pastoral problem. However the experience of parish priests throughout the country indicates that when lay people are informed of the pressing needs, when they are challenged to assume a mature role in the Church, when a program is well thought-out and organized and when an opportunity for adequate formation is given, they respond in numbers far exceeding all expectations. Godfrey Diekmann O.S.B., editor of *Worship,* offers a theological dimension to this question. He notes:

No one questions that parents are the primary teachers of our children and most especially in matters of religion. Even though they have received no or very little formal training in religion themselves, they are still the most effective religion teachers, for God gives them the grace of state which includes the grace of educating their children as worshippers in spirit and truth. . . .

Widening the argument, it can be said that theologically speaking the parish, in a very true sense of the word, is the Mystical Body in miniature. . . . As such it likewise has the obligation to educate its members in religion. And God certainly gives to this community, as He gives to the smallest family, the graces necessary to teach religion to its members. . . . Hence if there is no parish school, this means that in the providence of God there are undoubtedly sufficient adult members of the parish family to take over the necessary job of instruction, and these will be given graces and helps by God for this task similar to the graces and helps He gives to parents.[2]

An Historical Survey

The prevailing catechetical thought of each decade has determined the characteristics of teacher-training courses. Consequently, before we outline a program for the formation of lay catechists, we suggest a review of highlights of the American catechetical movement since the turn of the century. This will help put the current emphasis on personal faith and encounter in its proper historical setting.

Marcel van Caster gives us an insight into the development of the catechetical movement when he says that there are three periods in the maturation of the catechesis since 1900, namely instruction, formation and encounter. He observes that these steps follow the same chronological order in various countries although they may proceed at a different pace.[3] We submit that the present-day emphasis in the American catechetical movement on leading students to personal faith is part of the developing stream begun by religious educators during the past sixty years. Likewise, the lay teacher-training programs which will be proposed in this chapter and the next are actually a development of what has gone before and an expression of current catechetical thought.

The work of the Munich Catechetical Society is well known. Josef Jungmann describes how the writings of Herbart and Ziller were adapted by such leaders as Otto Willmann and Heinrich Steiglitz to the teaching of religion.[4] By the time of the Catechetical Congress in Vienna in 1912, European catechetical authorities were fairly well agreed on the method developed by

[2] Godfrey Diekmann O.S.B., "The Lay Catechist Is Here to Stay," *Syllabus, CCD Adult Education School,* Franklin, Minn. 1961, 41.

[3] Marcel van Caster S.J., "Teaching, Formation and Initiation," *Lumen Vitae* 16 (1961), 607.

[4] Josef Jungmann, *Handing on the Faith,* New York 1959, 179–182.

these leaders. In these early days religious education had as its first objective to make religious truth understandable. The content of catechesis was fixed and formulated in the catechism.

Almost immediately these European ideas were brought to America through periodicals and books and by students returning from abroad.[5] Lambert Nolle, an English Benedictine priest, wrote a series of articles for the *Catholic Educational Review* in 1914 on the formal steps in religious education. He laid great stress on the necessity of understanding the truths of the faith. He said that understanding, the second step of the Munich method, was the "central means of real education" and "the most important" step.[6] At the annual convention of the National Catholic Educational Association in 1915 William M. Costello outlined the main principles of the Munich method. He emphasized the importance of good teaching methods to help the catechist bring about in the student an understanding of religious truths. The main concern of American catechists during the second and third decades of this century was to popularize the Munich method and prepare teachers to do a more effective job in instructing children in the truths contained in the Baltimore Catechism.

Such writers as J. J. Baierl, Rudolph G. Bandas, Joseph B. Collins S.S., Aloysius J. Heeg S.J., Anthony N. Fuerst and Sister M. Rosalia M.H.S.H. were among the leaders of the movement to make the Munich method intelligible to American readers.[7] During the early 1930s another great catechetical leader appeared on the American scene, Bishop Edwin V. O'Hara. Bishop O'Hara pressed for the organization of the Confraternity of Christian

[5] The work of Father M. Gatterer S.J. on the Munich method called *Theory and Practice of the Catechism* was already published in translation in 1914.

[6] Lambert Nolle O.S.B., "The Formal Steps in Religious Education," *Catholic Educational Review* 7 (1914), 7–15, 227–239.

[7] Of special significance were J. J. Baierl's books: *Creed Explained, Grace and Prayer Explained* and *Commandments Explained* which appeared from 1919 to 1921 and were an adaptation of H. Steiglitz's catechetical writings.

Doctrine in every parish in the United States. Through the impetus given by the CCD and its National Center, catechetical congresses, regional institutes, leadership courses and lay teacher-training courses in doctrine and methods were set up in dioceses across the country.

It was during this period also that advances were made in the development of various teaching techniques: story telling, the art of questioning, the use of blackboard, pictures, charts and audiovisual aids, group work and discussion. The catechetical movement was influenced by the activities of the "learn by doing" school with its idea that children are formed not only by words but by life itself.

The first phase of the catechetical movement in America had been concerned with better instruction and using the best methods and techniques to help children understand the summary of Catholic doctrine as expressed in the catechism. The second phase emphasized Christian formation whereby students perceive the value of Christian truths for their lives. Application of religion to everyday life was stressed. New religion texts were written, notably the Christ Life Series by Virgil Michael O.S.B. and the *Spiritual Way* by Mother Bolton. The School Year Religion Course was prepared by the Confraternity of Christian Doctrine. It aimed at integrating bible and liturgy with the catechism and correlating doctrine and precept with life and conduct. It, along with the developed lesson plans prepared by the Mission Helpers of the Sacred Heart, became the official course of study for CCD classes in scores of dioceses. Another attempt to combine formation with instruction was made in the high school religion series produced by the Confraternity of the Archdiocese of Chicago.

These were only a few of the many influences paving the way for the third step in the maturation of the modern-day catechetical renewal in the United States, particularly as it affects the lay catechist. Now we are beginning to hear statements like the following: "The foremost purpose of catechetics is not to teach about God but rather to lead students to God" . . . "No teacher truly catechizes children unless they recognize through his teaching an actual personal call from God." As in other countries development of the first two phases has led to a catechesis in which personal faith and encounter enhance the elements of instruction and formation. The On Our Way Series for CCD children by Sister Maria de la Cruz reflects the beginnings of this third period in the maturation of North American catechetics.

As the catechetical movement develops, lay teacher-training courses need corresponding up-dating. There is need to reevaluate what is being done in the light of current insights made by distinguished catechists and theologians, religious psychologists and sociologists.

Personal Encounter in the Religion Lesson

What kind of training will best form the lay catechist into a faithful and effective messenger of God's Word? To a large extent the answer depends on the goal one wishes to achieve through the teaching of religion. Some wish to emphasize as the immediate objective the imparting of religious knowledge; others stress as primary and immediate the formation of dedicated Christians; still others assert that personal encounter between God and the student is what is to be sought. All three have an important position in the religion lesson and are to be taken into account in training the religion teacher.

A catechetical training program will be determined, to a large extent, upon which of the three is considered of primary and immediate importance, and upon the interrelation between these three. In regard to the objectives in teaching religion, François Coudreau states:

Current debate about the objectives of catechists reveals the existence of two quite different schools of thought on this matter. One of these schools emphasizes actual *instruction,* that is, the transmission of the content of revelation. It therefore seems to defend a pedagogy of object. The other school insists on the education or vital formation of the pupil, that is, his initiation into a way of life. It thus appears to be in favor of a pedagogy of subject. . . .

The basic error, of course, is that we should be obliged to choose between *instruction* and *formation.* It ought to be entirely evident that both pedagogical approaches contain much that is true and that a person ought not limit himself solely to one or the other point of view.[8]

From this one might surmise that the goal of religious education is an harmonious combination of instruction and formation. However closer analysis will show that a third element enters in; Marcel van Caster explains:

God speaks in the act itself of the catechesis. That is why the catechesis must be above all an *"initiation into the mystery of God who speaks to us,"* and especially God who speaks to us in Jesus Christ in His Church. The first initiation, or the most complete one, should make the listener enter into a real dialogue with God.[9]

In the teaching of religion a balance must exist between information, formation and encounter. The teaching of religion ought never stop at the mere transmitting of information, nor even at Christian formation whereby students perceive the value of Christian truth for their lives. Over and above these two there is the goal of personal encounter: the fostering and deepening of personal communion between God and the student.

The religion class itself must help lead the student into a conscious relation with God. Catholicism is not primarily a collection of truths to be accepted and professed, or merely a way of life. Above and beyond these things, it is the revelation of God personally coming to us in Christ and our approaching the all-holy God in the same Christ. It consists in a personal and inti-

8 François Coudreau P.S.S., "Introduction to a Pedagogy of Faith," *Shaping the Christian Message,* ed. Gerard S. Sloyan, New York 1958, 131.

9 Van Caster, op. cit., 609.

245

mate encounter between God and man. It is for this reason that leading catechetical authorities throughout the world emphasize:

> The aim of the catechetical apostolate is not knowledge as such, but LIVING FAITH—a faith which responds to God's call (message).[10]

> Catechesis does more than teach the doctrines of the Church; it wins men (children, adolescents, adults) for Christ and after Baptism further *unites* them to Him.[11]

> In the catechesis, a doctrine and life cut off from a meeting with God is just as unacceptable as a doctrine cut off from life or a life cut off from doctrine. Instruction and formation cannot be separated from the initiation. It is the latter that determines the degree of validity and the methods of use of the others. It would be wrong to wish to establish a theoretical instruction and a practical formation with the idea of adding an initiation into the dialogue with God. Catechetical methods must be thought out again beginning with the "initiation" . . . In a catechesis faithful to the Word of God, it is always a question of initiation, to which instruction and formation are subservient.[12]

> Scripture continually calls our attention to the purpose of the catechetical process, namely to bring us face to face with the Three Divine Persons. They speak to us, challenge us, ask us to respond to Them in faith. Scripture places us before Christ and the Spirit, not before mere ideas. . . . Throughout our presentation we must be faithful to this direct, person-to-person attitude which Scripture provides.[13]

This personal meeting in Christ between God and the student should not be thought of as something merely added to the end of an instruction. Nor should the religion lesson be viewed as only a preparation for the crowning encounter with

[10] Main characteristics of the catechetical apostolate, as summarized at the Bangkok Study Week (East Asian Catechetical Study Week) 1962. See A. Nebreda S.J., "East Asian Study Week on Mission Catechetics," *Lumen Vitae* 17 (1962), 721.

[11] Basic principles of modern catechetics drawn up by the International Study Week on Modern Catechetics, Eichstatt 1960. See J. Hofinger S.J. (ed.), *Teaching All Nations,* New York 1962, 394.

[12] Van Caster, op. cit., 610.

[13] Joseph Colomb, "The Use of the Bible in Teaching the Church's Faith," *Modern Catechetics,* ed. Gerard S. Sloyan, New York 1963, 19.

God in Christ which takes place in the liturgy through sacramental signs. In the religion class itself personal communion between God and the student is to take place—further disposing and acclimating the students for the crowning meetings with God in liturgy and life.

The historical development and evolution of the catechetical apostolate during the past fifty years might give the impression that first comes instruction, then formation and finally the personal meeting between God and the student. The reverse however is more correct. Communion with God ordinarily does not take place at the end of the religion lesson, but rather whenever God approaches through sacred signs (biblical, liturgical, witness or doctrinal signs). When the teacher of religion brings God into the classroom through one of these signs, it is God making himself known in this sign, leading the student into a dialogue with him. God coming through these signs disposes the student to adhere to a doctrine and to transform his mentality. Instruction and formation then are not so much conditions as concomitant effects of the meeting with God.

Thus the teaching of a doctrine, the forming of a Christian mentality and the disposing for a personal encounter with God go hand in hand. However it is the personal encounter and communion with God—his coming through sacred signs inviting students to approach him—which gives direction and life to the instruction and formation.

Initiation is the absolute task of the catechesis, concurrent with which are two relative tasks. Instruction and formation are in the service of initiation and must therefore take their orders from it. Occasionally they may receive the emphasis, but can never stand as absolute entities without reference to the dialogue with God.[14]

The goal of catechetics therefore is to initiate the meeting whereby God invites the student into personal communion with himself, thus opening the door which forms a Christian mentality

[14] Van Caster, op. cit., 614.

and which leads to the generous acceptance of the facts and truths belonging to the divine message.

The Three Divisions of Teacher-Training

If we accept the proposition that encounter with God is the immediate and primary objective in religious education, we will look for distinctive characteristics in the training programs which prepare catechists. We will expect the training to be an experience lived out by the religion teacher. Instead of merely providing knowledge about God and about religious pedagogy, the program, by design, will direct those being trained to discover Christ and their fellow Christians in Christ. Efforts will be channeled to grasping and experiencing how the all-holy God comes into personal contact with man and how man meets God in faith. This opens the way to a view of teacher-training which includes three broad divisions: 1) God meeting man; 2) man meeting God in faith; 3) transmission of God's message.

The first division of catechetical training, God meeting man, treats of revelation. God comes into personal contact with the believer in four marvelous ways. Through the *holy scriptures* God personally comes into our midst; in *liturgy* through sacramental signs he enters into personal communion with the believer; he uses the Christian community and individual Christians as *witnesses* through which he continues his personal intervention into men's lives. And finally he comes through the *Church teaching* under the guidance of the Holy Spirit.

An indispensable part of teacher-training is the study by teachers of religion of these signs by which God reveals himself. The study of scripture and liturgy is not a luxury in which to indulge only if time permits. It is the heart of religious education, for God's living Word, the Word-Made-Flesh, is enshrined in sacred scripture and in the holy sacraments. Without an adequate grasp of scripture and the sacramental signs through which God in Christ comes to his people in liturgy, the teacher of reli-

gion is severely handicapped. He unwittingly neglects the chief
treasures through which he might bring Christ into the classroom
to effect this interpersonal dialogue between God and the student.

The content of revelation, enshrined in the holy scriptures and
in sacred liturgy, should enjoy a preeminent position in teacher-
training programs. The East Asian catechetical Study Week reiterated this conviction when it stated:

> The emphasis is on content more than on method. With regard to
> content, the catechetical apostolate emphasizes concentration on the
> central theme of God's love accomplished in Jesus Christ (dead, risen,
> and living in His Church) and presented as a Gospel (good news
> oriented to life).[15]

This emphasis points to the necessity of teacher-training structured upon content rather than upon techniques and methodology. Teacher-training built on the bedrock of content with
method as its handmaid, rather than on methodology to which
are added courses in content, lays the foundation for achieving
the goal of personal encounter between God and the student.
This interpersonal communion in turn disposes the student to
adhere to the truth being taught and to a change of heart. In this
way the content of revelation leads to personal encounter, formation and instruction.

The content of revelation is unfolded in the biblical, liturgical, witness and doctrinal signs, giving the teacher of religion
a catechesis which is genuinely Christ-centered. Catechetical
training wherein the message is unfolded through these signs
disposes the catechist to turn more completely to Christ and to
approach God in and through him. It leads the religion teacher
not only to know but to experience in faith his personal involvement in the mystery of Christ, enabling him in turn to initiate
his students to the marvel of personal union with God.

The counterpart of revelation—God meeting man—is man's
response. This response indicates the second division of teacher-
training: man meeting God in faith. Man's approach to God

15 A. Nebreda S.J., op. cit., 721.

needs careful consideration in catechetical training programs. This implies that a total vision of faith be presented so that teachers of religion may grasp its personal, existential direction and may envision it as knowledge and commitment, both of which entail a conversion and lead to communion.

> Faith, in order to be truly personal and living, supposes an acceptance, a conversion, and a consecration . . . To believe is first of all to accept because faith, while it is adherence to truth, is at the same time and primarily an encounter with a person. . . . Our Lord is the object of our faith and He is not something but Someone. In all his teaching, the catechist must be careful to permit this reception of Christ by the one catechized and to ensure constantly the passage from the level of ideas to the level of persons.[16]

In this key section of catechetics faith is presented in its sweeping biblical-liturgical scope, as encounter with God, commitment, hope and obedience. In connection with this study of faith as communion with God attention is also directed to growth in faith at different levels: childhood, puberty, adolescence, adulthood. Happily most lay catechists, because they have families of their own, possess a ready-made school for gaining insights to the way children and young people grow in faith. Besides the understanding of faith which is given in the foundation courses of a teacher-training program, short continuation seminars can be offered to teachers of religion to offer them valuable insights into those things which help or hinder one's approach to God. These will be explained later in the chapter.

The third division of catechetical training focuses on the transmission of God's message. This division hinges on the first two, revelation and faith. Consequently the art of transmitting the message is studied in relation to personal encounter, with consideration given to God meeting man as well as man meeting God in faith. To this division of catechetical training belongs a study of the goal of catechetics, the stages in the process of faith, as well as the psychological and sociological factors in-

[16] F. Coudreau, op. cit., 144.

250

fluencing the communication of the message. The catechist must see clearly the aim or goal of religious education if he is to transmit God's message well. He ought to be familiar with the stages in the process of faith: pre-evangelization, evangelization and catechesis proper, and know the approaches related to each stage so that he may best reach the heart of the person being catechized. He must understand the way people think and act, therefore he should possess a basic familiarity with mentalities and milieux. This indicates the role of religious psychology, sociology and anthropology in a total formation program. In addition the catechist must acquire facility in ordering the message so that it may be more effectively communicated to those being catechized.

In a total program teaching techniques are no longer extrinsic appendages to the study of doctrine, nor do they become the heart of teacher-training. Instead they take up their proper role as handmaids in the transmission of the message. Those in the teacher-training program are to experience sound pedagogy while discovering the riches of the Christian message. The instructor should carefully introduce group dynamics, para-liturgies and those things which will enable trainees to experience their personal involvement in the mystery of Christ.[17] Moreover special attention should be directed to the main features of the psychological method, methods for best achieving communion between God and the students, lesson planning and practice teaching.

A Model Teacher-Training Program

In offering specific suggestions for the total training of lay catechists we are aware of obvious dangers. Circumstances vary greatly. Any model program will have to be adapted and modi-

[17] Examples of lessons structured in the form of para-liturgies are in Theodore C. Stone, *Christian Action:* "Teacher Manual for Grade Twelve," Chicago 1963.

fied according to existing conditions. The program suggested below may appear grandiose, too demanding, and therefore impractical. However to present the ideal is precisely what we have in mind; to form catechists who are *adequately* trained is our intention. Keeping this in mind we offer the following program, hoping it will provide helpful ideas to those responsible for the overall training of the religion teacher.

As the spokesman of Jesus Christ the teacher of religion has to present the genuine Christian message. If this is not done any amount of facility in skills and teaching techniques, and even superior ability in understanding the student, will fall short of its mark. We therefore suggest that the main emphasis in the foundation courses be on the content of revelation. An initial course and a follow-up course compose what we call the "foundation" courses. The initial course will concentrate on the mystery of Christ in sacred scripture, and the follow-up course will concentrate on the mystery of Christ in sacred liturgy. Together these two courses form the foundation of the training program.

The first section of the initial course will acquaint trainees with a global view of the catechetical apostolate, its aim and message. This can be achieved by having trainees survey a booklet like *The ABC's of Modern Catechetics* by Johannes Hofinger S.J. or *Communicating the Mystery* by Sister Michael O.L.V.M.

The course will then turn to an exploration of salvation history. The great deeds by which God intervenes in history should be examined in connection with their sacramental significance. Those in the course are to discover how the events of the Old Testament were re-lived and given new meaning by Christ, and how these same events are re-lived, made present and given fresh significance in our era of salvation by those who are in Christ.

Through this kind of exploration of the holy scriptures those who are being trained will more readily experience their involvement in the saving events of salvation history, and will begin to realize that they are a real part of the biblical story, even though they see themselves as a later chapter in the revelation of God's love for men. The discovery of their involvement in the mystery of Christ and in the wondrous events of salvation history will not be experienced by merely listening to occasional lectures on sacred scripture, or by mere survey of God's message. In the initial course those being trained need to be immersed in the holy scriptures. Like Ezechiel they must eat the book and taste how sweet it is (Ez 3:1–4).

We suggest that fifty to sixty hours be devoted to the course with at least three-quarters of this time given to exploring scripture. Depending on circumstances the course may be scheduled over a period of a year, with a two or two-and-a-half hour session held once a week. Such a course will afford volunteer lay catechists ample time to study and pray over the saving interventions of God unfolded in the scriptures. Such a course presupposes the homestudy and reading of selected parts of the bible, with as much time devoted to this as to class hours.

During class sessions the instructor's basic task is to highlight the sacramental significance of the biblical events being unfolded. He will also pave the way for better understanding by clarifying, as much as is needed, the literary forms being used. The instructor is to use a variety of means in presenting the lessons. This should not be a lecture course! Some sessions should be prepared in the form of a para-liturgical class activity in order to involve the trainees personally and to let them experience this form of lesson presentation. Trainees should be made to use their bibles in the class itself and should draw up their own religion notebook as the course progresses. Group dynamics, creative drama and other forms of class participation should be used in the unfolding of salvation history in order to involve trainees as much as possible in the learning experience.

Ideally, during the initial course, those being trained should not teach religion. This is to be a year of formation, observation and encounter with the mystery of Christ. Even when pressing needs and local conditions compel trainees to begin teaching immediately, the initial course should not be emasculated on this

253

account. Instead a special eight to twelve hour workshop on methods and techniques can be arranged for those being pressed into service. In order to be of immediate and practical help to the neophyte teacher the workshop on methodology ought to be divided according to the grade levels. In many places it would be advantageous to provide such a workshop before the beginning of each school year for all who feel the need for brushing up on these matters.

It would be helpful, during the initial year of training, for trainees to attend and observe actual religion classes on the grade level they plan to teach. Trainees can do this in their own parish or, if the school of religion is not in operation there, they may be able to sit in on a class in a neighboring parish. If possible the instructor should arrange that each trainee has a place at which he may observe an actual religion lesson at the grade level he intends to teach.

Even though trainees may not observe an expert teacher and an ideal classroom situation, many benefits will accrue. To obtain the best results we suggest that the trainee observe the same students and teacher over a period of six or more lessons. He will observe the weak points as well as the strong points in the teacher, take notes of how the pupils react and reflect on steps he would take to improve the lesson. During this time the trainee should study the text and teacher guide, and prepare weekly lesson outlines corresponding to the ones being taught in the class.

After the trainee knows the pupils the teacher may wish to invite the trainee to take over the next lesson. Such experience under actual conditions is invaluable. With careful planning so that each trainee has an assigned place for observation, much good can result. During the observation period several class hours of the initial course may be set aside to discuss the observations and problems of the trainees.

Early in the course trainees should select the grade level at which they plan to teach. They should be given the text and teacher guide for that grade. It will be highly advantageous for the instructor to spend a period or two on the techniques of lesson planning. At regular intervals and as part of the home assignment, he should designate a specified section of the text and guide for study and have trainees write out lesson outlines, which are to be subsequently collected and corrected.

Observation classes, homestudy of a grade level text and a limited amount of class hours devoted to the notion of faith and to the transmission of the message will provide trainees with a sufficient introduction to the second and third sections of catechetical training, i.e. the student meeting God in faith and problems of transmission. At this stage in their training it would not be particularly beneficial to give them more methodology. First they need an adequate doctrinal foundation and formation. For this reason it is important to reserve at least three-fourths of the class hours for the study of the mystery of Christ in sacred scripture.

Class hours and topic headings for the initial course in a total program of teacher-training could be arranged in the following manner. This is one of several ways in which to order the subject matter in keeping with the principles presented in this article. This course outline has been inspired by the work of José Calle S.J. of the East Asian Pastoral Institute, Manila.

Section One	Fundamental Principles of Catechetics and Catechetical Method
1	The aim of Christian catechesis: living faith
2	Essential elements of living faith
3	Obstacles to living faith
4	Main principles of pre-evangelization
5	The core of Christianity: a *message* an *historical* message a message *centered on a person*: Christ
6	The four ways of transmitting the Christian message
7–8	How to read the bible and its use in the classroom
9–10	Principles of catechetical method

255

Upon finishing the initial course trainees may receive a certificate of achievement. They are then expected to take the follow-up course to complete their basic foundation. During this second year of training, trainees are encouraged to begin teaching in their parish schools of religion. To delay them any longer would discourage some; moreover this practice teaching affords an opportunity for personal guidance during their initial year of teaching. As immediate preparation for teaching in the parish they may attend the special eight to twelve hour workshop on methods which has been mentioned previously and which may be offered prior to the opening of each school year.

The follow-up course continues the study of the mystery of Christ, but now in a liturgical setting. In the initial course the emphasis was on scripture, while in the follow-up course it is on liturgy. Or to be more precise the emphasis in both courses is on Christ—God's Living Word—first as enshrined in holy scripture and now as enshrined in the holy sacraments. Christ then is the foundation in the training of religion teachers. By introducing trainees to the sacramental significance of the saving events in scripture, the initial course prepares the way for the study of sacramental life in depth. In the follow-up course trainees will concentrate on the Mass, sacraments and the Christian response to God in the light of sacramental involvement in Christ.

Forty to sixty hours can profitably be allotted to the follow-up course. While most of the class hours will concentrate on the study of Christ in the holy liturgy, about one-fourth of the time ought to be devoted to other matters, especially to the second section of catechetical training, i.e. man meeting God in faith. Trainees should obtain a clear grasp of the personal, global and existential nature of living faith, and of the more common obstacles standing in the way of a person accepting Christ. In connection with this facet of training, those taking the course could be encouraged to make a cursillo sometime during the first two years of training. Class hours should also be set aside to discuss problems which trainees experience in their teaching assignments.

The chief tools used in the follow-up course will be the missal and ritual. The instructor is to employ a variety of ways to present the lessons, including para-liturgical class activities. Para-liturgical ceremonies related to the sacraments should be programmed to involve trainees more personally in the communal spirit of sacramental signs. The Mass and sacramental rites lend themselves to demonstration and offer ready-made opportunities

258

to introduce visual aids into the lesson. Here also a religion note-book should be kept by the trainees. And while learning of the different aspects of the Christian response to God's love, the trainees could also discuss life problems and values in various kinds of group discussions. This approach will allow trainees to experience different ways in which they in turn may be able to involve their students in the religion lessons.

Even after trainees have completed the follow-up course they ought not be left with the impression that they are now full-fledged teachers of religion. To avoid this impression a religion teacher diploma could be deferred until they have proven them-selves. There is a variety of ways to certify lay catechists. One suggestion is to award a certificate of achievement rather than a religion teacher diploma for the successful completion of the two foundation courses.

Opportunities should be provided for the catechists' continued formation and training. Lay catechists should be led to look upon their first years of teaching in the parish schools of religion as a continuation of their training. During these years they should be encouraged to participate in brief supplementary courses and seminars designed as part of the total training program. De-pending on the subject, seminars may run from six to twelve hours. They can be conducted in connection with diocesan institutes, in workshops and at any convenient time during the year. A variety of topics may be offered simultaneously since religion teachers experience different needs and interests. The availability of personnel and relative importance of the topic will determine how frequently a supplementary course is offered or repeated. Participants may be given a small certificate at the completion of each supplementary course, so that they will know their participation is being counted toward a religion teacher diploma.

As we noted above, a variety of courses should be made available to the religion teachers of the diocese. This is a wonderful way to rekindle dedication and zeal for their work in

259

the parishes. The following are topics which may be offered in short supplementary courses and seminars to help round out the catechists' training and provide brush-up work for those actively teaching in the schools of religion:[18]

The parables of Jesus
The mystery of Christ according to St. Paul
The exodus in bible and liturgy
Christ's passion as interpreted by each evangelist
Sacramental life in the gospel of St. John
The Church in the gospel of St. Matthew
Christian witness in the Acts of the Apostles
The sacraments: the acts of Jesus our Lord
The liturgical year—font of catechetics
Liturgy: an encounter with Christ
The Mass—liturgy of the Word
The Mass—eucharistic liturgy
The Eucharist and the worshiping community
History of the Catholic Church in the U.S.
Toward an apostolic and ecumenical approach to Church history
Making the ecumenical council meaningful to students
The Church: the sacrament of Christ
The Christ-concept of the Church
Current problems and the Church's answer
Commandments—a response of love
Problems of pre-evangelization of high school level
Formation of the Christian conscience
Christian social principles
Religion and race
Approach to dating, courtship and marriage
The challenge of the lay apostolate in the modern world
Introduction to religious psychology
Introduction to religious sociology
Counseling
Use of scripture in teaching (divide according to age levels)
Techniques of planning scripture services and participated Masses
Techniques for leading group singing
The art of story telling

[18] Many of the subjects listed here have been taken from institute programs of the CCD in the Archdiocese of San Francisco, which each year offers an excellent variety of supplementary courses for its teachers.

Principles and techniques of group dynamics (divide according to age
  levels)
Creative drama (divide according to age levels)
Creative projects (divide according to age levels)

The religion teacher diploma is to be a coveted prize for one
who has served our Lord in the catechetical apostolate, one who
has shown himself to be a faithful spokesman of Jesus Christ.
As an ideal we would suggest that this diploma be awarded only
to those who have completed the two foundation courses, have
taught five years in their schools of religion and have participated
in a minimum of eight supplementary courses.

Many will never receive this honor, but those who do will
bear the title with a genuine sense of accomplishment. Perhaps
most of the lay catechists in a diocese will remain only trainees.
Perhaps many will never be able to take the full training program. But if a total program is available, would it not encourage
many to seek further training? Moreover is it not wise for
those who are teaching Christ's message to look upon themselves as only trainees in the service of our Lord? One thing is
certain: a total program of catechetical training will present
more frequent opportunities for the catechist to nourish a deep
felt hunger in his heart—the hunger to enrich his spiritual life
and to become a more perfect spokesman for Jesus Christ.

In concluding we would once again reiterate that the above
program for training catechists is but a model to show how the
three sections of catechetical training—God meeting man (revelation), man meeting God in faith, the transmission of God's
message—can be incorporated into a workable program. It goes
without saying that details will be altered according to local
conditions; rural communities have special problems of their
own, etc. We believe however that the underlying principles
governing the development of the above program are valid and
necessary in all programs for training lay catechists. They are:

1) The teacher of religion needs a biblical-liturgical foundation—
a foundation structured on content.

2) The understanding of the mystery of Christ is best achieved through a program which studies God's Living—Jesus Christ—enshrined in the Holy Scriptures and in the Holy Sacraments (Liturgy).

3) Methodology and problems of transmission have an important place in the training of the catechists, but are subservient to and at the service of content, and should be so treated in teacher-training programs.

OUTLINE OF A MODEL TRAINING PROGRAM FOR LAY CATECHISTS

1) Initial course—doctrinal in emphasis—fifty to sixty hours, usually conducted over a period of one year.

2) Workshop on methodology—eight to ten hours—usually conducted on a weekend before the opening of the school year for those who will begin teaching.

3) Follow-up course—doctrinal in emphasis—forty to sixty hours, usually conducted over a period of one year. During this time trainees are teaching in their parish schools of religion.

4) Five years of teaching in a parish school of religion.

5) Supplementary courses—six to twelve hours each—a minimum of eight such courses required to qualify for a religion teacher diploma.

A Survey Course in Catechist Formation

SISTER M. VIRGINE M.H.S.H.

Introduction

No parish can afford to defer its religious instruction classes until it has catechists fully prepared to form children in Christ. The previous chapter outlined a program that is designed for the total formation of the lay catechist. By providing for enrichment at all levels touching on religious education the guidelines in the previous chapter serve as a model for adequate catechist formation. Such formation admits of no emasculation. How well the specialist in religious education knows this! The question is whether those who register for the catechist class take the same view of their formation. Can the distraught pastor who has no one to teach his CCD classes tomorrow afternoon insist on the complete program of teacher-training?

Chief among those who present themselves at the first catechist class meeting are the busy mother of eight or ten children, the professional man whose calendar would have him trilocate, the dependable parishioner who turns up for everything and the Catholic college graduate who is complacently comfortable in his knowledge of "theology." A first question any one of this group might ask is: "How long will the course run?" These adult laymen have come to pick up a few pointers so that they can "help Father out." They see no reason for an extensive and intensified training program. Neither do they desire to commit themselves to one.

What can be done to make these future catechists realize their need of a program such as that outlined in the previous chapter?

Advertising is successful if it creates a felt need. When the potential buyer is exposed to the clever slogan, the billboard scene or the TV demonstration he experiences a need for the product and a desire to have it. In a few brief statements Jesus brought the woman at the well to the point of begging for "living water," a reality that was unknown to her until then. The Lord's selling point was one of telling this woman of Samaria enough to make her realize that she was missing something. This essay will describe a survey course that is intended to give the adult layman a felt need for the full catechist initiation spelled out by Fathers Stone and Lucker. The content of the survey course must tell the future religion teacher enough to make him realize that he is missing something he needs to have. The survey course will also present, albeit sketchily, the total perspective of the Christian message for the student catechist who must be pressed into immediate service. This course will serve as the necessary introduction for those who must taste and see for themselves before they are willing to make a long term commitment to their parish catechetical program.

The survey course described in this essay will, then, introduce the candidate to the message he is to transmit and to the practical techniques he will employ in presenting it. It should arouse his desire for more.

It is understood that the priest, brother, sister or layman who prepares lay teachers of religion is himself an experienced catechist, one who is acquainted with the learning situation of the CCD parish school of religion. His grasp of present-day scholarship in catechetics, scripture, liturgy and doctrine is equalled by his ability to employ effectively the teaching techniques he suggests.

The potential catechist. The competent teacher, aware that learning builds on previous knowledge, informs himself of the students' backgrounds. In this regard the teacher of lay catechists meets a real challenge, for Christ desires to speak in some way through every adult no matter what education, age or experience he has. The Catholic layman who answers the invitation to preach Jesus to the public school child may be 18 years of age and fresh from high school or he may be approaching 65 and hold advanced degrees even to the doctorate. The prospective religious educator may have been exposed to Sunday school-catechism-rote-memory-work or he may be a product of sixteen years of Catholic schooling or a specialized program of doctrine, scripture and liturgy. He may be destined to staff a well equipped catechetical center that lacks no material advantage or he may be numbered among the seventy teachers of one parish who hold class in the homes of parishioners and teach over nine hundred children. He may be a veteran of the teaching profession or he may never have taught at all. In any event he will be impelled to lead others to live in Christ. In this desire the most heterogeneous mixture of student catechists finds fraternal union and strength.

Attitude re-formation. Before positive learning can take place it is necessary to uproot preconceived ideas the adult layman may have regarding religious formation and the purpose of the catechist class he is enrolled in. The teacher of religion teachers must be prepared to cope with the man or woman who expects to be given a "few pointers on catechism teaching" so that he can teach as he was taught. When the prospective catechist learns of the goals of religious formation he is at first amazed and then thrilled at his discovery of the advances made in the art of preaching Jesus. More seriously in need of understanding is the outlook of the busy teacher-by-profession who begrudges—and understandably so—the time he must give to "another methods course" or to practical helps to teach "another subject." The first class meeting should be enough to suggest to this teacher that the lay catechist course he is currently enrolled in will be neither of these. A sound exposition of the goals of religious education in terms of the "material" to be presented and the desired student response must precede any consideration of learning skills or organizational details.

The aim of religious education. The religious educator is an instrument in forming Christ in the students. He will put them in touch with the person of Jesus who calls them to know God as a Father and to live as his son. To love God as a Father is for the Christian to share life with the Son to whom he gives himself totally in faith. To bring students to a personal meeting with Jesus who is the truth, life and way to the Father, and to evoke their response in terms of a living faith, is the aim of religious education. What takes place then during the religion period will be far removed from a process limited to that of explaining the truths *about* God in one class and eliciting a recitation of them in the next. The teacher of catechists will lead the adult layman to make this distinction with unshakable conviction.

1. DESCRIPTION OF COURSE CONTENT

To accomplish the goal of religious formation the catechists need a clear understanding of the mediatory role of Jesus and his salvation-act in all its unity and historical sweep.

A) DOCTRINAL PERSPECTIVES

The following perspective of God's saving of man, which is the mystery of Christ, may be acquired by the student catechist during the survey course through teacher presentation, assigned reading or, preferably, both.

Salvation . . . as reality. The story of Christ who is our truth, life and way to the Father is none other than the history of divine sonship given, rejected, restored, lived. The Father's plan of giving himself to man and making man his son again is the

266

unifying factor that gives meaning to the events scattered over centuries of the Lord's actions with man.

In the divine self-gift God accommodated himself to the ways of men. God used the ebb and flow that marks the life of any people or of any individual to turn Israel—and through her all men—toward him. The Israelites had no monopoly on slavery or freedom or suffering or hope or even sin; the difference is that God was there. He not only permitted these experiences for his people, he deliberately brought them about (sin excepted) so that in these happenings the sons of Abraham would meet and respond to their God. And so God's gift of himself to man in the promise to Abraham, the events of the exodus, the covenant, the law, the prophets and the kingdom prepared man to receive the perfect divine self-gift in the Person of the Son who took flesh to dwell among us and restore us to Family life in the Father's house.

Man's return gift of himself to God was made perfect in the Son who united fallen mankind to himself and thus offered it *in him* to the Father through the passion, resurrection and ascension. Communication between God and man in Jesus is perpetuated by the Spirit, chiefly through the sacraments which the Church celebrates. From the Spirit man receives adoptive sonship which empowers him to give himself in faith to Christ and to love the Father with the Son's obedient Love. This is salvation, the reality.

Salvation . . . as message. The religious educator will present the reality of the redemption as a message addressed to the students in his care. Christ calls them here and now to enter into his redemptive act. Christian boys and girls will be motivated to respond to the Lord's invitation to live as a son of God. They will be prepared to recognize him and love him at every turn of their daily life because they have previously met him and acted in his Spirit with the Church at worship. It is the religion teacher's privilege to strengthen the Christ association of youthful members of the body so that they grow "in Christ" both at

267

the altar, where he speaks to the Father for them, and throughout the day, when he speaks to others in them.[1]

Salvation reality and message . . . understood by the adult layman. Far too few adult Catholics who enroll in the catechist class have a firm grasp of the mystery of Christ in its totality and unity. If the interrelation of concepts and the doctrinal stress of the above perspective are relatively new to the prospective catechist, then more time must be devoted to a development of some essential points. Treasures often missed are understandings basic to scripture, the liturgy in general, the Mass, the other sacraments and the commandments—all in their relation to catechetics. In the first lessons of the course the layman should discover the meager diet of his former life and be led to the rich nourishment of his spiritual birthright.

Thus if the student-teacher of religion considers the inspired writings as proofs of doctrine, as an accumulation of edifying stories one unrelated to the next, as a lifeless history of an insignificant semitic group which perpetuated a preparatory period no longer relevant now that Jesus has come—if this is his view (and it often is) then he needs to know that sacred scripture contains the continued story of God who acts to bring man back to him. It records the slowly swelling stream of divine activity through which God gave himself to all mankind in his self-gift to the Israel of old and—in a perfect manner—to the New Israel which is the People of God made his son again in the redemptive act of Jesus. The future religious educator needs to see that scripture conveys the Word of God, the life-giving message that touched the very heart of the People of God of the Old Law. It is the divine communication that is meant to be "kept in the Family" to touch the heart of the New People of God, meant to vivify us who like Mary of Bethany sit at the Master's feet to listen and to be nourished by the Word that

[1] Johannes Hofinger S.J., *Imparting the Christian Message,* Notre Dame 1961, is a valuable source from which the teacher may draw in unfolding the message to prospective catechists.

is Life. The catechist will know that the sacred writings make a spiritual looking-glass in which man can see himself in act— at his best and at his worst—in the lives of the men of the bible. He will use the perfect all-occasion prayers, the psalter, as God-given response to every life situation one can meet.

Once the future religion teacher experiences this training he will give to scripture its rightful place in religious formation so that the Word of God will be studied, prayed and lived by his students.

Often the Catholic layman is unaware that the liturgy continues what the bible describes. The Word-become-one-with-us carries on in sign the dialogue between God and man.[2] He does so because his Spirit dwells among us to bring us into the salvation-act of Jesus which is ever made present for us to take part in. For the one who leads boys and girls to faith in Jesus the Mass can be nothing less than the sacrificial banquet of the Family of God. The risen Lord as Mediator and High Priest calls us together to hear the Word of God, to respond to it, to enter into the covenant of the new law and to seal this love pact by eating the flesh and drinking the blood of the Lord. All this the religion teacher must be clear on.

In the sacraments the Christian meets the risen Christ who acts in sign to vivify, heal, anoint, nourish, forgive and instruct the members of the body and to gather them together in his worship of the Father. The commandments give outward expression to the new law written on the hearts of men. The new law is none other than the Holy Spirit who enables us to answer God's love with God's love. Never are the ten laws merely a code of conduct exteriorly imposed. The religion teacher is well aware of this fact.

Fundamental points such as these the prospective catechist is

2 For a clear exposition of communication via sign in worship, see Eugene A. Walsh S.S., "Worship is Sign-Language," *Sunday Morning Crisis,* ed. Robert W. Hovda, Baltimore 1963. The scholarship and popular approach of this collection of essays make them particularly valuable to the lay catechist.

expected to master before he can present Christ's message to others.

Salvation, reality and message . . . transmitted. The events by which the Lord worked salvation for man are recorded in sacred *scripture.* Their fulfillment in Jesus is made present in the *liturgy.* The effects of salvation shine forth in *Christian men and women* in whom Christ acts to relay divine love, especially to those ignorant of scripture or of the Church at worship. The truths of salvation are structured for theological precision by the Church in her *doctrinal formulas* and *synthesis.* Salvation, the reality and/or message, is thus transmitted by the Church:

in its inspired record, i.e. scripture;

in its reenactment, i.e. liturgy;

in its effects, i.e. Christian witness;

in its precise formulation, i.e. doctrinal statement.

Once the panoramic view of God's saving of man and the "four ways" of transmitting it have been presented to the lay catechist class the teacher may wish to analyze the Philip-Ethiopian episode, or one comparable to it, to bring out the four-pronged manifestation of salvation as it is contained in scripture, liturgy, witness and formula.

B) STUDENT RESPONSE

Response in faith. What does faith mean to the average Catholic layman? It is a theological virtue received in baptism to enable him to assent to a truth about God on the word of God revealing it. This is true of course. Unfortunately the concept of faith is limited to this definition for many Catholics. What more does faith mean? Faith means going all out for Christ, giving oneself to him to the point of holding nothing back. Faith means taking on Jesus' way of looking at things so that it becomes our way of looking at things. It means choosing him once and then struggling to choose him again and again as he comes in every crisis of daily life, each with its new demands.

Faith means so dying to all that is not Jesus and so living to all that is Jesus that he lives in us, the Son acting in the son to love his Father and all his Father's children. Faith means the gift of the Spirit, the Power that converts and transforms us. Faith lived until death lifts the veil onto an eternal possessing of God face to face.[3]

Can we lead our public school students to faith such as this? Let us look to Christ. He did! The teacher of lay catechists will lead his adult students to a fuller understanding of faith by showing them Jesus at work demanding and increasing the belief of *his* students, the twelve of them.

To what extent the Savior permitted the magnetic attraction of his divine personality to influence others no man can tell. We do know that no resistance to him could have existed had he been seen "as he is." But he was resisted and he was openly opposed, even to the point of crucifixion. The religious educator can take heart at the thought that the Lord taught under great handicaps. Despite this he provided opportunities for the apostles to grow in faith within a climate where faith could be nurtured. "Come apart with me . . ." "Let us cross over to the other side . . ." By withdrawing the twelve temporarily from the distracting elements of daily life Jesus strengthened their faith and equipped them to return to their environment better prepared to leaven it. The catechist who calls the youth of today to faith in Christ must create a climate that will encourage their spontaneous reply.

Climate of religion class. It is commonly agreed that life in Jesus is not to be *studied about* for one hour or so a week during the religion period and *practiced* for the rest of the week. Formation in Jesus permits no dichotomy of study versus practice.

---

[3] Faith as herein described does not exclude intellective elements. The academic integrity of the religion course is in no way diminished when the total man confronts the Person who transmits Truth itself. See on this point Father Nebreda's article, "Living Faith: Major Concern of Religious Education," 121–43.

Religious formation is a learning-living experience that takes place at the altar, in the home and during the religion period. What can be done to make the time spent in the classroom this kind of experience for the boys and girls who attend the CCD parish school of religion?

The physical setting of the room should admit of no distracting activities or decorations, no unnecessary interruptions or noises. The teacher's control, reverence and religious conviction will lend a prayerful—but not pietistic—tone to his presentation. He will provide opportunities for a response to the Lord through moments of silent prayer, reflective application and creative work done individually or collectively. In this sense the classroom setting may be thought of as a prepared environment but the atmosphere created should never be so regulated or unnatural as to preclude the continuation of the response in daily activity.

Most of all the teacher of religion does not gauge the success of his efforts, that is, the growth of the children in Christ, by examination results, valid though these be in their restricted use. Faith lived—and is this not the aim of religious formation?—is not subject to any standard of measurement we know of.

Discipline. The question of discipline is a major one in teaching children. This is especially true for the inexperienced lay catechist. Only one class period with the boys and/or girls is needed to convince the teacher that neither learning nor the desired student response will take place when a class gets out of control.

In some respects the very aim of religious education places the catechist at a disadvantage. The control measures of both public and Catholic school systems are for the most part not available to him. The teacher must be *Christ* to the students; he must lead them to a free giving of themselves to discipleship in Jesus— a response that cannot be coerced! If he is harsh, sarcastic or unjust, can he expect those children whose attendance lacks parental encouragement to continue to come to religion class?

What is worse, there is always the risk that the boy or girl subjected to such treatment will fail to distinguish in later life between the unjust treatment he received and the Christian faith itself which the teacher bore witness to—albeit somewhat poorly. Similarly prayers or catechism questions assigned to be written as *punishments* are never in order.

On the other hand no one student or clique may be permitted to disrupt the harmony of the class or inhibit learning for those who take growth in Christ seriously. All this must be understood by the teacher of the CCD class.

In addition to the above pointers, the student catechist should be assigned reading on the maintenance of discipline. He should observe competent teachers and note their handling of the class. He should inform himself of the administrative policy on discipline of the parish school of religion staff he will join.

Incidental teaching. Valuable class time need not be devoted to a full exposition of certain aspects of religious instruction. Such matters as classroom routine, the organization of the school of religion and the qualities of a religion teacher can ordinarily be covered by means of occasional remarks and assigned reading. Good reading is available. It must be done.[4]

There is nothing incidental about the unfolding of the human personality through progressive stages and its implications for the world of the Spirit. To plan for a detailed study of religious psychology however is to be more ambitious than the modest goals of a survey course in catechetics can permit. A token suggestion is to divide the class of student teachers into sections to discuss the psychology of the child and its significance in his religious formation. The basis for the grouping of the adults would be the child age level of particular interest to them. Teacher manuals often provide essential pointers that can be

[4] For an adequate treatment of these and related topics see Sister M. Rosalie M.H.S.H., *The Adaptive Way of Teaching Confraternity Classes,* St. Paul 1959, as well as the work done by Joseph B. Collins, *Confraternity Teacher's Guide,* Milwaukee 1960.

discussed against the background of the adults' observations of the age bracket in question.[5]

C) TECHNIQUE IN PERSPECTIVE

Is there a need for methodology in religious formation? Theorists who expect method to take care of itself are as unrealistic as theorists who let methodology govern teacher, student and content. The proponents of either position betray a shortsighted view of catechetics at the practical level. Any adult who has suffered in silence and courtesy from the lecturer who was master of his material but the only one to appreciate it knows that more than knowledge and zeal for the kingdom is required to make a religion teacher. Children have neither the verbal restraint nor the courtesy of adults. Their attention must be actively and constantly elicited. This is especially true when attendance at CCD parish schools of religion steals from their playtime! The catechist must strive to emulate the Master's adeptness at engaging the total person in a learning activity that leads to growth in Christ. In so doing he will give to methodology the place given it by *the* Teacher who reveals himself and the Father to man.

The planned lesson. Christ's dealings with the men and women of his time both as individuals and as members of an ethnic group are so perfectly adapted to the psychology and needs of the learner that the reader of today may be deceived by it. One could easily mistake the Lord's ability for "beginning where the student is" for a casual play-it-by-ear approach that requires little forethought. But there was nothing fortuitous

---

[5] A valuable study of the contributions of depth psychology to the field of religious formation is found in a work by Marc Oraison, "Some Light from Depth Psychology on Adolescence," *Modern Catechetics,* ed. Gerard S. Sloyan, New York 1964; Robert P. Odenwald, *Your Child's World from Infancy through Adolescence,* New York 1958, gives a comprehensive exposition of child psychology for the average reader. More advanced works include Marc Oraison's *Love or Constraint?* New York 1961, and special issues of *Lumen Vitae* devoted to religious psychology: 2, 1947 and 2, 1961.

about the Savior's encounters with the men of Palestine! Through the genius of the catechist Jesus' meeting with our boys and girls will be as natural and as planned as his meeting with Zaccheus, the woman at the well, the father of the epileptic or the inquiring lawyer.

An analysis of any of these meetings will reveal a pattern of activity which contains several elements: 1) an introduction or preparation; 2) an action that reveals and invites; 3) a response.

The introductory action or statement begins with something of present concern to the participants. "Zaccheus, hurry down, I'm coming home with you" (Lk 19:1–10) "Give me (something) to drink" (Jn 4:1–42). "What are you arguing about among yourselves?" (Mk 9:13–29). "What is written in the law?" (Lk 10:25–38). "Do you want to get well?" (Jn 5:1–16). "Who touched me?" (Lk 8:43–49).

The initial step alerts the participants to the presence of Christ who then (second element) engages them in a personal way to bring them into his Father's saving plan for man. This done the Lord then elicits the desired response (third element). ". . . I restore fourfold." "Sir, give me this water. . . . Now many of the Samaritans of that town believed because of the word of the woman who bore witness . . ." "I do believe; help my unbelief." "Go and do thou also in like manner."

In some instances Jesus indicates the response that should have been made. "O you of little faith, why did you doubt?" (Mt 14:22–34).

In any planned lesson the preparatory step or orientation should be used to the extent that it alerts the students to Jesus who is about to speak to them. In the second step the Lord's deeds are brought to life so that through his dealings with Zaccheus, the woman at the well, the distressed father and the inquiring lawyer he acts here and now with Jim, Mary and Bill. The boys and girls of today experience the helplessness of the unloving son and the forgiveness of a merciful Father; they thirst for "living water" which they have learned to value; they

275

desire to love Christ in their fellowman—in a word, they respond to Jesus who calls them to the life he reveals.

Pithy doctrinal statements are rarely missing in the Lord's public ministry but few of them can be identified by the modern educator as the "summary of the day's lesson" he expects to find. One need look however no further than the credal formularies of the early Church to discover the role of the doctrinal statement in summing up teaching on the Mystery we live by. The catechist should plan for an organizational exercise to sum up the material given in each lesson.

A preparation, a presentation of Christ who speaks to us (through Old Testament or New, in sacramental celebration or in his human witness), a response and a summary are the basic components of any lesson planned by the religious educator. These elements of a lesson should be presented by the instructor to the student catechists both in theory form and through demonstrations. For maximum benefit the instructor should have "live" demonstrations with children of the desired grade level being taught in the presence of adult class members.

Use of scripture. How precisely will the instructor in religion effect the meeting of Jesus with Bill, Mary and Jim of his present CCD class? The teacher of catechists can best demonstrate this meeting by *his* use of scripture.[6] He will let the Lord speak for himself.

For the older boy and girl this meeting means direct contact with the Word of God. There is no better way for youthful members of the body to become listeners of the Word as it is proclaimed in the sacred liturgy than to be listeners of the Word as it is reverently read during the religion class. Silent, reflective reading of the bible at home may follow if the youth has acquired a taste for it through silent, reflective reading of scripture

[6] The Catholic layman should be aware of some of the problems related to the use of scripture. A study to be recommended for its clarity and non-technical approach is the essay on literary form done by Lawrence Dennemiller S.S. See "God Speaks in Human Ways," *Worship* 36 (May 1962), 380–86.

done during the religion period. Likewise appreciation for the Word in act, which is the sacramental reenactment of Jesus' salvific deed, will be nurtured through para-liturgical celebrations that culminate a unit's work for the CCD class.

A direct experience with the inspired writings does not preclude the paraphrasing of the text or the retelling of the event in story form, especially to the smaller child. Neither would one neglect the value of the Christian witness whose life is the story of Christ. "Lay bare the life of any Christian who lives in love and you see there all of Christ and all of time."[7]

Specific skills. Lessons on the skills or aids employed in the lesson plan, such as the art of questioning, of storytelling, the use of analogy and audiovisualization, should not be divorced from the content they are meant to convey. The teaching on these skills provides an opportunity for reviewing and deepening the doctrinal perspectives that are given in the first part of the course. An exposition of the principles governing a particular technique could be followed by a study of the technique as it was or is employed by Christ, by the Church in her liturgy and by the writers of the religion course to be taught to the children —all done only to the extent that the technique itself merits such attention.

The following is an example of this procedure as applied to the art of questioning:

1) An exposition of the principles basic to the art of questioning:
discussion on the reasons for questions:
mention of basic do's and don't's in questioning as applied to religious formation.

2) An examination of Christ's use of the question technique:
to check factual knowledge—"whose image is this?"
to lead to self-appraisal—"Can you drink the chalice whereof I shall drink?"

[7] Gerard S. Sloyan, "God's Secret Design Summed Up in Christ: The Heart of Catechizing," *The Bible Today* 7 (October 1963), 415.

to test understanding—"Who do men say I am?" "Who do you say I am?"

to evoke commitment—"Will you also go away?"

3) A reference to questions used by the Church in sacramental worship:

to lead to self-appraisal—"Do you know them to be worthy?" (holy orders).

to test understanding—"What does faith offer you?" "What do you ask of the Church?" (baptism).

to express commitment—"Do you renounce Satan?" (baptism). "Do you take this man for your lawful husband?" (matrimony). "Do you promise reverence and obedience to me and my successors?" (holy orders).

4) A study of leading questions used in the religion course: This procedure may be used for storytelling. Less time need be spent on audiovisualization and apperception.

Analysis of the religion course. Once the prospective religion teachers have grasped the basic principles for planning a lesson they are ready for an intensive analysis of the religion course that is designated for use in their CCD parish school of religion. A thorough study of this course will equip them to identify basic teaching principles and to condense or expand the material as time requires it. The teacher of catechists will lead those he instructs to discover what in the developed matter needs to be adapted to the specific Christian milieu of the children to be taught. At no time should the text rob the catechist of the creativity he must exercise as this person here and now working with these boys and girls. Substantial fidelity to the suggested lesson for the day is required; slavish adherence to it is abhorred.[8]

---

[8] An analysis of the course should include reference to doctrinal concepts treated above. For instance those who have the fourth grade teacher's manual of the On Our Way Series by Sister Maria de la Cruz H.H.S. might refer to it when work on the commandments is done in the catechist class, or to the eighth grade manual of *Religion Lessons for Catholic Living* by the Mission Helpers of the Sacred Heart when studying the reenactment of the Christ-event in the liturgy.

In conclusion: the present writer has made a practice of questioning student catechists at the completion of such a course as is here described. "Before taking this course would you have considered enrolling in the catechist preparation classes had you known that several years of study were involved?" The answer most often is a definite "No!" "Do you now want additional courses of great depth and concentration?" The answer is an emphatic "Yes!"

Notes on Contributors

Paul Brunner S.J. is a member of the East Asian Pastoral Institute, Manila, and the author of *These Are the Holy Words, A Mass Commentary.*

José Calle S.J., also associated with the East Asian Pastoral Institute, is in charge of religious education for all public high schools in Manila.

Bernard Cooke S.J. is Chairman of the Department of Theology at Marquette University, Milwaukee, and a frequent contributor to theological journals.

Andrew M. Greeley, Senior Study Director of the National Opinion Research Center at the University of Chicago and assistant pastor of Christ the King Parish, Chicago, is the author of several books, including *And Young Men Shall See Visions.*

Johannes Hofinger S.J., Director of the Eastern Asian Pastoral Institute, is the editor of the catechetical review *Good Tidings.* He is the author of *The ABC's of Modern Catechetics* and edited *Teaching All Nations.*

Raymond Lucker, Professor of Catechetics at St. Paul Seminary, St. Paul, is the Director of the Confraternity of Christian Doctrine program for the St. Paul Archdiocese.

Alfonso Nebreda S.J., a Professor of Religion at Sophia University, Tokyo, is the author of several books, including *Landmarks for a Pre-evangelization.*

Frank B. Norris S.S. is Professor of Dogmatic Theology and of Catechetics at St. Patrick's Seminary, Menlo Park, California. He has contributed to *Worship, The Bible Today* and other periodicals, and is the author of *God's Own People.*

John J. O'Sullivan is Professor of Sacred Scripture at St. Paul Seminary, St. Paul, and is active in catechetical work for the St. Paul Archdiocese.

William Reedy is Director of Catechetics for the Wm. H. Sadlier publishing company in New York. An author, lecturer and teacher,

281

he is also an executive member of the New York Archdiocesan Religion Teachers Council.

William Sherzer is Dean of students at Sacred Heart Seminary, Detroit, and Chairman of the Liturgical Commission of the Archdiocese of Detroit.

Sister M. Carol Frances B.V.M., a frequent contributor to *Today, Worship* and other magazines, is Chairman of the Department of Theology at Mundelein College, Chicago.

Sister M. Virgine M.H.S.H., author and former Lecturer in Catechetics at the Catholic University of America, is presently associated with the Confraternity of Christian Doctrine program in the Detroit Archdiocese.

Gerard S. Sloyan is Chairman of the Department of Religious Education at the Catholic University of America and President of the National Liturgical Conference. He is the author of *Christ the Lord* and *The Three Persons in One God,* and edited *Shaping the Christian Message* and *Modern Catechetics.* He is also the editor of the "Foundations of Catholic Theology Series."

Richard Sneed O.S.B., President of and Professor of Sacred Scripture at St. Gregory Abbey Seminary, Shawnee, Oklahoma, has contributed to *Catholic Biblical Quarterly, The Bible Today, Theological Studies* and other periodicals.

Theodore C. Stone, author of *Christian Action,* is assistant director of the Confraternity of Christian Doctrine Program for the Chicago Archdiocese, and a member of Loyola University's Institute of Pastoral Studies.

Index